Roman Catholic Nuns in England and Wales 1800–1937

A Social History

BARBARA WALSH

IRISH ACADEMIC PRESS
DUBLIN • PORTLAND, OR

First published in 2002 in by
IRISH ACADEMIC PRESS
44 Northumberland Road, Dublin 4, Ireland

and in the United States of America by
IRISH ACADEMIC PRESS
c/o ISBS, 5824 N.E. Hassalo Street, Portland
Oregon 97213–3644

Website: www.iap.ie

British Library Cataloguing in Publication Data

Walsh, Barbara
    Roman Catholic nuns in England and Wales, 1800–1937: a social history
    1. Monasticism and religious orders for women – England – History – 19th century
    2. Monasticism and religious orders for women – England – History – 20th century
    3. Monasticism and religious orders for women – Wales – History – 19th century
    4. Monasticism and religious orders for women – Wales – History – 20th century   5. Nuns
    – England – Social conditions – 19th century   6. Nuns – England – Social conditions – 20th
    century   7. Nuns – Wales – Social conditions – 19th century   8. Nuns – Wales – Social
    conditions – 20th century
    I. Title
    271.9'00942'09034

    ISBN 0-7165-2745-6

Library of Congress Cataloging-in-Publication Data

Walsh, Barbara, 1932–
    Roman Catholic nuns in England and Wales, 1800–1937: a social history/Barbara Walsh.
        p. cm.
    Includes bibliographical references and index.
    ISBN 0–7165–2745–6 (cloth)
        1. Monasticism and religious orders for women–England–History–19th century.
    2. Monasticism and religious orders for women–England–History–20th century.
    3. Monasticism and religious orders for women–Wales–History–19th century.
    4. Monasticism and religious orders for women–Wales–History–20th century. I. Title.

BX4220.G7 W35 2002
271'.90042'09034–dc21   2002069089

Typeset by in 11.5 pt on 13.5 pt Dante by
Carrigboy Typesetting Services, County Cork
Printed by MPG Books Ltd, Bodmin, Cornwall

Contents

LIST OF PHOTOGRAPHS

LIST OF MAPS

ABBREVIATIONS

DVDP: Daughters of Charity of St. Vincent de Paul
SSHJM: Sisters of the Sacred Hearts of Jesus and Mary
SND: Sisters of Notre Dame de Namur
SSP: Sisters of St. Paul the Apostle

Foreword

IN 1873 J.N. MURPHY published his *Terra Incognita; or, the Convents of the United Kingdom* with the intention of conveying 'information on a subject about which much ignorance and prejudice prevailed'.[1] Even as we enter the twenty-first century there is still considerable ignorance about the life and work of nuns. Nuns are often ignored by historians of religion, and historians of women have only recently come to study the remarkable history of women religious. Nuns have for too long been understood as submissive figures in a patriarchal and hierarchical church. The dynamism and innovative nature of their early structures and work have only begun to be appreciated. It is perhaps timely that Barbara Walsh's study of the origins and service provided by female religious communities in England and Wales has found its way into print. More than a hundred years after the publication of *Terra Incognita*, Dr Walsh provides us with an immensely detailed and readable social history of convents in England and Wales from the nineteenth to the early twentieth century. It is a necessary contribution to the history of female religious communities.

The impact of convents on the social, economic and political life of England and Wales is a much neglected subject in British social history. The richness of convent archives for a study of social history has yet to be fully recognised by historians. Research in such archives is not solely a means of examining the lives of nuns, of exploring the internal physical, spiritual and emotional spaces where these women lived their lives. Through convent archives we can also study the history of society generally. We can uncover, amongst other things, the history of health, welfare and educational institutions of all types. We can also, to some extent, examine the lives of individuals who came into contact with religious communities whether as children or adults, as users of services, or providers of money and funding, or as representatives of higher authorities. The material stored in convent archives holds the history not only of religious congregations but also of the wider society.

Dr Walsh examines the place of Roman Catholic nuns within the broad context of nineteenth- and early twentieth-century society. These religious

1 J.N. Murphy, *Terra Incognita; or, the Convents of the United Kingdom* (London, 1876), 2nd ed., p. vii.

communities were popular among women, attracting many entrants wishing to live a spiritual and professional life. Roman Catholic religious communities had historically been mainly contemplative, but women who formed and entered religious communities in the nineteenth and twentieth centuries were seeking an active life of service. Nuns managed and organised many institutions. They were believed to be uniquely capable and qualified for 'caring work' and were often attractive workers because their labour was cheap. The founders of these religious communities were women of vision and substance. Innovation was a key word in the work of nuns. They ran and often funded a multitude of welfare institutions ranging from orphanages and schools to hospitals and asylums. They ran businesses and managed complex financial arrangements. Nuns were almost always forward looking and innovative in their work. The contribution of lay women to these institutions was significant to their success. Through the extensive regional development of convents nuns also formed networks of support within and beyond communities and parishes. Dr Walsh's detailed survey work brings to our attention the regional pattern of convent expansion and reveals that their range of social services was unprecedented in scale. The extensive tables and appendices in this study provide information on recruitment and, for historians of emigration, uncover the extent to which Irish women entered religious communities in England, a much-neglected aspect of emigration history. Religious women could and did have a profound effect on the Catholic Church and the services it offered its adherents. The attractions of convent life for women were many. It provided an alternative to marriage; allowed women of ability to have careers in a possible multitude of enterprises, and it granted single women a status denied them in secular society.

Catholic religious generally have received a bad press in the last decade or so. Honest and open relationships between religious and laity have not been a feature of Catholic life through the centuries. The Catholic Church currently faces many difficulties, some arising from its secretive and self-protective structures. The poor image of religious today tends to hide the idealism and dedication of many individual religious, men and women, and their service to community life and to society at large. The institutionalisation of religious life arguably became its greatest weakness. This book provides us with an insight into how that weakness developed but also uncovers the valuable contribution these female religious communities made to society. As a result of Dr Walsh's work convents are no longer 'Terra Incognita'.

MARIA LUDDY
University of Warwick
July 2002

Acknowledgements

THE RESEARCH ON WHICH this book is based was undertaken as a doctoral thesis and it is appropriate that I acknowledge again with thanks and gratitude the enthusiasm and care of my supervisors in the University of Lancaster: Mike Winstanley, Michael Mullett and Bill Fuge, all of whose critical comment and wise guidance ensured a successful outcome.

I acknowledge the encouragement and help received from many other sources. In respect of the research drawn from original material contained in four convent archives, I was privileged to have been allowed to examine and draw data from confidential and sometimes sensitive material and I would like to thank the following for their unstinted help, advice and generous hospitality, all of which I have greatly appreciated: Sister Anne Cunningham, SSP, Sisters of Charity of St. Paul the Apostle, Archive Office, Selly Park, Birmingham; Sister Jean Bunn, SND and the late Sister Anne Burke, SND, Sisters of Notre Dame de Namur, Provincial Archive Office, Woolton, Liverpool; Sister Mary Kelly, SSHJM, Sisters of the Sacred Hearts of Jesus and Mary, Archives Office, Chigwell, Essex and Sister Margaret Mary, DC, Daughters of Charity of St. Vincent de Paul, Archive Office, Provincial House, Blackrock, Co. Dublin. These archivists provided me with an enormous amount of assistance and, in appreciation of the confidentiality of their convent archives, I have endeavoured to maintain an appropriate level of discretion in the use of this material while at the same time revealing much needed statistical and demographic information. I am also grateful to Sister Zeala, OSU, Ursuline Convent, Lancaster; Sister Judith Greville, DC, Archive Office, Provincial House, Mill Hill, London and Sister Pauline Cahill, St. Michael's Convent of Mercy, Clacton-on-Sea for their generous assistance in response to my queries.

My grateful acknowledgement is extended to many other people and libraries for their unfailing courtesy and help. These include: the duty staff at the Lancaster University Library; Father Robbie Canavan and the late Sister Ruth Duckworth, DHS, Talbot Library, Preston; Anselm Nye, Queen Mary & Westfield College, University of London; Deirdre Quinn, former librarian of the Central Catholic Library, Dublin; the National Archives of Ireland, Dublin; the Dublin and Irish Collection in the Gilbert Library, Dublin and the National Library of Ireland, Dublin. I would also like to acknowledge the usefulness of the contacts made through the Catholic Archive Society, and the Women's History Association of Ireland.

In the preparation of the book for publication, I am grateful for all the assistance and advice received from Irish Academic Press. My special thanks to Dr Maria Luddy, University of Warwick, for writing the foreword and for her truly inspirational encouragement.

I would also like to put on record my appreciation of the encouragement and support received from many old and new friends in Lancaster, Dublin and elsewhere, not forgetting my extended family of cousins in Preston. Last, but not least, I would like to acknowledge and thank my family here in Dublin, not only for their enthusiasm for my endeavours, but for their patience and forbearance during my intermittent absences from home.

CHAPTER ONE

The Veiled Dynamic

IN THE NINETEENTH and the early twentieth century thousands of young women chose to live in all-female, Roman Catholic religious communities in England and Wales, either as active sisters, who engaged in work as teachers, nurses and social carers, or as contemplative nuns with a hidden vocation totally dedicated to prayer. No easily accessible, correlated, quantitative research exists and little is known of the scale and scope of these convent-based activities. The aim of this book is to explore the nature, extent and achievement of women's religious institutions which could be classified as 'active', in particular their response to the changing needs of the Roman Catholic community, and the factors which influenced their growth.[1] This chapter introduces the topics to be covered more fully in later chapters, the sources that have been used and problems to be encountered.

In 1800 there were nine orders or institutions of Roman Catholic religious communities of women.[2] The majority of these were pre-Reformation communities of nuns which had returned from exile in Europe in the late eighteenth century. The following fifty years saw the gradual build up of new foundations or the arrival of active communities of sisters. By mid-century the number of congregations or orders had grown to thirty-one, with a network of a hundred convents spread out almost evenly between London, the Midlands and the North. The number of active communities of nuns and sisters increased steadily as the century progressed. London and the South-East were favoured, but there was also expansion in the North-West, especially in Lancashire. By the turn of the century there were 105 communities operating out of 469 convents and this growth continued well into the twentieth century, so that by 1937 there were 175 orders and congregations operating out of 956 convents. Although the greatest number was to be found in London and the South-East, convent-based undertakings had existed in all but one county in England and three in Wales.

That the nineteenth and the early twentieth century witnessed this unparalleled expansion has received little attention from historians. Yet these religious communities owned or were responsible for a wide range of socially-integrated services. They provided or administered many hundreds of schools at every level of education. They ran and staffed institutions which provided social care: orphanages, asylums and hospitals, residential homes for children, homes for single women, the elderly and those with special needs. Convent-organised nursing services provided for both the wealthy and the poor in their own homes. Convent-based social services offered support and care of the needy and sent their sisters out into city slums to care for families and to provide help and support for women and children.

Women who spent their lives engaged in such work as members of a religious community are rarely mentioned in general studies of social history, or even in the voluminous literature on women's history which has appeared since the 1970s. It is also the case that women who entered English convents to become teachers or nurses or social workers have never been recognised as having been part of the increased profession-alisation of women of all denominations who were engaged in providing a wide range of social services during the late nineteenth century. Their contribution to the fabric of late Victorian and early twentieth-century social life has been regarded as of little interest except as part of the history of religion or, more narrowly, the history of the English Roman Catholic church. For the most part unrecognised and rarely acknowledged by contributors to general works, their existence, if mentioned at all, has been often relegated to a brief footnote. This might be excused on the grounds of the lack of accessible statistical material on convents. Religious congregation archivists, on the whole, are only now beginning to recog-nise the historical importance of such material.[3] Observations by social historians therefore are inclined to be vague, even dismissive ' . . . the number of women in Roman Catholic religious orders, mainly as teaching sisters, *was small but growing*' [author's emphasis].[4] Prochaska, *Women and Philanthropy in Nineteenth-Century England* (1980), in his assessment of Catholic-run philanthropic and charitable undertakings, for example, could only estimate (or more probably greatly underestimate) the figure of 5,000 for the number of women in 'sisterhoods and nunneries' directly involved in these charitable endeavours in 1893, and he did not specify any individual communities or undertakings.[5] Commentary on the social history of nursing also omits to recognise early nursing standards originated in the training regimes of religious communities.[6]

Even more intriguing, leading commentators on the development of the Roman Catholic Church in England have either ignored or shown mere token recognition of the contribution made by these women to the emerging Catholic community.[7] Only within the collection of scholarly essays edited by Beck, *The English Catholics 1850–1950* (1950) has there been any serious attempt to set the record straight. Three of the contributors present a view of nuns and sisters as viewed from inside the church: John Bennett, 'The Care of the Poor'; W.J. Battersby, 'Educational Work of the Religious Orders of Women, 1850–1950'; and Edward Cruise, 'The Development of the Religious Orders'.[8] However, in none of the foregoing was there any attempt to provide a quantitative analysis of the religious communities or to shed light on their patterns of growth and development in the several regions of England and Wales. Susan Mumm noted a similar lack of interest in Anglican sisterhoods by 'those who study the history of the Victorian Church of England and historians of women's culture and experience'.[9]

In general studies of women's social history recognition of the work of nuns and sisters, if included, continues to be often reduced to just one or two famous names and well-known congregations.[10] Until now it has been easy enough to explain away such omissions by alluding to the serious lack of collated research findings for authors seeking data. For example, Jo Ann Macnamara, *Sisters in Arms: Catholic Nuns through Two Millennia* (1996), while claiming to be the 'first definitive history of Catholic nuns in the Western world', gives relatively little attention to developments in nineteenth-century England and Ireland.[11] Likewise, the hypothesis presented by Mary Heimann, *Religious Devotion in Victorian England* (1995), omits to acknowledge the enormous contribution made by the nuns and sisters working in hundreds of schools to the revival of many devotional practices. She leaves the sisters very much on the sidelines and, apart from a scattering of sometimes unflattering anecdotes is, for the most part, content to rely on the inclusion of references to the ubiquitous Janet Erskine Stuart and Cornelia Connolly.[12]

Substantive work on women's religious communities in England has been undertaken by Susan O'Brien.[13] Her perceptive and important studies of several orders and congregations in Victorian England have opened up many avenues to explore and provide useful corroborative evidence which has been drawn upon in several chapters here. Useful, too, is the work of Maria McClelland, *The Sisters of Mercy: Popular Politics and the Growth of the Roman Catholic Community in Hull, 1855–1930* (2000), in which she examines the realities faced by one foundation of Sisters of Mercy.[14] Papers presented at the Catholic Archive Society conferences and subsequently published in their annual journal also offer useful and interesting aspects, information and contacts. This society's contribution in providing a vehicle to help and advise religious archivists to gather and preserve their communities' material is an invaluable asset for the success of future research.

The intense growth of religious community life for women in Ireland during the nineteenth century was similar in many ways to developments taking place in England and Wales, and Irish women's history for the same period is well served by a number of well-researched studies which can provide useful corroborative material.[15] Two definitive works are Caitriona Clear, *Nuns in Nineteenth-Century Ireland* (1987), in which she drew attention to the neglect of social and ecclesiastical historians and Maria Luddy, *Women and Philanthropy in Nineteenth-Century Ireland* (1995), who has placed the work of women within religious institutions at the core of philanthropic development in that country.[16]

The expansion of the religious life in North America, which owed much to input from Ireland, continues to inspire the interest of scholars from the United States and their findings complement and add to our knowledge, especially in respect of the methods used for the recruitment of aspirants.[17] However, we know virtually nothing about the factors which influenced the expansion and development of convents and their activities in England and Wales.

To a large extent, of course, the successful growth of these women's religious orders and congregations in England and Wales was drawn along with the driving force of faith and fervour which saw the English Roman Catholic Church gaining strength, wealth and power throughout the nineteenth century and beyond. At the same time, political events and successive waves of anti-clericalism in Europe from the 1870s onwards brought about a considerable influx of exiled religious communities. These nuns and sisters sought to be assimilated into the more tolerant climate of English society and needed to find some means of generating an income to provide them with financial security. Many turned to providing convent boarding schools, nursing services, convalescent homes and laundries.

However, this book is neither a study of the power of faith nor an in-depth examination of the relationship of religious communities of women *vis-à-vis* the English Catholic Church, nor a detailed investigation of how women organised and managed convent life. While women who chose to embrace the religious life would most certainly have entertained a great desire to spread the Roman Catholic faith through 'good works', in addition to aspiring higher personal spirituality, religious fervour was not the sole influence responsible for the growth of the convents. There is evidence of important social, economic and politically-based inter-locking factors which generated and influenced the great vitality, breadth and diversification of convent-based activities.

The mid-nineteenth century saw a changing social climate and the developments in government-led health and welfare policies. There was a need for the English Catholic hierarchy to provide services for an expanding Roman Catholic population which, even after the Great Famine of 1845–51, was being further swollen by continued immigration of Irish Catholics. This situation had prompted the Catholic episcopate to make regular appeals to communities of nuns and sisters for assistance and help with parish work, particularly in the running and staffing of schools, which were seen as playing a crucial role in stemming the falling away or 'leakage' from the Faith in the next generation. An immediate and far-reaching response was required in respect of the 1870 Education Act and the changes in Poor Law legislation which cut back on outdoor relief for the poor.

Towards the latter end of the nineteenth-century, however, the Catholic population of England also developed as part of an increasingly wealthy, middle-class and suburbanised society. This had led to a greater preponderance of Catholics in the economically strong service sector in the south-east of England and in the conurbations of some of the larger northern cities. Middle-class Catholics in all areas created a demand for increasing numbers of convent-run private day and boarding schools, nursing services and convalescent homes, particularly on the south coast. Not confined to Catholics, however, was the popularity of exclusive 'high-class' education for the sons and daughters of 'gentlemen' in locations near to London, which profited the congregations with links to France. There is evidence that convent-based activities were never confined to serving members of the Catholic community. The high standards and strict discipline within convent schools for girls were popular and they catered for many non-Catholic pupils. Religious-run hospital and nursing services advertisements were aimed at all denominations and creeds. This indicates that, on the one hand, if the nature and characteristics of the work or 'apostolate' of Roman Catholic women's active religious communities were not attuned solely to serving the needs of the Catholic population, this provides one answer to why there were so many convents outside the

'Catholic North'. On the other, it indicates that the Roman Catholic population may have been considerably greater, in fact, and rather more nationally diffused than official sources estimated. Catholics lower on the social scale who relied on the health and social care services provided by the convents and whose children made use of the free schools were not all necessarily committed to regular attendance at church services and, being classed as 'lapsed', thus escaped inclusion in parish statistics. It is interesting, therefore, to explore in more detail some of these secular reasons to correlate convent growth with the expansion of social services and the changing regional distribution of wealth and population in English society from the mid-nineteenth to the mid-twentieth century.

Central to this is a concern with the practical aspects of this growth. What type of work did the convents undertake? How widely dispersed were convent networks throughout England and Wales? How did they organise sufficient finance for survival? From where did they find enough young women to staff their expanding services?

The success of the response of the religious communities to social change was partially due to the financial strategies which convents employed to remain economically viable and to provide the resources with which to engage in new undertakings as needs arose. Despite their often initial struggles with poverty, religious communities devised methods of generating income and providing free care for the poor through operating two-tier fee systems in schools, hospitals and nursing services and by providing exclusive and expensive education for the more wealthy segments of society. Congregations also invested funds deposited with them as members' dowries, or which were made available for their use as endowments. Religious communities thus came to wield considerable purchasing power within the expanding services sector of the late nineteenth and the early twentieth century. The personal fortunes of members who were heiresses in their own right were often spent on the development of a congregation's apostolate. Moreover, the expansion of communities and the setting up of new 'houses' and additional convent-based activities often relied on the assistance provided by the generous financial and practical help and support of members of the Catholic laity. New converts to Catholicism were particularly anxious to contribute. Wealthy and well-connected 'Old Catholic' families were traditionally closely involved in helping the convents. A great deal of more modest support came from well-wishers from every walk of life, many of whom were women.

How important was the contribution of the convents to the development of social services in the nineteenth century? The first strand of evidence for the vitality and importance of women's religious communities is signified by the sizeable growth in the number of orders and congregations as demonstrated by their expanding convent networks. Often starting from impoverished circumstances, the increasing financial strength of these institutions allowed them to engage in an ever-widening range of convent-based undertakings and social services. However, the success and viability of these activities is linked to a second strand of evidence – a plentiful supply of young women willing to embrace the religious life.

The availability of numbers of young aspirants to the convents was crucial to the development and staffing of schools, institutions and nursing and social services, and the desperate need of the congregations for recruits has been identified as an important pull factor. It can be demonstrated that many girls who entered were drawn from Ireland or from the Irish diaspora in England, Wales and Scotland. In Ireland alternative employment for farmers' daughters, other than an arranged or 'matched' marriage, was non-existent, and the socio-economic pressures that existed in the 'strong-farmer' class of post-famine rural Ireland, therefore, created an unremitting push factor. The bourgeois value-systems that existed in these relatively well-off, rural, Irish families presented a set of conditions that offered girls not only a career path that promised the status of a professional teacher, nurse or social worker, but also the spiritual means to achieve what they believed was the highest accolade of God's grace and blessing. The recruitment of Irish girls to convents in England was pursued diligently and with great skill by congregations, aided and abetted by schools, persuasive literature and the exhortations and approval of their families. Speculation remains with regard to what extent large numbers of recruits to the religious life drawn from Ireland should be explained or viewed *vis-à-vis* high female emigration figures and there is sufficient evidence to suggest this is a topic which may benefit from additional research.

There were also considerable numbers of English-born entrants to convents, but it was more usual for congregations to procure entrants from their own convent schools and convent-run, teacher-training colleges, a method which created a self-generating or 'in-house' source of recruitment. English aspirants, therefore, showed less inclination to migrate the long distances undertaken by Irish girls desiring to enter, and, on the whole, chose a community that was local or familiar to them from their schooling. The case studies examined will reveal the socio-economic background of English entrants to be mainly drawn from the urban middle class. Throughout the discussions we need to bear in mind, however, that there are a number of issues related to the concept and definition of 'nuns' and the problems associated with sources available for their study.

While common usage gives the title of 'nun' to all women embracing the religious life within the Roman Catholic Church (and the Anglican Church as well), the correct terminology distinguishes between the nuns in religious orders whose members take solemn, lifelong vows, and congregations of sisters who adopt the more simple vows of poverty, chastity and obedience, to which is sometimes added 'care of the poor'.[18] The rule of a community that has simple vows allows its members to engage in work as teachers, nurses or social carers outside the convents. These types of community are categorised here as 'active sisters'. There is also a small number of congregations, self-designated as 'mixed', which endeavour to combine the rule and lifestyle of a contemplative order of nuns with that of the active sisters. In many ways almost indistinguishable in their work from that of the communities of active sisters, this latter category has been identified as mixed in order to distinguish these congregations from the small number of orders of nuns whom I have described as contemplatives, whose lives were dedicated to prayer.[19] These distinctions are important and a glossary of the terms used is provided in Appendix I. This book is mainly concerned with members of religious institutions who were active or mixed sisters, so they are generally referred to in this way in preference to the blanket term 'nuns'. Religious institutions, religious congregations and orders and religious communities are terms which have been used interchangeably.

Apart from some peripheral references, I have also chosen to leave aside any discussion of the class divisions found within many orders and congregations which make distinction between choir and lay members. In such communities choir nuns and sisters were regarded as having been drawn from a higher social group and were thus given professional duties befitting their background. Lay sisters were often enrolled as cooks and cleaners to undertake domestic duties. It should be clear that the efficient running of any large household at this time, either secular or religious, was totally reliant on an endless round of chores performed by servants and a convent household was no different from a large country house or a middle-class villa in this respect. However, the distinction between choir and lay sisters was not universally applicable to religious communities and, in fact, began to decline towards the end of the period.[20]

Dating the origins of a community can also be problematical. A modern foundation of a community of religious sisters (that is, since the seventeenth century) most usually occurred when a small group of similarly-minded women came together, under the inspiration of one of their members, to engage in some form of active or charitable work. Roman Catholic religious foundations such as these might function informally for many years, even decades, before their members were given permission to apply for, and receive, official approbation of their status by the Holy See. This lengthy procedure presents occasional problems when making reference to the activities of some communities before their official foundation date.[21] Religious institutions of women also required the support and direct involvement of a senior churchman who would be thereafter usually named in association with a community's establishment.[22] There are a number of other minor qualifications relevant to the categorisation and analysis of the congregations and orders working in England and Wales in the nineteenth and the twentieth century and these are provided as notes to Table 1 in Appendix II, where all the Tables are assembled. A further problem that has been encountered in the researching of the religious life for women has been the confusion arising from so many communities sharing similar or even identical names and activities, while being wholly distinctive and separate organisations. As one writer put it, 'The position is confusing in the extreme . . . there are no fewer than eight Orders of Sisters of Charity, four congregations of Sisters of St. Joseph, besides a number of different Congregations of Dominicans and Franciscans of the Third Order.'[23]

In preparing quantitative data, therefore, reliance has rested on several different sources which, when consulted and compared, provided acceptably accurate access to identify arrival dates, locations of convent buildings and the work and rule of each of the similarly-named communities. These and other sources are cited and discussed in the chapters on the growth of congregations and the regional development of convent networks.

Different problems are associated with more specific material drawn from convent personnel records and archives. These records themselves need to be regarded in the same light and with the same sensitivity as are confidential family papers and thus treated with respect for the retention of an appropriate level of privacy. They are also highly selective, both in terms of their survival and the information which they contain. With regard to convent accounts and financial matters, these have not been widely trawled by others engaged in this field of research and, therefore, collaborative data have been particularly difficult to obtain. Evidence presented to illustrate examples with regard to the business of running a convent has required sensitivity in regard to confidentiality. Again, the nature and the extent of four communities' records which have been explored in detail are discussed in more depth in the appropriate chapters.

In addition to dedicated religious sources, however, this book has also drawn extensively on one major secular source, particularly to explore patterns of recruitment. This is the Irish decennial census, most particularly the returns relating to 1901 and 1911 for the counties of Limerick, Tipperary and Wexford. Accessible in manuscript form, the 1901 and the 1911 enumerator's sheets include information on housing classification and descriptions of farm buildings in addition to naming the occupants of each household, thus allowing for the socio-economic assessment of farming families. Rural districts in Ireland utilise townland designation in addition to parish boundaries and this format draws attention to the many instances of extended family clusters within townlands which are reflected in the evidence showing reliance on kith and kin recruitment within the congregations studied.[24] Convent personnel records relating to periods earlier than 1901 are hampered by the fact that virtually all archives in the Public Record Office of Ireland before this time were destroyed by fire in 1922. However, other recognised primary sources which include the Primary or Griffith's Valuations of 1847–64 and several trade directories have been used to supplement the lack of census data in identifying the birthplace of recruits from Ireland. The tenacity of generations of post-famine, rural, family clusters which survived to hold on to their land, usually rented but later owner-occupied, make this technique feasible.

The following chapters closely reflect and expand on this discussion. General patterns of growth are dealt with first and the arrival or new foundation of congregations and orders from 1800 until 1939 is outlined. This is followed by some observations on the main areas of work undertaken by religious communities. The significance of where and when networks of convents came to be established is then examined to provide an interpretation of the scale and the patterns of regional development. Matters concerning the finance and control of convents are then considered. Finally, expansion on and data drawn from the membership registers of four case studies provide an examination of how the growth of convent numbers and convent-based activities was reliant on and sustained by large numbers of recruits to the religious life.

The conclusion considers the potential significance of this research for our understanding of a variety of historical areas.

CHAPTER TWO

The New Religious Communities

To UNDERSTAND THE scale and the scope of the contribution made by the work undertaken by the communities of nuns and sisters in England and Wales from around 1850 onwards, some thought must first be given to what was happening in the decades leading up this time. This chapter, therefore, begins with an outline of how women's religious orders and congregations which had been officially suppressed for the most part since the Reformation, were later re-established or founded as new institutions. Their rate of growth, the location of first foundations and some factors affecting the reasons for their arrival will be discussed. The significance of the regional and sub-regional distribution patterns of these institutions' convent branch houses will be the subject of closer focus in Chapter 4.

There is no definitive quantitative study of nuns and sisters on which to either base or contrast the hypotheses presented. In an ideal world, existing research drawn from the archives of every individual Roman Catholic women's religious order and congregation working in England and Wales would have been the most appropriate source for providing indisputable quantitative data. No such comprehensive research figures exist and, in their absence, the absolute numbers presented here have been drawn from a number of published texts of the period. My findings, therefore, should be read as providing an acceptable working indication of the patterns of scale and development of conventual life in England and Wales across the period under consideration.[1] To simplify the process, several autonomous convent communities, such as the Sisters of Mercy, the Ursulines, the Benedictines, the Carmelites or the Poor Clares, have been treated initially as one single named institution for the purpose of calculating the arrival or foundation of orders and congregations.[2] Rather more difficult to handle were the individual communities of Dominicans, Augustinians and Franciscans which had often originated from different branch foundations in Europe or came into being as new English communities. Although often with similar titles and rule, most of these, where possible, have been dated as new and separate arrivals for the reason that they continued to be operated and administered separately. Care has been taken to distinguish between second and third orders, where appropriate.[3]

It should be noted that the more important numerical count of these communities' convent networks will remain unaffected by this process.[4] The resulting analyses raise not only a number of issues to be considered here but may also provide a base for future research.

In 1800 nine women's religious orders or congregations resided in England and Wales (Table 2). These communities occupied twenty-one convents.[5] Thurston does not indicate whether the convents he lists contained orders of contemplative nuns or congregations of active sisters.[6] It may be taken that the majority of them were communities of enclosed nuns since only one of the communities can be clearly designated as being established with the specific intention of providing a religious life for active and unenclosed sisters.[7] Designation of the first mixed community is less certain but it seems reasonable to let it stand.[8]

Many of the orders of nuns *in situ* by 1800 had origins dating back to the early middle ages.[9] These communities had been dispersed with the dissolution of the monasteries at the time of the Reformation and the nuns had sought shelter in Europe, although retaining close links to the English Roman Catholic community. Several subsequently returned in 1794–96 as refugees from the French Revolution, aided by English Catholic families of high social standing who were instrumental in assisting their resettlement.[10] Although embracing a contemplative lifestyle some, but not all, of these early nineteenth-century convents continued a tradition of educating a small number of female pupils within their walls.

By contrast, however, additional congregations of nuns and sisters in England and Wales after 1800 consisted mostly of active communities. In the two decades following the Catholic Emancipation Act of 1829 eleven additional active communities arrived in England from France, Belgium, Italy and Ireland. Many of these sisters came at the request of the clergy and bishops who were struggling to provide pastoral care for a Roman Catholic community which had been overwhelmed by the effects of the Irish famine between 1845 and 1851. Thousands of near-destitute Irish Catholic immigrants sought refuge and work in English industrial cities and towns.[11] The English-born Catholic population was also increasing at this time, especially by the growing number of converts from the Church of England as a result of the popularity and influence of John Henry (later

Cardinal) Newman and the Oxford Movement which came to prominence in 1839–45.[12]

By the time of the restoration of the English Catholic hierarchy in 1850 there was a total of twenty-three women's religious communities in England and Wales, of which eleven were fully active. The following seven years saw the arrival or new foundation of eight more. By 1857, therefore, the number of communities in England and Wales stood at thirty-one orders or congregations.[13] Ten were contemplative orders and there were sixteen congregations of active sisters, and five which may be designated as mixed (see Tables 3 and 4). Three active communities had sent sisters from Ireland. Five may be regarded as of English foundation; the remainder had come from Europe.

What is most striking (Tables 2 and 3) is that it was not the traditional Catholic North which accommodated the original arrival of the greatest number of communities, but London and the South-East and, to a less extent, the South-West.

As to the national indices of the proportion of active, mixed and contemplatives, there are already signs of an increasing bias towards active congregations by 1857. In 1857 over 51 per cent of all congregations and orders were active sisters, 16 per cent were mixed and 32 per cent were contemplatives (Table 5).

BACKGROUND TO THE NEW COMMUNITIES, 1830–57

The earliest arrivals included some communities of nuns and sisters who particularly sought the freedom to undertake all forms of social care in the community by providing teaching, nursing and practical support for the poor. Between 1830 and 1850 the arrivals of active congregations of sisters were principally those communities with a primary interest in providing education at several levels. The Faithful Companions of Jesus came to London in 1830. Founded in Paris a decade earlier under Jesuit direction, these active and unenclosed sisters opened schools for the poor in Somers Town in 1830 and a boarding school for 'young ladies' in Isleworth in 1841.[14] Some Presentation nuns (an Irish order founded by Nano Nagle) travelled from Cork to Manchester 1836 to set up schools for the poor there.[15] They were the first of the new arrivals of many Irish women who would dedicate their religious lives to work and to settle in the north of England.

In 1839, in response to an appeal from Bishop Griffiths in London, some English women who had trained with the Irish Sisters of Mercy in Cork returned here to establish a community in Bermondsey. (The Sisters of Mercy were an active congregation founded by Catherine McAuley in Dublin in 1830.)[16] The superior of this community, Mother Clare Moore from Cork, later led the party of fourteen Mercy Sisters who, together with the Sisters of the Faithful Virgin from Norwood, nursed with Florence Nightingale during the Crimean War, 1854–56.[17] She had seriously considered becoming an Anglican nun herself at one time. She held the sisters in high regard, writing later, ' . . . what training is there compared to that of the Catholic nun?'[18] Other nursing volunteers to the Crimea would, in due course, establish religious congregations devoted to the care of the sick.[19] Much of the increasing professionalisation of nursing as a respectable career for women resulted from the high standards and rigorous discipline set in place by women's religious communities in the first half of the century.[20]

The Sisters of the Good Shepherd established a House of Refuge for women in Hammersmith in 1841. Founded in Angers in France in 1835, these religious were dedicated to providing institutionalised care and rehabilitation for girls and women.[21] Communities of the Good Shepherd had grown rapidly and extensively throughout Europe and provide an example of nuns who, having taken solemn vows, combined the active life with enclosure.[22]

Other notable and significant foundations of women's communities arriving before the re-establishment of the English Hierarchy in 1850 included the Sisters of Notre Dame de Namur from Belgium (founded in 1803). Some sisters from this active and unenclosed congregation had been invited to Penryn, in Cornwall, in 1845 by the Redemptorist Fathers in order to help with schools and parish work. Cornwall was but a stepping-stone to London, for within two years the sisters were persuaded by the Redemptorists to transfer their work to Clapham, where it was felt there was greater need for their expertise.[23]

Cardinal Nicholas Wiseman, the senior Roman Catholic prelate of England and Wales and Archbishop of the London diocese of Westminster (1850–65) was keen to support the provision of good education for middle-class girls. Encouraged by his interest, the Society of the Holy Child Jesus, an English-founded congregation was established in 1846. Their founder was the American-born Cornelia Connolly.[24]

The Society of the Sacred Heart was an institution also dedicated to the provision of higher standards of education for upper- and middle-class girls. Founded in Paris in 1800 with the help of the Jesuits, these sisters established their first school in London in 1842.[25]

The Sisters of Charity of St. Paul the Apostle (Selly Park) were originally a branch of an active and unenclosed French community, founded in Chartres in 1704. Invited to Banbury in 1847 by a local cleric and friend of Cardinal Wiseman, they immediately began recruiting locally for additional sisters to work in the industrial areas of the Midlands and the North. In due course they were to become one of the largest congregations to provide schools and welfare care for the poor. They later became a totally independent English community.[26]

The re-establishment of the Catholic hierarchy of England and Wales had faced the new bishops with a number of problems. There was the continuing urgency to provide and minister for an expanding Catholic population which needed churches, schools, nursing and welfare care for the poor. Although no longer driven by the immediate effects of famine in Ireland, there was still a steady stream of Irish Catholics seeking work and settlement in England and Wales. In addition, the reverberations of the Oxford Movement continued to bring in many new converts, which was thus a positive factor, especially in terms of the newcomers' enthusiasm in providing financial support for the building of churches and schools and in the provision of property and other contributory support for convents and convent-based undertakings.[27]

The new bishops gave priority to the rapid establishment of 'missions' under the jurisdiction of the new English dioceses.[28] Anxious to press forward with the work of providing pastoral care, the bishops and clergy turned for help to those communities of nuns and sisters which they knew were prepared to respond to whatever was required of them. Senior clerics had close links with Europe. Having studied and trained there, they were aware of and familiar with the pastoral work undertaken by active women religious in France, Belgium and Germany. Thus it was only to be expected that invitations were issued to European sisters to come and lend assistance.

O'Brien has theorised that many priests and bishops, despite the 'great sense of urgency . . . did not believe that the church's needs could be met by the newer and relatively untried Irish and English initiatives', looking instead to French sisters who 'came from a culture . . . educated English people admired and was certainly preferred to that of Ireland'.[29] The validity of this argument might be questioned for the reason that it is based only on doubts expressed in the records of one of the congregations she has examined. Her view begs the question of why all French congregations relied so heavily on the recruitment from Ireland or of second-generation Irish immigrants.[30] It might be suggested that, while some prejudice towards Irish women members certainly did exist within a number of French communities, it had little effect on the enormous distribution and input of the Irish within religious communities on the whole. The Sisters of Mercy, for example, who, albeit operating as autonomous convents, continued to rely on their close links with an Irish foundation and were to be found in almost every county of England and Wales.[31] This hardly suggests a significant element of reluctance on the part of the priests and bishops who invited them. It seems likely that those members of the English hierarchy who had Irish connections knew that the women's religious institutions were already contributing much of value in the development of education and welfare care in Ireland and were keen to issue invitations to Irish sisters to supply similar support in their own jurisdictions.[32]

In the north of England a congregation from Dublin, the Irish Loreto sisters (an independent offshoot of the Institute of the Blessed Virgin Mary) set up schools in Manchester in 1851.[33] In the same year four Ursuline sisters from Tildonk in Belgium arrived in London. Like so many of the communities who had come to open schools the Ursulines had few financial resources and were at first lodged in the slums of Eastcheap before eventually moving to Upton.[34] In Stroud in Gloucestershire, Mother Teresa Matthews founded a community of Dominican Sisters in 1855. Their apostolate was also dedicated to the education of girls.[35]

During the later decades of the nineteenth century many more congregations arrived from Europe or were established by Englishwomen. Patterns of choice continue to show a distinct preference for the southern counties of England as a location for these foundations.

LATER ARRIVALS AND FOUNDATIONS, 1857–1937

Between 1800 and the mid-1930s, 175 orders or congregations of nuns and sisters came to be established in England and Wales. Of these, newly arrived French communities were clearly in the majority (see Table 1), although there were several from Belgium, Germany and other European countries. There were fifteen congregations founded by Englishwomen and three new foundations of Irish origin. The dominant feature throughout the nineteenth century was the regular influx of European congregations. At times these became a flood. Many, indeed, had arrived as a result of a direct invitation of senior churchmen or through recommendation or connection with male missionary orders such as the Redemptorist Fathers, the Passionist Fathers and the Jesuits.[36] However, a great number of new congregations and orders came to England and Wales of their own choice, often as exiles from political strife in Europe.[37] In many respects, England was regarded as a haven of tolerance and a precedent had been set already by the earlier arrival of religious refugees of the French Revolution. In the 1870s several communities sought the safety of England in the aftermath of the Franco-Prussian War. Bismarck's *Kulturkampf* (1871–87) and the Falk Laws of 1873, which sought to suppress completely the influence of the Roman Catholic church in Prussia, also precipitated the expulsion of a number of religious communities which subsequently established themselves in England.

Although too many to mention individually, a few examples of European *expatriate* communities who were early arrivals in the second half of the century may be cited. For instance, two separate communities of the French nursing sisters of Bon Secours came to England and were established in Liverpool (1867) and in London (1870). They supplied a range of fee-paying, home nursing services for the rich, while at the same time nursing poor patients free of charge. The Servants of the Sacred Heart of Jesus, whose members included German, French and Irish women, fled to London from Paris in 1870 and continued their work of caring for homeless girls in the East End. These sisters eventually expanded into providing specialised nursing and education for mentally-handicapped children.[38] In Sussex, by 1870, a community of Augustinian sisters from Bruges had established residential care for mentally ill adults.[39]

Not all new congregations at this time emanated from France, Belgium or Ireland. Five new English active foundations were formally recognised between 1858 and 1877. In 1859 a London-Irishwoman, Margaret Hallahan, founded the Dominican Third Order in Stone in Staffordshire. She was supported in this by an enthusiastic champion of women's religious life, Bernard Ullathorne, the Catholic Bishop of Birmingham (1850–88), whose diocesan administration extended across Warwickshire, Staffordshire, Oxfordshire and Worcestershire. In Stone these sisters were responsible for a hospital, schools and an orphanage.[40]

In Manchester, the year 1863 marked the formal foundation of Elizabeth Prout's Sisters of the Most Holy Cross and Passion. Established with considerable struggle and initial local clerical hostility in 1850, her primary aim was to offer a life of spirituality for working-class women and so seek 'religious life for its own sake not as a means of working for the poor or of stabilising a social work'.[41] Despite these lofty aspirations, the sisters soon found it necessary to take over the running and staffing of schools in order to provide themselves with the income necessary for survival.

The year 1868 saw the foundations of two more English active communities. The Poor Servants of the Mother of God were established in London by Fanny Taylor (a former nurse in the Crimea), with the help of Lady Georgina Fullerton and Cardinal Manning.[42] These sisters' apostolate was dedicated to care for the poor and, later, had for their particular emphasis the provision of free hospital nursing. In the same year, the establishment of the Franciscans of the Five Wounds (Mill Hill) came about under slightly different circumstances in that its foundress, Mother Francis Basil, and five original members were former Anglican nuns. Following their conversion to Rome, they set up schools in Mill Hill in London with the active encouragement and support of Cardinal Manning.[43] In 1877, Mary Potter, with the help of Bishop Bagshawe, began her foundation of nursing sisters, the Little Company of Mary in Nottingham.[44]

The final quarter of the century saw no lessening in the number of new arrivals or foundations. The majority of the newcomers to these shores continued to be of European origin, mostly French, with a sprinkling of Belgian and German congregations. Just one new Irish community arrived. These were the Irish Sisters of Charity, founded by Mary Francis Aikenhead in Dublin much earlier in 1815 to provide relief of the poor.[45] The Dublin sisters came to Rock Ferry, Birkenhead, in 1890 where they set up a rescue home for women at the invitation of the Bishop of Shrewsbury, Dr. Knight.

In the eighty-year period, 1857–1937, out of a total of 175, the majority of nuns and sisters were communities of active and mixed congregations (see Table 5). During this time, just ten new foundations of strict contemplative orders were established compared to the 144 additional active or mixed communities. In the final two decades of the nineteenth century at least fourteen of the incoming active and mixed sisters concentrated solely on education in the form of boarding and day schools for 'young ladies'. Three of the newly arrived active congregations arriving at this time ran fee-paying nursing services or convalescent homes for well-off patients which subsidised the provision of free nursing to the poor. The remainder of active or mixed congregations established between 1877 and 1897 provided services for the poor in one form of another, either in schools or in welfare care.

The new English communities founded during the final quarter of the century – all active communities – had each adopted a Franciscan rule which allowed them to engage in practical welfare undertakings. While church bureaucracy dictated that the support and direction of senior members of the hierarchy continued to be crucial at the time of establishment, it can be recognised that the true impetus generating the foundation of these new English congregations was a number of exceptionally talented and determined women. The new communities were: the Franciscan Missionaries of St. Joseph, founded by Mother Francis Ingham in Manchester under the auspices of Bishop Vaughan in 1883;[46] the Franciscan Minoresses, established by Sister Mary Francis Murphy with Cardinal Manning's approval, which began caring for the poor in Long Acre in London in 1888;[47] the Cardinal was also directly supportive of Mary Manning's founding of the Littlehampton Franciscan sisters (later renamed the Franciscan Missionaries of the Divine Motherhood). These opened an orphanage in Hampstead in London in 1895.[48] The Franciscan Sisters of the Holy Ghost, also dedicated to working with the poor, were founded in Manchester in 1897 while Bishop Vaughan was the Bishop of Salford.[49]

Accounts of the formation of the Sisters of St. Joseph of Peace contain some controversy. Described by Steele, Hohn and Anson as having been founded by Edward Bagshawe, Bishop of Nottingham (1874–1901), with Mother Mary Evangelista Gaffney's assistance, these 'official' versions of the early history of the sisters are now recognised as having contained a disingenuous writing-out of the controversial Margaret Anna Cusack (the nun of Kenmare).[50] Research has now rehabilitated the true story of her role.[51] Evidence suggests that Bishop Bagshawe was a prelate with a high concern for social justice for the working-class poor.[52] Ten years earlier he had been sympathetic in assisting Mary Potter in the foundation of a congregation of nursing sisters, the Little Company of Mary (1877), although, later, they had a difference of opinion over policy and control of the community.[53] The extent to which Bagshawe had been highly influenced and impressed by the writings and radical feminist ideas of Cusack has only recently been recognised. Not altogether surprisingly, he later drew upon himself the disapproval of the more conservative elements within the hierarchy.[54]

The most extensive influx of communities of nuns and sisters occurred in the decades between the turn of the century and end of the First World War. Why this was so was due, once more, to political events in Europe. The majority of these congregations came from France, having been effectively banished through Combe's educational laws of July 1904 which 'forbade members of religious orders to teach. Their houses were to be shut within ten years. The teaching orders were to be dissolved and liquidated.'[55] For these congregations England was once more a safe refuge, with London or the South-East still the most preferred choice of initial location. Of the forty-five foreign congregations who arrived between 1900 and 1910 only five newcomers made their first foundation in the north of England.[56] As will be shown in Chapter 4, the subsequent growth of convent-based undertakings in the North can be attributed in the main, therefore, to the expansion of the early established congregations and not to a surfeit of foreign incomers.

In order to provide themselves with the means of subsistence, the majority of the incoming communities subsequently opened schools. But the secularisation of French life had also included the phasing out of religious who were hospital nursing sisters so that, by 1907, almost all had been replaced by laywomen.[57] Such communities sought refuge in England and provided for their financial upkeep by offering home nursing services and convalescent homes. At least nine of the incoming congregations arriving after 1897 were nursing sisters. It should be stressed that neither in providing nursing nor high-class education were members of women's religious institutions solely dealing with the Catholic community. Their services were advertised in the *Catholic directories* as offering care for all, Catholic and non-Catholic alike.[58]

Nursing communities, unlike the educational congregations which came to be concentrated in London and the South, settled first in a much wider variety of locations which included Lancashire, Worcestershire, Cumberland and Staffordshire. Only four or five of the newcomers who arrived between 1898 and 1917 can be seen to have had a particular dedication to caring for the poor, although, as will be indicated later, many active sisters had an opportunity to be aware of the needs of poor families through their work in schools. In many instances practical support was offered in a covert manner in order to retain confidentiality on both sides.[59]

Following the First World War there was a striking decline in the number of orders or congregations arriving or being newly established. This contrasts with the buoyant growth and widening distribution of convents – branch houses of existing established communities – which was taking place at this time (see Chapter 4). Unlike the earlier arrivals, invited here by the English bishops or clergy or self-exiled from the Continent, the fifteen congregations which set up houses here between 1917 and 1937 would seem to have been established specifically for recruitment purposes, especially for girls willing to undertake overseas missionary work as religious. Two of the new congregations provided nursing services and five were specifically missionaries. Three congregations ran homes for guests or homeless girls. Only one community chose the North-East as their first location and these were a group of sisters from Belgium who set up a home for elderly and convalescent ladies in Durham in 1934. The remaining five newcomers were engaged in the provision of schools. The most favoured type of religious institution continued to be communities of active sisters, a trend already well advanced by 1857. The number of orders embracing a contemplative and non-active religious lifestyle, which had been much in the majority in 1800, had declined to 32 per cent of all religious communities by 1857 (see Table 5). The following decades saw this proportion continue to drop steadily: 19 per cent in the 1870s, 14 in the 1890s and 11 in 1917. By 1937 only 10 per cent of women's religious congregations or orders were those of strictly contemplative nuns.[60]

Detailed study of developments within the dedicated contemplative orders lies beyond the scope of this book and, therefore, comment will be restricted to noting that these monastic communities of nuns remained relatively insignificant in numerical terms from the mid-nineteenth century onwards.[61]

The geographic locations for establishments of each fresh arrival of women religious throughout the period under review is an important factor to consider in terms of patterns of development. There is evidence of continued preference for women religious to choose London and the South-East as the initial location for a new foundation (see Table 3). Northern industrial cities and towns saw the arrival of newcomers after the 1850s only rarely, despite the fact that the North-West, the North-East and Yorkshire were traditionally considered as the Roman Catholic heartland. Population maps for the Catholic community validate this premise.[62] However, it is quite striking that as analysis of absolute numbers has proved, the 'Catholic North' after 1877 contained neither the highest number of religious congregations nor, as we shall see, the largest number of branch houses or convents, and there are a number of reasons why London and the South-East led the way in attracting new foundations, both foreign and native.[63]

One important factor was the extent to which the successful establishment of incoming foreign or newly founded English communities was reliant on the active support of the English Roman Catholic bishops and clergy or the superiors of male religious orders. Considerable influence was imposed by leading prelates who occupied the Metropolitan Roman

Catholic See of Westminster. Church historiography has recognised that the hub of power for the English Catholic Church lay in London. 'It is from London – since 1850 – that Catholic England is, if not governed, controlled.'[64] Clearly, much of the earliest initiative and encouragement of religious communities of women to set up social services and care of the poor was due to the direct input of Cardinal Wiseman. He was keenly aware of the need to address matters of welfare within his pastoral jurisdiction. Chronic poverty and deprivation existed side by side with extreme wealth. In November 1850 Cardinal Wiseman wrote: 'Close under the Abbey of Westminster there lie concealed labyrinths of lanes and courts, and alleys and slums, nests of ignorance, vice, depravity and crime, as well of squalor, wretchedness and disease; . . . haunts of filth which no sewage committee can reach – dark corners, which no lighting board can brighten.'[65]

The Cardinal had a direct input into the establishment of the Poor Sisters of Nazareth in London in 1851. Their convents or Nazareth Houses, which in due course spread throughout England Wales, provided homes where the sisters cared for destitute children and old people of both sexes. In 1861 Wiseman's continuing concern for work with the slum dwellers of London led him to invite a French community, the Little Sisters of the Poor, to work in his archdiocese. These sisters, active in Brittany since 1838, had received formal approval in 1842. They visited the poor in their own homes, where they nursed the sick and provided care for families and old people. Funding relied on alms collected by the sisters.[66]

Wiseman's successor, Cardinal Manning (1865–92), continued this concentration of support for the practical contribution made by communities of nuns and sisters based in the London dioceses of Westminster and Southwark.[67] Deeply concerned with matters affecting social justice for the working classes, 'God forbid that we should be looked upon by the people as Tories . . . or as the servants of plutocracy instead of the guides and guardians of the poor', Manning saw the work of the women's religious institutions as a key element of pastoral care.[68] He once said to a friend, 'If I were a woman I would be a nun [*sic*] of Nazareth House.'[69]

Cardinal Vaughan, who succeeded Manning in 1892 as Archbishop of Westminster, is reputed to have had little patience with Manning's support for social issues affecting the working classes.[70] Yet the number of new orders and congregations settling under Vaughan's diocesan jurisdiction continued to increase, suggesting that other reasons, possibly financial and economic, should be taken in account when assessing the popularity of London and the South-East of England.

In addition to the influences of leading prelates, practical factors were at work. One consideration is that London and the south coast provided easy access to sea links to European ports and this was an obvious advantage, especially in the case of many of those congregations which retained close ties with a mother house in Paris or Rome. Other equally practical factors derived from the increasing economic dominance and wealth of London and the south-east of England. These and other social and economic considerations will be examined when we investigate the proliferation in the branch houses and convent networks which were generated by the arrival or foundation of new congregations.

Finally, some thought may be given here to the extent of the involvement and official approbation of the English hierarchy. These male clerics formed an integral part of the mechanism which allowed a new foundation or arrival to be established in the first place, and, as far as was possible, controlled. Unlike the Anglican sisterhoods which were less constrained by hierarchical pressure, the Roman Catholic congregations and orders have been perceived as existing very much under the dictate of Church direction.[71] To a great extent this is correct and significant, because every religious community had to receive a bishop's permission before opening a house within his diocese. The local bishop's responsibility encompassed both the spiritual and the financial oversight of the convents within his jurisdiction. Under Canon Law he would have 'visitation' or inspection rights, usually on an annual basis, to ensure that a community's constitution rules were being compiled with and that material and spiritual needs were being correctly attended to. However, in reality, several congregations, especially those with strong financial assets and/or a European mother house, could wield a considerable level of independence of action, despite being under the official surveillance of the bishop. Those congregations which had recourse to a cardinal protector, for example, could appeal direct to Rome, if necessary. Others had alternative means of lessening restrictive pressure. If a local prelate were intransigent or if serious disputes arose a community of sisters could, and did, threaten to move to another diocese and a more benign administration. An ability to engage in tactful and diplomatic manoeuvres was an attribute required of many of the religious superiors who cherished ambitions to expand their convent-based undertakings. Working relationships between the mother founders and superiors and individual bishops and clergy in the subsequent development and expansion of orders and congregations, however, present a number of complex issues to be looked at later.

FACTORS AFFECTING THE GROWTH OF ORDERS
AND CONGREGATIONS

In Chapter 3 we shall be examining the work undertaken by religious communities in greater detail and, subsequently, the extent to which the location of convent branch houses was dictated, not only by the nuns and sisters' apostolate identified and pursued by individual active and mixed congregations, but also how movement was influenced by the response to local needs and conditions. However, here it will be useful to introduce and discuss some of the broader external factors which contributed to the expansion of the communities' involvement with developing social needs. These factors included: the increase of the Catholic population and its changing composition; legislation applicable to the education and the response of the Catholic Church to it; and developments within the state's involvement in welfare and nursing health provision.

In all these factors it is important to be aware of an existing underlying perception that much of the response and attitudes may have been due to 'the need of the Catholic Church to develop community structures which would foster solidarity among her members'.[72] This sociological inter-pretation carefully traces back to the impact of the Reformation and 'the process of secularisation of Europe' begun by the French Revolution on ' . . . the Catholic ideal of the relative autonomy of the family and of inter-mediate groups, developed originally in the medieval socio-economic order, [which] became a means of defence for the Catholic Church against the encroaching advance of the secular state'.[73] In other words, the English Catholic community, both lay and clerical, were wary, if not sceptical, of reliance on the benefits of state-funded aid. The result was that, as will be shown, the religious communities and their expanding convent networks were well-supported financially in their efforts to respond to the changing needs of the time.

The Growth of the Catholic Population

Cardinal Manning, the Archbishop of Westminster (1865–92), has been quoted as believing that 'eight-tenths of the Catholics in England are Irish', and that he had spent his life 'working for the Irish occupation of England'.[74] His view remains, none the less, an unconfirmed impression rather than an established fact.

Calculating the proportion of Irish within the Catholic community of England is fraught with difficulties. The Religious Census of 1851, although recognised as being broadly indicative of church attendance for Catholic services, for the reason that Sunday Mass attendance was obligatory for practising members of the faith, would have missed out on the large grey area covering the non-practising but nominally Catholic Irish who still looked to the church for practical help in terms of social need and for spiritual solace in times of crisis.[75] In addition, before considering the number of 'Irish' in England and Wales, it is acknowledged that if second-generation Irish are taken into account, numbers would be higher, although equally hard to validate. Estimates put the Catholic population of England and Wales at nearly 700,000 in 1851, of which Hughes reckons a quarter of a million were what he describes as 'of English stock', that is, of old English Catholic background and not incomers from Ireland.[76] Jackson calculates the percentage of the population that were Irish-born stood at 3 per cent in 1861, dropping to under 2 by 1891, and to 0.9 per cent by 1931.[77] Collins, on the other hand, suggests there was rather more diffusion of Irish settlement than has been previously believed, but concedes that just under half of all Irish-born immigrants lived in the four biggest cities of London, Liverpool, Manchester and Glasgow in 1841, and that 'this concentration was maintained throughout the nineteenth century'.[78] Davis holds that there were two patterns: one a concentration of Irish in the worst parts of Victorian cities, living a life apart; the other, more predominant and less highlighted, that of Irish assimilation alongside English neighbours. He describes the view of the Irish 'as living in urban squalor as symbolised by Little Ireland in Manchester' as unrepresentative of Irish settlement in Britain.[79] Liverpool, Manchester and London received large numbers of immigrants, but there was also a considerable diffusion of the Irish within other English towns and cities and much greater integration and dispersal than was generally thought to have occurred. Davis cites the research of Lynn Lees, 'who found that the Irish were present in every census district in London'.[80] Whether the pattern of distribution for convents, outside of London, Liverpool and Manchester, should be seen as serving distinct clusters of Irish Catholics or not has been raised earlier and the answer is not clear-cut. When the broader indices of regional growth are examined it may be suggested this may only be so in relation to some of the seaports such as Cardiff and Bristol, and it should be borne in mind that not all Irish immigrants were of the Catholic faith.

In the wider context of the assimilation of Irish Catholics into the church in England, it was apparent to the bishops by the 1860s that the majority of the immigrant Irish were not holding on to their Catholic faith with the enthusiasm that should have resulted from Cardinal Cullen's rigorous ultramontane practices aimed at modernising the Irish church. One of the driving forces behind the urgency to set up Catholic schools was the realisation that many of the poorer migrants from rural Ireland, still steeped in beliefs emanating from the old Celtic church mixture of orthodoxy, folk magic and superstition, were 'nominally [Catholic but] growing up forgetful of their duties', prompting fear of 'leakage' so that the next generation would be completely lost.[81] Much of the early expansionary pattern of convent growth in England from 1850 onwards, therefore, can be seen to have come about in response to the need for schools for an increasing Catholic population, many of whom were these poor, working-class Irish in the industrial cities. But this conclusion cannot continue to be applied to developments which took place later on in the century.

Educational Developments

The second half of the nineteenth century witnessed an expansion of education for the poor. For many of the active religious, the passing of the Education Act of 1870 precipitated an even greater involvement in education and an increase in the number of convents providing schooling. The Catholic hierarchy, eager to provide more 'mission' (parish) schools, in common with the Church of England and the Nonconformist denominations, had become embroiled in the controversy that raged over the secularisation of government-assisted elementary schooling. Cardinal Manning, although opposed by some of the bishops, was in favour of negotiating government grants for education. He held the view that elementary schooling should not have to rely on private charity alone, but that children of all denominations had a right to receive help from the state.[82] It was mainly through his efforts that increasing numbers of Catholic schools came to be built and the expansion of convent numbers at this time can be directly attributed to the willing response of the active teaching congregations to provide teaching staff. The building of a new school often included the provision of convent living quarters for the sisters in charge, but not necessarily large and imposing convent complexes. As a Sister of St. Paul the Apostle has commented, 'We worked in often poor and small schools, parish schools. They didn't belong to us. We lived in terraced houses among the poor, not in big convents . . . .'[83]

A further consequence of the 1870 Act was an acceleration in the provision of training colleges for Roman Catholic lay teachers run by women's religious congregations. John Murphy, writing in 1873, noted the report of the Committee of the Privy Council on Education for 1870–71 and cited the findings of Scott Nasmyth Stokes, Her Majesty's Inspector of Roman Catholic Schools in the North-Western Division of England.[84] Out of an estimated Catholic population of just under two million, Stokes calculated that there were about 300,000 Catholic children of primary school age. His report argued that even a provision of one trained teacher for each 100 scholars meant that 3,000 teachers were urgently needed.[85] There is no need to speculate who filled the gap. The greatest response came from congregations of women religious who were increasingly relied on to guide and instruct new pupil teachers in hundreds of classrooms and to establish teacher-training colleges.[86]

The following decades saw established, active congregations engaging in a consolidation of their earlier undertakings, especially those convent-based activities concerned with schools for the poor and the education of orphans or children in institutional care. Teaching congregations continued to open new schools or to expand into the higher levels of education by upgrading existing facilities at the same convent address or by opening branch houses in new areas.

One interpretation of these developments in Catholic education has been identified as 'the endeavours of English Catholics to develop subsocietal institutions to preserve their [self-perceived] subculture by segregating the young in educational terms through the maintenance of a separate denominational education system.'[87] However, as shall be shown in Chapter 3, a considerable proportion of convent-run school places were, in fact, taken up enthusiastically and supported by non-Catholic pupils.

Welfare Developments

Increases in the number of convents in mid-century may be attributed also to the increased attention given by active sisters to other areas of welfare work. An Act of 1862 to 'provide for the Education and Maintenance of Pauper Children in certain Schools and Institutions' was extended by further legislation in 1866 and 1868. This increasing attention to 'problem' children prompted among the Catholic hierarchy a deep concern over the danger of Catholic children 'losing their faith' if placed in the care of secular or non-Catholic institutions. Catholic reformatory and industrial schools were deemed necessary and many convents were built to accommodate the sisters who took charge of this work. The government was already well accustomed to placing responsibility and giving payment for such services in Ireland. Peckham notes that 'a precedent for state salaried nuns had been set in the 1830s in Ireland and that the Reformatory Act of 1858 allowed *per capita* payments to be made for the operation of workhouse hospitals, reformatories and industrial training schools.'[88]

In the 1860s and the 1870s government policy enforced an even stricter interpretation of payments distributed under the 1834 Poor Law. Convent relief work for the poor as a result came under increasing pressure. The flourishing of convent-run welfare care services would have provided some recompense for what Harris has called 'the dramatic drop of direct relief to the poor'.[89] Victorian commentators were wont to distinguish between poverty as a regrettable by-product of economic growth and pauperism as a social disease brought about by too much reliance on charitable support. Although Levitt comments on the ' . . . many workers [who were] reaping the rewards of economic progress' by this time, he has calculated that there were still between 3 and 7 per cent of the population of England and Wales classed as paupers in 1869. He also points out that in the mid-1870s the workhouse test was being even more ruthlessly applied, and especially so to mothers with illegitimate children.[90] This would have had a particular significance for the expansion of the convent-run Houses of Refuge or Mercy for women 'penitents'. William notes, 'In the five years from 1871 to 1876, 276,000 paupers or almost one in three of those on outdoor relief were cleared off the relief roles.'[91] However, although official levels of 'pauperism' dropped, the poor continued to avail themselves of other forms of charitable assistance, such as the sisters' soup kitchens, workrooms, night shelters and refuges.

After the end of the century the number of active sisters' convent-based relief services for the poor levelled off, possibly because in the decades following 1900 legislation by Liberal governments increased state aid for the working-class poor. The 1906 Education Act had included provisions for school meals, the Workmen's Compensation Act came in the same year and old age pensions were introduced in 1908. Unemployment and Health Insurance followed in 1911. Thus certain levels of chronic distress were being alleviated by the state rather than by private or voluntary charity. Moreover, by 1909 levels of official pauperism had all but disappeared and remained only in small pockets at levels of about 2 or 3 per cent.[92]

The changes in economic conditions and welfare for the poor could not have been the only reason for the slowing down of the rates of convent expansion in the twentieth century. The provision of schools and care for the needy were not their only apostolate, however, there were also extensive nursing services in operation. It is doubtful whether the changed social standing of the nursing profession had any effect, although Mumm has suggested that several of her Anglican sisterhoods withdrew from providing nursing in the late 1880s because it had become 'a respectable secular profession', observing that 'the introduction of Jubilee Nurses into the East End [of London] in 1887 was the signal for at least one community to withdraw from local hospital work'.[93] For Roman Catholic nursing sisters, however, the emergence of secular district nurses was not perhaps of such importance since by the end of the century active sisters were increasingly involved in the provision of hospital nursing services and had moved forward to undertake specialist residential health care for children.[94] The influx of nursing and teaching sisters from France in the first decade of the twentieth century obviously also had a considerable impact in terms of the extra numbers of trained women available. So it would seem that a shift in the emphasis of the purpose and function of active sisters provides a more reasonable explanation of the slowing down of conventual expansion in some regions. By the end of the nineteenth century fewer new convents were established in areas of low economic growth, particularly in slum areas and deprived working-class neighbourhoods.

ENGLAND AS A BASE FOR THE DRIVE TO EXPAND OVERSEAS MISSIONARY ENDEAVOUR?

Although it may be seen as having an oblique bearing on the interaction and engagement of religious responding to social need in England and Wales, the enforced exile of many European religious communities in England brought about an unexpected bonus for congregations whose apostolate looked further afield. Clearly, a base here brought about easier access to and recruitment of English-speaking sisters who could be sent to the missionary outposts in Africa, Australia, India and elsewhere in the Empire. Many communities of religious were also expanding in the United States of America and Canada, especially from the late 1890s onwards and into the first half of the new century. By 1912 almost three-quarters of the hundred or so European religious congregations or orders *in situ* at that time in England and Wales had some link overseas. As will be shown in Chapter 3, convent-generated income derived from running schools and nursing services in England and Wales was often the source of much needed funding and support of their colleagues abroad on 'foreign missions'.

CONCLUSION

The arrival or establishment of foundations of religious institutions for women in England and Wales from 1800 onwards reflected to a large extent the expansion of religious life for single women that was taking place in Europe. Factors such as the granting of Catholic emancipation in 1829, the Irish Famine years 1845–51 and the restoration of the English hierarchy may be seen as contributing to the growth and development of the Roman Catholic population, especially in British industrial towns and cities. The introduction of changes in respect of the Poor Laws and new legislation for education and social care created a need for more nuns and sisters to undertake responsibility for these areas of work. The establishment of several new English religious institutions for women in addition to invitations proffered by English churchmen to French and Irish congregations to provide assistance helped to create an adequate response to the needs of an expanded English Catholic community.

An important additional dimension to be seen in the last quarter of the nineteenth and the first decade of the twentieth century was the increasing anti-clerical political pressure imposed on the activities of women religious in France and Prussia. This brought about a dispersal and movement of many European religious communities to seek exile in England and Wales, and it may be recognised that their arrival created the greatest rise in number of religious institutions. Evidence suggests that the majority of new or incoming religious orders and congregations settled first in locations in or near London and the South-East in preference to the traditional northern Catholic heartland. While many of these newly established foreign communities were dedicated to the care of the poor, an increasing number also provided educational and nursing services for sectors of the Catholic community which had become suburbanised and middle class. Non-Catholics too made regular use of their schools and nursing services. A base in England for congregations actively engaged in sending sisters to work on the missions abroad was an advantage not only in terms of the recruitment of English-speaking sisters but also as a useful source of funding.

In the next chapter we shall discusses the nature, the volume and the significance of the religious communities' professional and philanthropic endeavours.

CHAPTER THREE

The Work: 'A Practical and Most Philanthropic Utility'

One thing that many honest people are apt to overlook, namely that the convents have nearly all a purpose of practical and most philanthropic utility.

Manchester Guardian, 1875[1]

ALTHOUGH FOR THE most part unacknowledged in studies of social policy and welfare provision in nineteenth-century Britain, the work undertaken by women within Roman Catholic religious communities of nuns and sisters extended to all regions of England and Wales and affected all classes of society. The purpose of this chapter is to provide some idea of the nature and extent of their engagement in education, nursing and social care.

Changes in the poor law in the mid-nineteenth century allowed government to draw back from accepting direct responsibility for what were seen as the ills of society and reliance was laid instead on the back-up provided by a proliferation of newly-established lay and religious charitable institutions. It was not uncommon for middle-class and upper-class Victorian English women to become actively involved in 'good works' in philanthropic societies, and women members were, to a large extent, mainly responsible for their successful organisation, day-to-day operations and fund-raising activities.[2] For Roman Catholic young women such direct involvement previously 'frowned upon as methodistical and unladylike' probably became acceptable when it was conducted in the habit of a religious.[3] The evangelical enthusiasm of the churches in the nineteenth century sparked off great rivalry and the saving of minds and bodies could, and did, at times become undisguised proselytising on all sides. Each of the churches fretted when their 'faithful' strayed and rejoiced when new 'converts' were embraced. Active sisters working within schools and social care services formed the foot soldiery of the English Catholic hierarchy in this regard, and, in common with all other denominationally-driven undertakings, their underlying desire to demonstrate by example what they perceived as the 'true' Christian teaching may be acknowledged as being an important driving force. This motive is clearly evident in the biographies of women who had dedicated themselves to the religious life. Mary Potter, founder of the Little Company of Mary, for example, chose nursing as the work of her community because 'it embraced two motives – the salvation of souls and the alleviation of suffering'.[4] This desire for an expression of their spirituality fuelled the energy needed to seek practical ways of alleviating poverty, sickness and ignorance. The poor and the children always came first. As a member of the Sisters of St. Paul the Apostle explained:

> We picked up coal on the shore and used it to light people's fires. We used Sisters' salaries to buy food for the poor . . . We visited the sick. We fed people at their doors and took in their washing . . . After 'retiring' I did almost twenty years working among the old, the poor and lonely. They were the best years of my life.[5]

The English hierarchy were motivated by the anxiety that the Catholic faith should be preserved in future generations. Therefore much of their effort in supporting religious communities was intended to enlist their practical help in providing schools and institutionalised child care in order to stem what they termed 'leakage'. Not all senior churchmen were of Cardinals Wiseman's and Manning's generosity of heart, however, in caring for the physical as well as the spiritual needs of their flocks. In fact, the social policies of Cardinal Manning, which extended support and encouragement to active sisters carrying out this work were viewed at times with dismay by some bishops.[6] Bishop Vaughan of Salford, for example, once voiced criticism of Manning's admiration for William Booth and the Salvation Army. The view prompted a rebuke from the Cardinal, who felt that Vaughan was only 'interested in souls not bodies'.[7]

The work or 'apostolate' of active and mixed Roman Catholic communities of women was shaped and grounded by the disciplinary mechanisms of their rule. Their work may be designated under three broad headings: education; social or parish work; and nursing care. However, it often came about that these activities overlapped with each other in varying degrees, often expanding and shifting in emphasis over time. Thus, unlike the absolute numbers of convents which is to be presented in the next chapter, neat quantification of the volume of each area of the work undertaken is not a feasible exercise until more research has been conducted.

For the present, therefore, it is possible to present only tentative indications from the available evidence.

The range and the scope of the work of nuns and sisters have been rarely recognised or acknowledged in general works on social history. Attention has been already drawn to the uncertainty of the observations on the philanthropic work of religious institutions by Obelkevich and Prochaska.[8] A similar lack of acknowledgement in works concerned with ecclesiastical history and women's social history in England and Wales is also evident.

It might be expected that the social history of the nursing profession would provide some recognition of the religious institutions which established professional nursing practice, standards and terminology. However, potential links to strict disciplinary practices and training imposed by (mostly French) eighteenth- and nineteenth-century Roman Catholic orders and congregations have been almost universally overlooked in the literature.[9] Celia Davis credits the support given to Elizabeth Fry and the 'Protestant Nursing Sisters in Whitechapel' by 'the Dowager Queen Adelaide and the Bishop of London in 1840', adding that 'the Oxford Movement was awakening in the hearts of earnest women the desire for definite religious work . . . in a life dedicated to the care of nursing of the sick'.[10] Roman Catholic hospitals and their training of nurses, however, are not mentioned. The romanticised story of Florence Nightingale's initiative in allowing a few 'nuns' from London to nurse with her in the Crimea is now viewed less favourably by historians of the profession. It is never mentioned that four of the Catholic sisters were later formally honoured by Queen Victoria in recognition of their valour and dedication.[11]

Social histories of nursing concentrate on the reform of the deplorable standards to which secular nursing care had descended in early nineteenth-century England. Only one writer notes that the practice of setting out hospital beds in parallel lines had origins that 'might be traced more to the customs of monasteries than to any early theories of ventilation.'[12] And the same author adds a footnoted qualification elsewhere to excuse the omission of reference to convent origins by noting that ' . . . the medieval religious orders [might be regarded as] the true antecedents of the nursing profession, [but] quantitative information is not available about their role . . . '[13] So, while there has been a peripheral level of awareness, it has been largely dismissed because of misconceived views of the function of Roman Catholic nuns and sisters and a genuine ignorance of their contribution to nursing services, training and hospital administration in nineteenth-century England.[14]

It is striking that studies of the Irish in Britain contain little or no acknowledgement of the dedication of the religious institutions in providing nursing, welfare care and education for Irish immigrant families.[15] Their commitment over the years may be recognised as having benefited second- or third-generation Irish communities.

Yet, some indication of the scope and the scale of the work of these women and their individual endeavours can be found in the many published histories and the private archives of congregations and orders. Such material, however, is both daunting and unwieldy to use except for very close-focused studies and cannot be used to build up quantitative surveys. There are as many similarities as there are variations in how convent communities organised their lives and work. Research concerned with the lives of some religious congregations in nineteenth-century England has gradually opened up the area, however. Susan O'Brien has studied several English and French nineteenth-century congregations established in England and Wales.[16] Susan Mumm's findings and comments, although dealing with Anglican sisterhoods, provide some further clues about the work of the Roman Catholic institutions.[17] Her thesis devotes two chapters to 'Community works' under the headings of nursing, healing, teaching, rescuing and protecting.[18] Hope Stone's thesis on the Foundresses focuses on the work of both Anglican and Roman Catholic communities of women.[19] Caitriona Clear and Maria Luddy are invaluable sources for comparisons of the areas of work engaged in by convents in Ireland because there are many instances of a congregation working under similar conditions in Ireland, England and Wales.[20] Thus the broad outline of the work of nuns and sisters can be discerned. This survey includes examples drawn not only from my own case studies but from the findings of others.

Some of the most reliable and accessible information may be found within contemporary publications which were intended as guides for intended aspirants to the religious life. These incorporated a précis of each order and congregation and it is possible to corroborate material drawn from the compilations of Murphy, Steele, Hohn and Anson and the handbooks of charitable undertakings issued by officially approved church publishers such as Burns and Oates and the Catholic Truth Society.[21] The advertising sections of contemporary annual *Catholic Directories* are also informative. The archdiocesan and diocesan statistical segments in the directories also provide listings of charitable efforts, schools and other institutions, but there are many omissions, ambiguities and inconsistent designations to be found and figures compiled from this source should be read merely as indicators unless corroborative evidence can be used.[22] However, because of the two-tier system operating throughout the educational and nursing services of religious institutions, which allowed for fee-paying services side by side with free or subsidised charges, even these findings remain inconclusive because of the difficulty involved in the identification of charitable or free services.

How we might attempt to identify and categorise the overlapping nature of the undertakings engaged in by the majority of congregations and orders is indicated in the lay-out of Table 6. Some qualification is required in relation to these data because these calculations cannot be taken as faithfully representing the precise volume of each type of work undertaken, since congregations were of differing size. The work of religious may be described as falling within four broad headings:

- those primarily engaged in education, but whose apostolate was, on occasion, combined with the provision of limited nursing and social services;
- communities primarily concerned with social work and care of the poor, but which would provide schools and nursing services, when and if necessary;
- congregations of sisters founded specifically to nurse or provide medical and hospital care; and
- orders of contemplatives, of which a few might offer a limited amount of education or other care within their enclosure.

The categories should not be seen as exclusive but as an attempt to present the major priorities of each congregation. Relatively few concentrated solely on one single, chosen activity but adapted an apostolate which could combine, for example, their role as educationalists with nursing and social work.

Discussion of primary areas of activity begins with education. Later, snapshot studies of three large congregations in 1887, will illustrate how their engagement embraced a number of overlapping services to combine school duties with social care and nursing in the community.[23] This is followed by a brief survey of social work and health care.

EDUCATION

Elementary, Middle and High Schools

The provision and staffing of elementary schools formed the greatest volume of work engaged in by nuns and sisters. In Chapter 2 it was suggested that, to a great extent, the proliferation of new congregations (and consequently the expansion of convent networks, see Chapter 4) was a result of their response to Forster's Education Act of 1870 and the increasing call for new elementary schools for an expanding Catholic population. However, the congregations of sisters categorised in Table 6 as having been primarily engaged in education taught in schools at every level. Initially most congregations began by providing free 'poor' or elementary schools for girls and small boys and mixed parish schools with classes for boys and girls.[24]

It is difficult to suggest even a tentative figure for the number of schools run by religious communities. John Murphy, in *Terra Incognita* (1873), attempted to calculate and analyse the primary school system for the whole of England and Wales in the early 1870s. His findings, although painstaking, are inconclusive because the evidence he drew on was restricted to the 383 Catholic schools in receipt of state grants at that time.[25] Linscott's research indicates that the growth of elementary schools in Lancashire, for example, was as steady and as sustained as the increase of convent numbers. She cites the Roman Catholic diocese of Salford (a small, but highly industrialised area encompassing the Hundreds of Salford and Blackburn in Lancashire), where 'the numbers of Catholic elementary schools rose from 350 in 1870 to 1066 in 1900'.[26] Throughout the nineteenth century there were many convent-run private schools, both free and fee-paying, which remained outside the government grant system and were therefore unaccounted for. A rough indication of the increase in Catholic school numbers is probably congruent with the increase of convent numbers because almost every new convent had a school or schools attached. When an additional school was provided it was most often one that catered for a higher grade of pupil – a direct response to 'major influences on the development of girls' schooling over the years' which was being fuelled by 'currents of social opinion'.[27] Felicity Hunt comments in her introduction to *Lessons for Life: The Schooling of Girls and Women 1850–1950* (1987) that 'the complications of social class in an education system rooted in a solid class structure helped to dictate the educating and socialising experience of girls'.[28] There were few religious congregations which did not perceive and respond to this growing demand for secondary education. Convents established middle schools for girls, both day and boarding pupils, and high schools to university entrance level – if only for the practical reason that fee-paying schools provided a secure income for the community and subsidised the pupils who were taught for free. As Gillian Sutherland has commented, referring to the early twentieth century, 'secondary schools were now established as the royal routes to both gentility and respectability, routes which by definition only some could take'.[29]

The latter half of the century saw an increase in the provision of exclusive, high-class boarding and day establishments for 'young ladies'. Young boys were catered for in some boarding and day schools. Such pupils were described as the 'daughters and sons of gentlemen'. The advertising of convent boarding schools placed great emphasis on the health of the children entrusted to their care. Bracing air, extensive grounds, farm produce and a good train connection to London were attributes which seemed as important as their preparation for Oxford and Cambridge examinations, conversational French and needlework. The convent boarding schools often catered for pupils whose parents worked in the colonies and advertised that the accommodation of children could be continued during the school holidays. Mother Superiors strove to emphasise the broad curricula and modern facilities to be found. For example, one prospectus cites a 'Demonstration Kitchen and completely fitted Chemical Laboratory' for classes in science and domestic science; private bedrooms for pupils and a large gymnasium and well-heated swimming bath.[30] Usually set in large grounds, these schools offered outdoor games and holiday and term-time occupational pursuits which included lawn tennis, croquet, hockey, horse-riding, swimming, dancing and Swedish drill: '[we] give a complete and thorough education on modern lines, filling pupils for the higher positions in the world now open to educated women'.[31]

Analysis of the distribution of Roman Catholic, high-class, convent boarding schools in the period immediately after the First World War reveals that out of 187 advertised in the 1920 edition of the *Catholic Directory*, over half were located in London and the South-East. In all regions, socially 'superior' addresses predominated, such as Ascot, Bournemouth, St. Leonards on Sea, Torquay, Scarborough, Southport, Harrogate, Cheltenham and Salisbury.

Clearly, convent education may be seen as complying with Hunt's claim that, 'the role of the girl's secondary schools established in the late nineteenth and early twentieth century was to prepare girls to become the wives of the bourgeoisie'.[32] To which may be added the recognition that convent schools also presented practical role models for girls contemplating the choice of an alternative lifestyle as a religious sisters – a dimension to be discussed further in Chapter 6.

CONVENT SCHOOLS, &c.

ST. DOMINIC'S CONVENT,

Luton, Bedfordshire.

BOARDING SCHOOL FOR THIS DAUGHTERS OF GENTLEMEN.

Within 25 minutes of London. Healthy situation. Large playgrounds. Superior education. All modern accomplishments. Pupils prepared for public examinations.

BOARDING SCHOOL FOR YOUNG GENTLEMEN under twelve adjoining the Convent.

Apply to the Rev. Mother Prioress.

BENEDICTINE MONASTERY,

St. Mary's Abbey, East Bergholt.

No school. The Religious devote themselves to Prayer, the Solemn Celebration of the Divine Office, Study, and Manual Labour, according to the spirit of the Rule of St. Benedict.

For particulars, apply to the Lady Abbess, St. Mary's Abbey, East Bergholt, Suffolk (Station, Manningtree).

ALDEBURGH-ON-SEA.

URSULINE CONVENT.

Sound Education given by French and English Sisters. Special care is taken to meet all modern requirements. Lessons in Drawing, Painting, Music, Dancing, French and Needlework.

The Convent overlooks the sea, and is situated in its own grounds. Air bracing and restorative. Five minutes from the G.E.R. Station. Lady Boarders received. Moderate terms.

Special care given to young children.

Apply to Rev. Mother Superior.

FRENCH CONVENT, LOWESTOFT,

Boston Lodge.

Boarding School for Young Ladies conducted by the French Sisters of the Immaculate Heart of Mary.

This Convent is offering a high-class education including French, Latin, English, Music, Singing, Painting and Fancy Work. Pupils are prepared for Oxford and Cambridge Examinations.

Boston Lodge is situated in very extensive grounds and close to the sea, thus having the most healthy and bracing sea air possible. Application may be made to the Rev. Mother, or the Rev. ALEXANDER SCOTT, The Presbytery, Lowestoft.

SEE INDEX, pp. 477-479.

ST. MARY'S CONVENT,

The Elms, Cambridge.

(A branch Convent of St. Mary's, Micklegate Bar, York.)

Pupils are prepared for the University Higher Local, Local, Royal Academy of Music and South Kensington Examinations. The staff consists of registered Religious assisted by Masters and Mistresses holding higher certificates.

Every facility is afforded the elder pupils to attend lectures and visit the numerous places of interest in and around Cambridge. Special arrangements are made and separate rooms provided for students over seventeen years of age who wish to follow a particular line of study.

CONVENT OF THE SISTERS OF NOTRE DAME,

Northampton.

BOARDING SCHOOL FOR GIRLS.

This School will repay a visit. All the appointments are of the best and thoroughly up to date. Pupils are prepared for the Oxford Locals and for the Higher and Lower Certificate of the Oxford and Cambridge Joint Board. In order to obtain an independent test of efficiency, the School is examined, inspected and reported on every year by an examiner sent down by the Oxford Delegacy, and his reports have hitherto been excellent.

For particulars apply to the Sister Superior.

1. A typical selection of high-class boarding schools, 1909

CONVENT SCHOOLS, &c.

ST. MARY'S PRIORY,
St. Mary Church, Torquay, S. Devon.

Boarding School for the Daughters of Gentlemen. The course of studies comprises all branches of a higher education. Pupils prepared for the Oxford or Cambridge Local, also Associated Board of Royal Academy and Royal College of Music, and Royal Drawing Society's Examinations. The Climate has proved specially beneficial to children. Tennis court and large playground; country walks and sea bathing. Separate bedrooms for the elder girls. Lady Boarders received.

For particulars, apply to Rev. Mother Prioress, as above.

CONVENT OF NOTRE DAME,
Plymouth.

RECOGNISED SECONDARY SCHOOL.

Pupils are prepared for the University Locals, the Royal Drawing Society, the Royal College and Royal Academy of Music, the National Fröbel Union Society's Diploma, and also for the Teaching Profession.

CONVENT OF THE HOLY FAMILY, EXMOUTH.

Under the Patronage of His Lordship the Bishop of Plymouth.

Select Boarding School for Daughters of Gentlemen, in the healthiest part of the town, with special advantages in Modern Languages. Children are able to talk French after three months' residence. Pupils prepared most successfully for Oxford Local Examinations, Royal Academy of Music, and Drawing. Staff of qualified Teachers. Careful attention paid to the health and deportment of each pupil. Gymnasium, Swimming, Tennis, Basket Ball. Entire charge of pupils whose parents are abroad.

Apply, MOTHER SUPERIOR.

CONVENT OF THE PRESENTATION OF OUR LADY,
Palace Gate, Exeter.

Boarding School for a limited number of young ladies. Day Scholars also received.

The Course of Studies comprises the usual subjects, special attention being given to Needlework and Conversational French. Professors of Dancing and of Calisthenics attend. Pupils may be prepared for the Oxford Locals and Music examinations.

Large and cheerful class-rooms fitted with up-to-date appliances. Beautiful grounds containing Tennis and Croquet lawns, etc. For particulars, apply to the Lady Superior.

URSULINE CONVENT.
North Down Hall, Bideford, North Devon.

Excellent scholastic course: French, Music, Drawing, etc., at moderate charges for Boarders and Day Scholars. Pupils prepared for Oxford and Cambridge Local, also R.A.M. and L.C.M. Examinations. Near Sea and Westward Ho! Golf Links.

2. Selection of high-class boarding schools for the daughters of gentlemen, 1920

While not contradicting the belief that the growth of the Catholic middle class increased demand for higher levels of education, a striking characteristic of convent education for girls was the number of pupils catered for who were not Catholic; as others have noted. O'Brien comments that, 'For some respectable Anglican parents, the "otherness" of Catholic convents, including their French connections, was a positive source of attraction.'[33] Her impression is that this trend increased, a conclusion also reached by Summerfield's study of girls' schools in Lancashire between 1900 and 1950.[34] Expatriate religious communities recently arrived from Europe who set up convent boarding schools did have, of course, the distinct advantage over other educational establishments in having the ability to specialise in providing the children of non-Catholic parents opportunity to acquire 'the purest French accent, the same advantage as in Paris, as well as fluent conversation and special lessons on French literature';[35] but it would seem that some religious superiors, in view of the need to attract non-Catholic pupils, also took care to provide what might have been a measure of reassurance in regard to the description of the non-specific, denominational character of the Christian values taught: 'The aim of the school is to combine a Christian influence and the life of a refined home with sound up-to-date education.'[36]

However, the rise in the number of Protestant children in Catholic schools was not confined to the demands of a small number of the elite upper class or the daughters of the social-climbing middle classes. In 1892 it was noted that, 'In [the schools in] Banbury, the proportion of children stood: Catholic 139, non-Catholic 250; hereby exhibiting a preponderance of Protestant children of nearly 2:1.'[37] One explanation of why this should be so might be found in the numerous reports of school board inspectors who, on the whole, found excellent high standards in the schools run by religious, despite the meagreness of their grants. In 1871, in a school converted out of a former stable for the Ursulines in Upton, an inspector found it to be 'conducted with much care and the instruction is well given'.[38] Yet Sturman reveals that there were serious problems subsequently encountered by the sisters here in their early days. Although aspiring to high standards, they had few resources and many financial worries, and, by 1876, had drawn the criticism of inspectors, 'not about the teaching, which was consistently praised, but about the conditions under which it was given'.[39] Upton was a very poor area and how the sisters managed to obtained funds to make improvements to the heating and lighting of the classroom is unclear, but evidence suggests that it came from the community itself and the Upton Council, who 'regularly visited the school'.[40] When a new classroom was opened in 1879 it was described by inspectors as 'excellent' and 'tastefully decorated'.[41] Twenty years later, an inspector's report on the same school commented that, 'this is a remarkable pleasing Infants' School. The children are bright, happy and intelligent. The little ones evidently obey their teacher because they love her . . . their school life is just what the school life of the young ought to be, full of warmth and sunshine.'[42]

Some indication of a similar congregation's engagement in providing several levels of education is set out in Table 7. The data have been drawn from the records of the Sisters of Notre Dame de Namur (SND), working out of an extensive convent complex in Liverpool. This evidence clearly shows that, although this congregation gained a reputation for the provision of higher education at secondary and university level, in fact, they expended much of their energies in providing for children in their poor schools which became government-aided elementary schools.[43] The Sisters of Notre Dame de Namur taught over six thousand elementary pupils on average each year and several hundred at the higher levels, with an emphasis on continental languages and ladylike attributes, but also including practical classes in subjects such as science and geography. The records for SND entrants in the late 1880s contain instances of sisters with teacher-training qualifications in advanced science long before these was usually taught to girls. After the turn of the century, when greater employment opportunities were opening up for girls, they pragmatically added shorthand and typing to well-rounded curricula that included art, music, science and French.[44]

At the junior level, too, these sisters were willing to experiment. Having deployed the Froebel method since the 1880s in their infant schools, Linscott notes how an enterprising teacher made the acquaintance of Madame Montessori in 1923. The meeting resulted in a pilot scheme that was subsequently put in place incorporating this method with her own ideas.[45]

The archives of the SND contain many examples of HM School Inspectors' praise for teaching practice in the convent schools. The confidential report of an inspector from the Board of Education visiting the Notre Dame convent in Leeds in 1921, for example, stated that, 'The sisters have a happy knack of maintaining excellent discipline with no apparent effort and an atmosphere of cheerful orderly activity prevails throughout the school.'[46]

Fahey, albeit in the context of Irish convent schools but equally applicable to those in England, has clearly identified the reason HM

Inspectors approved of the ethos of the schools run by religious. He concluded that ' . . . [nuns'] educational message was not overly political, its emphasis on "moral instruction" taught a respect for civilised convention and through that, a respect for established authority, both civil and religious'.[47]

Training Colleges and Pupil Teachers

The provision of training colleges for Catholic teachers was an increasingly important aspect of the educational work of some congregations. The SND were foremost in this field, having opened the first successful college in Mount Pleasant, Liverpool in 1855.[48] Linscott claims that 'Namur had evolved a pattern of training which anticipated later developments', having initiated a 'serious contribution to secondary education [for girls] eighty years before the State became concerned with it and more than twenty years before Miss Buss opened the North London Collegiate School'.[49]

The demand for teachers ensured that other congregations came to operate similar training colleges. In 1874 the Society of the Sacred Heart had established their training college in Wandsworth; by 1905 the Sisters of Mercy Training College at Endsleigh was being modelled on the lines of Mount Pleasant.[50] In 1910 the Sisters of St. Paul opened facilities in Birmingham.

Many teaching congregations also operated a system for pupil teachers which allowed a bright girl with modest means to pursue a course of preliminary training as a monitor in their schools at the same time as continuing her own education. Successful candidates were then offered places or scholarships to one of the Catholic teacher training colleges. Linscott has given us an outline of how the SND arranged their own pupil-teacher scheme, which was felt to be some improvement on the monitorial system, 'thirteen year olds were promised training by undertaking a five year apprenticeship for college by teaching and studying under the direction of some qualified head-teacher. They taught in school during the day and were themselves taught in the evenings and on Saturdays.'[51]

How successful these pupil-teacher schemes were may be measured by a survey of pupil teachers from Lancashire, Cheshire and north Wales for the years 1863–70 undertaken by John Murphy and published in 1873.[52] Murphy's report shows that within these years elementary schools from this region produced 182 pupil-teachers who emerged to take up teacher training from fifty elementary Catholic schools in the area. Just over one-

IN 'THE PRACTISING SCHOOL', A STUDENT IS GIVING A GRAMMAR-LESSON, ANALYSIS AND PARSING,
TO A CLASS OF GIRLS; AN S.N.D. LECTURER IS OBSERVING THE LESSON FROM BEHIND THE PIANO!

3. A pupil teacher at work in the classroom, 1892

Source: Sister Jean Bunn, SND, 'The archives of Notre Dame de Namur in Britain',
The Journal of the Catholic Archives Society. 13 (1993), pp. 3–12. Taken from George Lambert's
illustrations for V.C.H., 'A visit to Notre Dame Training College (Liverpool) in
The Catholic Fireside, Vol. XIV, No. 4 (April 1892).

third (34 per cent) were administered and staffed by secular or lay teachers, while two-thirds were run by eight different congregations of active religious. Pupil numbers were estimated at almost 13,000, but very possibly this figure would not have taken into account the half-timers and those attending night classes or Sunday schools.[53] (See Table 8.)

The Liverpool-based SND may be viewed as a leading example of this larger type of teaching congregation and it is possible that Murphy chose the North-West for this reason. How typical his report may be taken of the situation in, say, central London in 1871 is, however, difficult to judge. The dynamic which fuelled the intensity and urgency of providing schools for working-class Catholics in the North-West, which we shall discuss in Chapter 4, will reveal that the initial growth of convent numbers took place earlier across all the northern counties than in the south of England and that the convent-based undertakings were at first concentrated on providing social care and schooling for the poor. Although London had also seen early arrivals of communities with an apostolate that was dedicated to care for the poor, I have suggested that the nature and characteristic of convent expansion in the economically richer South-East became more affected by increasing demands for 'middle-class' and exclusive 'high-class' convent schooling. Suburbanisation and the *entente cordiale* fostered and popularised a wave of fashionable Francomania, which manifested itself in many ways including the desire of polite society to acquire the ability to converse in French.[54] So it is not surprising that so many convent schools capitalised on this fashion, especially as the majority of congregations and orders enjoyed the advantage and opportunity afforded by links with the Continent. This was particularly so in respect of many newly arrived, exiled communities who needed to find methods of generating an income (discussed in Chapters 2 and 5). Furthermore, in Chapter 6 it will be demonstrated that the recruitment of English-born girls to the religious life relied heavily on numbers drawn from convent day and boarding schools. So we should consider whether the steady pursuit and maintenance of high standards of tuition in these schools thus carried an additional focused, if not altogether hidden agenda: that of the perpetuation of the system?

Orphanages, Industrial Schools and Reformatories

Women who had taken religious vows, in addition to working as teachers in the schools, also undertook the care of children committed to orphanages or industrial and reform schools. According to information provided by the *Catholic Directories*, the number of these institutions run by communities of sisters rose from eleven in 1857 to probably about eighty in 1937. Detailed data are set out in Table 9, but what appear to be changes in the description of reform schools, industrial schools and homes for children and girls in these official diocesan listings after the turn of the century create an unsatisfactory blurring of these institutions.[55] Statistics drawn from the Inspectors' Annual Reports for Certified Reformatories and Industrial schools for Roman Catholics do not indicate which of these institutions were run by religious communities of women (see Table 11) and it may be taken that responsibility for some of these relied on male religious orders or lay Catholics. However, some measure of corroboration is possible from figures drawn from information contained in the *Handbook of Catholic Charitable and Social Works*, published in 1912. These data are set out in Table 10.[56]

It is striking how many convent communities took on responsibility for orphans. The care of 'foundlings' had been a tradition for many religious institutions, especially congregations of Sisters of Charity and secular commentary has recognised the inspirational role played by St. Vincent de Paul in Paris whose *Hospice des Enfants Trouvés* was endowed by Louis XIV in 1670.[57] In England, by the mid-1850s, there were five orphanages listed in the *Catholic Directories* as being attached to convents. The number of such institutions grew rapidly, to approximately twenty-six by 1877, thirty-nine by 1897 and fifty-seven by 1917, before falling marginally to just under fifty by 1937.

The increasing number of institutions catering for orphans not only reflects a growing concern for abandoned and parentless children, but also draws attention to the fact that there was no lessening of the social stigma attached to illegitimacy. While not overlooking cases of the loss of both parents, it may be surmised that the majority of these convent-cared 'orphans' were the children of single mothers whose 'respectability' and family's reputation would have been irreparably damaged by the arrival of a child out of wedlock. The extent to which Roman Catholic religious-run orphanages ran adoption services for childless couples in England and Wales would be an interesting area of research to pursue further. It may be seen, too, that the policy of sending batches of orphaned children as immigrants to Canada and Australia for the opportunity of 'a better life' in the colonies was favoured by many secular and religious organisations and there were many Catholic societies set up to assist such emigration. In retrospect, this solution to the problem of the growing numbers of 'orphans' is now questioned as having been neither ethical nor desirable, although it was considered quite acceptable in its day. Many convents were involved in these schemes in one way or another. The Sisters of St. Paul, for instance, through their connection with the Coleshill-based Father Hudson Homes for Children, became involved in the amalgamation of the existing Catholic emigrant societies into one body in 1904. By 1907 these sisters had set up a receiving home for the children in Ottawa.[58] Data on children who were sent away as orphans are still being collected by the Catholic Child Welfare Council, but it is thought that between 1860 and 1930 more than 100,000 children were despatched from England in this way. Of these, over 30,000 went to Canada. Ten per cent of those who went to Canada were Catholic.[59]

In addition to caring for orphaned children and others in need of homes, communities of nuns and sisters were also foremost in undertaking responsibility for the Roman Catholic Church's response to legislation affecting children who came before the law courts. Initially, reformatory and industrial schools had been established in the 1850s and 1860s by the Sisters of Mercy, the Daughters of Charity of St. Vincent de Paul and the Good Shepherd nuns as a result of the Reformatory Schools Act of 1854 and the Industrial Schools Act of 1857.[60] This legislation allowed voluntary bodies to open schools for children who might otherwise have been committed to prison. The religious affiliation of workhouse children was legislated for in 1859 and a further Act in 1862, amended in 1866, allowed poor law boards to send pauper children 'to some school established for the reception, maintenance and education of children of the religion to which such child shall be proved to belong'. Bennett comments that 'the legal position was thus favourable to the Catholic child, providing Catholics were willing and able to open and staff schools'.[61]

Invalid Children and Those with Special Needs

The two decades up to 1917 saw the religious orders and congregations also being increasingly involved in issues related to children's health, especially in regard to providing segregated residential schooling and nursing care for invalid children. Several congregations were already providing institutional care for such children when an Education Act legislating for 'open-air' schools for delicate or sick children came into force in 1907. The Act 'empowered local authorities to appoint school medical officers and to provide open air schools for children who by reason of impaired health need a change of environment or cannot, without risk to their health or educational development, be educated under the normal regime of ordinary school'.[62] This paved the way for further convent initiatives. The drive to provide for what today are termed 'children with special needs' was enthusiastically promoted by Catholic educationalists and others who were particularly concerned with the 'problem of the feeble minded'. An article in *The Crucible* in 1910 claimed that '5 per cent of the entire population of Great Britain are feeble-minded'. The writer, Alice Vowe Johnson, called for legislation to allow for the establishment of residential schools and farm colonies 'situated in healthy open country, far from human habitations'.[63] Foremost in residential educational care for invalid children were the Servants of the Sacred Heart of Jesus who had already opened 'a home for mentally defective children' in 1901.[64]

In 1910 the Chigwell sisters (SSHJM) opened a similar residential school in Liverpool, which was quickly followed by second one in 1915 and then by several others. The Daughters of Charity of St. Vincent de Paul, whose 'home for crippled children' in Clapham had been founded in 1907, transferred their operations to Pinner as an 'Open Air School and TB Hospital' for children in 1912. In addition, the Sisters of the Poor Servants of the Mother of God in Brighton, the Daughters of the Cross in Margate and Much Hadham, the Sisters of Mercy in Eltham and Clacton-on-Sea, the Sisters of Providence in Herne Bay, the Dominican Sisters in Notting Hill and the Little Company of Mary in Isleworth, to name but a few, were active in expanding the field of child health care.[65] Many of these establishments were situated on what were then the outskirts of London, in rural areas within the Home Counties or on the south coast. Such locations were particularly suited to convent activity devoted to health care and nursing. That the numbers of convents moving in or re-establishing themselves in seaside or rural locations continued to increase, therefore, is no surprise. Such developments illustrate the point that active religious congregations were not slow in their response to changing social needs. They were prepared to be innovative and quickly responded to the opportunities that opened up.

One of the earliest activities of the Daughters of St. Vincent de Paul (DVDP) was the institutionalised care for the blind and the deaf and dumb which they began to provide in 1870. This was before the Education Act of 1876, which made provision for compulsory residential schooling for blind children, and long before legislation for deaf and dumb schools came into being in 1893. This congregation's responsibility for the operation of these institutions existed throughout the period reviewed here.

ST. VINCENT'S OPEN-AIR HOSPITAL AND SCHOOL FOR CRIPPLED BOYS AND GIRLS

Eastcote, Pinner.

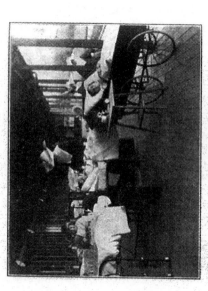

The object of this work is to provide home care, education and training for crippled boys and girls. There is accommodation for 115 boys and 20 girls. Medical and surgical attention is a leading feature, as nearly all cases of crippling are susceptible at least of amelioration. The "open-air" treatment is a special feature. The Hospital is under the care of the Sisters of Charity of St. Vincent de Paul, and is certified by the Home Office and Board of Education. It is approved by the MINISTRY OF HEALTH as a Sanatorium for children suffering from surgical tuberculosis. For terms and form of application, apply to the SISTER SUPERIOR. Contributions towards the maintenance and building funds are urgently solicited by, and all particulars may be obtained from, the

SISTER SUPERIOR, Sisters of Charity,

St. Vincent's, Eastcote, Pinner.

Telephone : Pinner 59.

ST. GERARD'S CHILDREN'S ORTHOPÆDIC HOSPITAL,

Coleshill, near Birmingham.

Hospital for Children suffering from Tubercular and other Joint Diseases, Infantile Paralysis, etc., under the care of the Sisters of Charity of St. Paul. Certified by the Board of Education and Ministry of Health. Efficient staff of Sisters for day and night duty. Individual teaching conducted in the wards by special trained Sisters. A fully-equipped Massage Medical Gymnasium and Electrical Department. Open-air treatment afforded under the most advantageous conditions. Ward patients, 45/- per week : private patients, three guineas upwards.

Orthopædic Surgeons: Mr. Naughton Dunn, M.A., M.B., Ch.B., Mr. Malkin, M.D., Ch.B., Mr. Moir, M.B, Ch.B. *Medical Officers:* Dr. B. E. Wall, M.D., Oxon, Dr. Bosworth Wall, M.B., Ch.B. *Dental Surgeon:* Mr. Elliott, L.D.S., R.C.S., F.Z.S.

Secretary: Right Rev. Mgr. Hudson.

☩

J. M. J.

SISTERS OF BON SECOURS,

166 Westbourne Grove, London, W. 11.

Under the patronage of His Eminence the Cardinal Archbishop of Westminster.

The Sisters of Bon Secours are trained, and nurse the sick, rich and poor, of every creed, at their own homes.

For further particulars, apply to the Rev. Mother, above address.

ST. MARY'S CONVENT,

Shanklin, I.W.

The Sisters of Mercy receive Religious of all Orders who require change of air after illness or the hard work of Schools, and delicate Sisters, whom a few months in the salubrious climate of the Isle of Wight may restore to perfect health. Daily Mass in the House.

G G

4. Open air hospital for children and other nursing services, 1926

CONVENT OF THE MOST HOLY SACRAMENT,

35 Brompton Square, S.W.

Ladies received as boarders. Home for Governesses.

Lessons given in Foreign Languages, Music, Singing and Painting.

English Branch of the International Catholic Association for the Protection of Girls.

For particulars apply to the Rev. Mother Superior.

ST. ELIZABETH'S HOME FOR DISTRICT AND PRIVATE NURSING,

172 Renfrew Street, Glasgow.

The above was founded in January 1893, to provide trained nurses to attend the sick poor in their own homes, free of charge.

Donations and Subscriptions are much needed.

There is also a Home for paying patients and a staff of private nurses.

Application to be made to Miss White, Matron.

CLAREMONT HOUSE,

St. Albans.

Home of Rest for Women, under care of the Sisters of Mercy. Within easy access of London. Fine country walks around; nice air.

Charges, from 8s. a week and upwards. No distinctions of creed.

Full particulars from the Sister-in-Charge, Claremont House, Alma-road, St. Albans.

SISTERS OF CHARITY OF ST. VINCENT DE PAUL,

11 St. John Street, Edinburgh.

St. Ann's Home for respectable Girls out of Situation and in Business.

Terms from 6s. weekly. References required.

THE SISTERS OF THE SACRED HEARTS OF JESUS AND MARY,

CHIGWELL, ESSEX.

The Members of this Institution afford Homes to Orphans and Poor and Feeble-minded Children of both sexes. They superintend Hospitals and Homes for Penitent Women. They accept the direction of Public Elementary Schools, and the training of young girls as Pupil Teachers.

For Particulars apply to the Mother General, The Convent, Chigwell, Essex, or to the Superioresses of any of the following branch houses :

St. Pelagia's Homes : Limehouse, Highgate, Tottenham, and Rotherhithe.

The Sacred Heart Home, Mount Vernon, Liberton, Edinburgh.

The House of Providence, West Dingle, Liverpool.

St. Mary's Home, Charlotte Street, Glasgow.

The Cottage Hospital and Elementary Schools, Aberdare.

The Hospital and Elementary Schools, Old Cumnock, N.B.

The Hospital and Dispensary, Daliburgh, South Uist, Hebrides.

The Ophthalmic Hospital, Chigwell, Essex.

The Orphanage, Workroom and Elementary Schools, Rothesay.

St. Mary's Orphanage, North Hyde.

Special School for Feeble-minded Children of Both Sexes, certified by the Board of Education on March 27th, 1902, Field Heath House, Hillingdon, Middlesex.

The Cathedral School for Boys, Oban.

The Elementary Schools, Sudbury, Suffolk.

The Elementary Schools, Chideock, Dorset.

The Training Home for Pupil Teachers, 25 and 27 Tredegar Square, Mile End, London, in connection with the Guardian Angels' Schools, Mile End, and the Good Shepherd Schools, Stepney.

House of Providence, Durran Hill, Carlisle. Home for Homeless Women.

---

5. Sisters of the Sacred Hearts of Jesus and Mary and other nursing services, 1907

OVERLAPPING ACTIVITIES: SCHOOLS, CHARITY
NURSING AND SOCIAL WORK

We may now examine how some overlapping of undertakings occurred in response to local needs, such as when a community undertook the organisation of poor schools, Sunday schools or night classes for women, day-crèches, institutions and orphanages. The activities of three congregations of sisters of charity in the year 1887 have been selected to illustrate the overlapping of activities in education, nursing and social care which these active institutions undertook[66] (see Table 12).

In 1887 the sisters of charity of St. Paul the Apostle (SSP) may be considered as primarily a teaching congregation which had expanded into ancillary undertakings. With a membership of just under 400 sisters at this time, they had responsibility for eighty-three mixed boys' and girls' parish schools and nineteen girls' parish schools, of which seventy-seven included facilities for infants. They also ran twenty-three select middle-class boarding schools. A home for workhouse boys, a hospice and a night school were additional operations.[67]

Between 1847 and 1937 these sisters opened and staffed at least 127 parish elementary schools in the Midlands and the North at one time or another. During this time, night schools, half-time pupils and a system for pupil-teacher training were also provided. Forty-seven of their convents were engaged in parish visiting, providing social care, nursing and other relief. By the first decade of the twentieth century the sisters' home for workhouse boys had expanded into what was to become a large convent complex in Coleshill, Birmingham. Here were contained several different operational units for the nursing care and education of invalid and homeless boys and girls.[68]

In 1887 the Daughters of St. Vincent de Paul (DVDP), in addition to their dedicated parish work among the poor which took the form of visiting, caring and nursing, also staffed twelve orphanages, industrial and reform schools for boys and girls, nine day schools under government grant, two middle day schools and a hospital. They operated an asylum and school for the blind and another for the deaf and dumb. Other undertakings included six night schools and training workshops, three crèches for infants of working mothers and a home for business girls and pupil-teachers. As one of the larger active communities working in England, they continued to expand dramatically well into the twentieth century by becoming involved and responsible for many kinds of institutional care.[69]

By the second decade of the twentieth century the DVDP had charge of fifty-three institutions and taught in forty-eight elementary schools. By 1924 they were responsible for works and associations within seventy Catholic parishes.[70] In their distinctive habits and *cornette* headgear the 'French sisters', as they were often called, were familiar figures in the back streets and slums of many cities (see Plates 6 and 7).[71] For the most part, the cloaks, long skirts and veiled bonnets worn by other less recognisable active sisters did not stand out quite so clearly. Indeed, in comparison to the everyday garb of widows or the sombre dress adopted by women of other denominations who also engaged in good works among the poor, the nuns and sisters out in the streets were not overly distinguished by their dress.

The Sisters of Mercy provide the last example of overlapping activities which combined education with social work and nursing (Table 12).[72] These sisters' convent-based activities also increased well into the twentieth century until they constituted the largest, albeit autonomously administered, convent network.[73] In 1887 they were already engaged in providing forty-one elementary and infants' schools and twenty-four schools described as catering for superior and middle-class pupils. They had responsibility for nine orphanages, which included industrial and reform schools. By this time they were operating six Houses of Mercy for women and one night refuge in addition to a training school for servants, five night schools and workshops, and a home for business girls and pupil teachers. They also operated one hospital.

In the inter-war period there were almost 1,600 professed Sisters of Mercy working in England and Wales (to which must be added over 200 in novitiate training). They were educating and taking responsibility for 40,000 children, over 800 of whom were orphans or in care. These sisters also nursed almost 500 hospital and sanatoria patients, including war veterans. By 1931 there were well over 300 girls resident in their Houses of Mercy.[74]

Congregations with multifaceted apostolates such as the three examples above contributed to and were involved with the broader social care needs in each diocese. The extent of this activity has been outlined in Tables 9 and 10. The calculations drawn from the *Catholic Directories*, although marred by some inconsistencies and changes in the categorising of some children's homes and the reform and industrial schools, present defined patterns of growth and development of social services, while a clearer snapshot of the volume of Catholic charitable and social work, laid out in

The Roman Cahtolic Cathedral
of St. John's, Salford
Source: W.A. Shaw, *Manchester Old and
New*, Vol 2. (London, 1894), p. 137.

Oxford street, Manchester
Source: W.A. Shaw, *Manchester Old and
New*, Vol 2 (London, 1894), p. 136.

6. Daughters of Charity of St. Vincent de Paul go about
their business in Salford and Manchester in the 1890s

7. Dispensing bread: Daughters of Charity of St. Vincent de Paul, 1916

Source: RTE Photographic Library Archive,
Photograph from the Murtagh Collection Dublin.

Table 10 and relating to one year, 1912, illustrates that most Catholic charitable endeavour at this time was in the hands of women's religious congregations. A large measure of their energies was devoted to the institutional care of orphans, prostitutes ('fallen women'), the 'aged poor' and various health problems inherent in children brought up in conditions of poverty. At a time well before the concept of 'political correctness' had been coined, it is striking that there were no such qualms about using direct language to describe some of the charities: 'Home for Children with Scalp Diseases', 'Home for Deformed and Incurable Girls', 'Home for Defective Children' and 'Home for Inebriate Women'. To be in receipt of charity in 1912 was to be faced with a harsh and realistic terminology.

Members of religious congregations were particularly concerned with providing social services for working girls and women, especially in safeguarding single women who found themselves out of regular employment. In the late nineteenth century finding a job as a trained domestic servant was still seen as the best option for girls who needed to earn their living and, into the early decades of the twentieth century, large numbers of convents offered training to girls as servants or supplied shelter to girls who found themselves unemployed, colloquially described as servants 'out of place'. Having somewhere to go for shelter, if dismissed, was particularly important before the mid-1930s when unemployment insurance was not available to servants. At one end of the social scale, the sisters of Mercy supplied training in domestic and laundry work and set up sewing workshops for destitute girls so that they might later earn their living, and, at the other end of the scale, established hostels and homes for 'respectable' girls working in business as clerks or shop assistants. The accommodation provided by the convents assured the safety and protection of single girls living away from home who might otherwise find themselves friendless or vulnerable to abuse.

The administration and staffing of soup kitchens, night shelters and the daily visiting and relief of the poor also took up much of the energies of congregations of Sisters of Charity. Although impossible to quantify, the visiting and covert work in poor working-class and slum areas was widespread and accounted for a large proportion of the social services provided by religious.[75] The need to relieve the distress of the poor was not confined to Victorian Britain, however. In the inter-war period considerable levels of poverty in industrial cities and towns still existed. In the 1930s over 17 per cent of the working class on Merseyside lived below the poverty level. Southampton had 20 per cent and 'even in prosperous

Bristol' there was almost 11 per cent.[76] Congregations such as the Little Sisters of the Poor, with a convent in most cities and towns, made visiting and relief of the poor in urban areas their particular apostolate, but many of the congregations of active sisters who staffed poor schools often undertook similar social care and parish work in addition to their duties as teachers. The volume of this unofficial social work, contributed by what were often known as the 'walking nuns', is only now being recognised because today's members of religious organisations are far less reluctant to make specific reference to their past efforts. For example, the Mercy Sisters give an account of Yorkshire in the 1880s:

> Poverty was very great in Sheffield at that time . . . and, as the sisters were without regular income, a fee-paying Private School for middle-class families was opened to provide basic needs for themselves and enable them to help the poor they had come to serve. Visitation of the sick and poor in their homes was done in the evenings and at weekends, groceries and clothing being discreetly distributed.[77]

PRE-SCHOOL CARE

Day crèches for the infants of millworkers and other women were one of the community services provided by the DVDP, whose apostolate was primarily dedicated to social care. However, it is puzzling to find the identification and listing of day crèches for infants to be quite small, indicating, perhaps, that this service was officially largely under-acknowledged. Possibly many 'infant' schools in industrial towns, particularly those run by the Sisters of Mercy and the Sisters of St. Paul (SSP) were more akin to modern 'play-groups' which took in children at a younger age than the regular schools. There are indications, too, that the provision of day care for babies was not confined to these so-called 'Sisters of Charity', there were many other congregations actively but quietly involved.

An example from 1873 encapsulates this need. A circular described as 'recently issued by a Dominican Reverend Mother Prioress in a manufacturing town in England', cited by Murphy, explains just one facet of these sisters' work in that town:

> For the greater part of the last seven years we have had a Crèche for babies. In this school we receive infants from six weeks old, and take charge of them from six o'clock in the morning until six in the

evening. They are the children of poor working women, who are employed all day in the factories, or at other manual labour. Our object is to save these poor children from the want of wholesome food, exposure to the damp and cold of the street and from the terrible effects of the bad nursing of mere children. Often, too, they are left in the charge of old women, who, to escape the trouble of these infants, dose them with opiates, sometimes poisoning them to such an extent, that even if they recover, their brains are injured for life. We are now engaged in building a large and well-ventilated room for these poor little ones . . . [78]

CONVENT-ADMINISTERED INSTITUTIONALISED CARE: ASYLUMS, HOMES AND HOSPITALS

The formalised organisation of social care spawned the growth of large asylums and institutionalised hospital nursing. Government-funded assistance for charitable enterprise had been much increased towards the end of the century and Prochaska has calculated that, by 1891, there were 200 charitable institutions receiving state aid, including many that were Catholic.[79] The growing number of Roman Catholic, convent-based complexes which ran large asylums and institutions were themselves reliant on bureaucratically-run power structures that had developed to manage the increased demand for this type of formalised social care. Of necessity, many of their operations had become larger and more institutionalised. What Foucault has called 'the swarming of disciplinary mechanisms' was hardened within convent schools, orphanages, hospitals and asylums and led to conditions which, if judged by today's standards and not by those of the past, appear over-repressive.[80] The treatment meted out to those who were perceived as social outcasts was invariably strict and often harsh, whether they be 'fallen women', illegitimate or abandoned children, or social misfits of any age or with any physical handicap.

In Chapter 2 we noted that changes in legislation affecting the Poor Law had a particular impact on the welfare of single women with children. Although indoor institutional care had gradually improved from the 1870s onwards, Thane points out that there was ' . . . a serious reduction in aid especially to the elderly and single mothers who had been the chief recipient of outdoor relief'.[81] Certain religious communities filled this gap, although this category of care is difficult to define because most of the relevant figures are buried within the statistics for 'homes for women and

THE SISTERS OF CHARITY.

9 Lower Seymour-street, Portman-square, London, W.

The following charitable works are under the care of the Sisters, and all are supported by voluntary subscriptions : A *Crèche* or Day Nursery for infants ; an Orphanage ; a Home for young business girls ; an Elementary Day School for girls and infants.

The Sisters give breakfasts to the poorest of the children attending the parochial Day Schools during the winter months.

The poor of the parish and those of St. Charles', Ogle-street and Warwick-street, are relieved and visited at their own homes, and receive religious instruction by the Sisters.

Needlework is done by the Orphans ; and the Sisters will be grateful if ladies will patronise this work, by having under-linen and children's clothes, &c., made at the Convent.

Gifts of old clothes for men and women, &c., will be gratefully received.

Yearly subscriptions and donations, however small, will be thankfully accepted, and can be sent to the Very Rev. Canon Gildea, D.D., Spanish-place Presbytery, W. ; or to Sister Joseph Costello, 9 Lower Seymour-street, Portman-square, W.

ST. MARY'S ORPHANAGE FOR GIRLS,

Richmond-Hill, Leeds.

Manager—The Bishop of Leeds.

Treasurer and Secretary—The Right Revd. Dr. Cowgill, Bishop of Olenus, Bishop's House, Leeds.

The Sisters of Mary Immaculate receive orphan and deserted girls under fourteen years of age, educate them along with the children of the parish, in St. Mary's Schools, and train them in all branches of domestic duties.

Application to be made to Rev. Mother Superior, as above.

Donations and subscriptions are earnestly solicited. Cheques and P.O.O. may be made payable to Mrs. Mary O'Dea, St. Mary's Convent, Leeds ; or to the Treasurer.

SISTERS OF MISÉRICORDE

(OF SÉEZ)

St. Vincent's House, 49 Queen-Street, Hammersmith, W.

The object of this Community is to nurse the sick at their own homes, whether rich or poor, Catholics or others.

For further particulars, apply to the Rev. Mother, as above, and at "The Firs," Lower Caversham, Oxon.

THE SISTERS OF CHARITY OF ST. VINCENT OF PAUL,

Carlisle-Place, Victoria-street, Westminster.

(Near the Victoria Station).

Under the patronage of the Archbishop of Westminster,

The House of Charity contains the following works : an orphanage for girls over two years of age, work-room, and a middle-class day school for girls ; classes of preparation for first Communion, and catechetical instruction on Sundays for girls also ; a night-school for men and boys ; and the daily visiting and relieving of the poor and sick of the two parishes of Westminster, one of the most destitute parts of London.

As these works are supported by voluntary offerings, and the greater number of the children are entirely left on the Sisters' hands, they are compelled to appeal for help, that they may carry on their work.

Yearly subscriptions, however small their amount, would be gladly accepted, and can be remitted to the Sister Superioress, Carlisle-place, Victoria-street, Westminster.

Plain and fine needlework executed in the work-room ; also embroidery and artificial flowers for churches.

A Soup Kitchen has been opened for the benefit of the poor of the two parishes, for which subscriptions in kind or money are most earnestly requested.

ST. JOHN'S INSTITUTION FOR THE DEAF AND DUMB,

Boston Spa, Yorkshire.

Under the charge of the Sisters of Charity of St. Vincent of Paul.

The above Institution is the <u>only</u> Catholic School in England for the Deaf and Dumb.

Catholic parents, having deaf children, should apply to the School Authority to send them to St. John's Institution, and not to any Protestant school. By the Elementary Education (Blind and Deaf Children) Act of 1893, the School Authorities have power to pay the cost of maintenance, clothing and education in the above Institution.

Particulars of Admission obtained from the Secretary.

Special accommodation and board provided if required.

According to the Act of Parliament, 1893, the Managers are required to raise about £2000 each year ("one third of the expenses of maintenance") from private sources.

Subscriptions and donations are therefore necessary for its continuance, and are earnestly requested.

Illustrated Report, with list of subscribers, sent post-free on application to the Secretary, Rev. Edward W. Dawson, Boston Spa, R.S.O., Yorkshire.

---

8. A selection of charitable undertakings, 1907

girls' and do not surface as 'mother and baby homes' until the first decades of the new century (see Table 9). In fact, the Sisters of the Sacred Hearts of Jesus and Mary had already expanded their apostolate to open one of first mother and baby homes in London in 1890 and they went on to open another, non-denominational home in Liverpool in about 1897.[82]

Asylums for the rescue and rehabilitation of prostitutes and other 'unfortunate women' identified as 'penitents' also witnessed steady growth (see Table 10). The *Catholic Directory* of 1857 notes two 'Houses of Refuge' and there are at least twenty-five similar establishments listed by 1937.[83] The incarceration of women in institutions and asylums was affected by the Mental Deficiency Act of 1913, which 'permitted detention of feeble-minded unmarried mothers dependant on poor relief'.[84] Harris has drawn attention to the curious silence of feminists when this legislation was enacted, commenting that 'women child-care workers and asylum attendants played a prominent role in the campaign which gave rise to this measure'.[85] Nothing is known of the reaction, if any, of the religious congregations of women who were engaged in this work, but they would not have been unaware of the debate and the problems inherent in providing for the protection of vulnerable women without imposing total incarceration.

The provision of sheltered care for the aged was conducted mainly by the sisters of Nazareth and the Little Sisters of the Assumption. They were active in many towns and cities and the number of their homes steadily increased. Here again, statistics extracted from entries listed in the *Catholic Directories* (Table 9) fall somewhat below the numbers cited in the 1912 *Handbook of Catholic Charities and Social Works* (Table 10), but not sufficiently as to distort emerging patterns of activity. By the first decades of the twentieth century there were anything from twenty-five to thirty homes for poor and elderly people in operation. Such institutions were, of their nature, relatively hidden from public view and of individual smaller scale.

In contrast to communities engaged in education or social work there were few congregations which were engaged solely in the administration and/or staffing of hospitals, nursing services and convalescent homes. Although difficult to isolate with precision, it would seem that the number of religious orders and congregations specifically dedicated to nursing the sick increased from just one in 1857, to ten by 1897 and fifteen by 1937.[86] However, it is possible that the number of places run by these few specialist nursing communities was quite considerable, especially in respect of convalescent and home nursing care. Calculations drawn from the *Catholic Directories* (Table 9) indicate that a total of twenty-two hospitals and nursing or convalescent homes were being administered by religious by 1917 with seven more by 1937. In 1912 (Table 10) The *Handbook of Catholic Charities and Social Works* listed fourteen hospitals and twelve convalescent homes.

Hospital and nursing care services run by religious were established in many parts of England and Wales. Some of the larger hospitals became foremost institutions in the medical world. For example, the Sisters of Mercy's Hospital of St. John and St. Elizabeth in St. John's Wood, removed there in 1899, began its existence in 1856 in a house at 46 Great Ormond Street, London, almost immediately after the sisters returned from the Crimean War.[87] Next door in the street, was Dr Charles West's now world-famous Children's Hospital, opened by him some four years earlier in 1852.[88] It is not recorded whether, in their early days, they had much contact or exchange of views with the hospital next door for, although established to serve the poor and later described as caring for 'incurable female' patients, in 1864 the sisters had almost half their fifty beds allocated to a children's ward which was equipped with toys and hobby-horses.[89]

Hospitals run by religious were also established to serve and be supported by their local community. For example, the Providence Free Hospital, in St. Helen's, Lancashire, established by the Poor Servants of the Mother of God in 1882, was described in the 1890s as ' . . . the only free hospital in the town [with] surgical and medical cases received of all creeds. There are also paying wards.'[90] The method of dedicating income from fee-paying wards together with doctors' and surgeons' fees to subsidise free medical and nursing care was not, of course, unique to hospitals and nursing services conducted by religious. The system was commonly practised in secular-run hospitals.[91] Likewise, in the large measure of financial support they received from local committees and wealthy patrons (see Chapter 5) religious-run hospitals also differed little from secular-administrated medical care. However, advertisements in the *Catholic Directories* for nursing services and hospitals almost always made mention of the ethical standards employed by religious in caring for 'rich or poor, Catholics or others' without distinction.[92] Other congregations specifically engaged in nursing and hospital administration were the Bon Secours Sisters, the Little Company of Mary, the Sisters of Misericorde and several communities of Augustinians, some of whom specialised in caring for mental maladies.

A drawback to the greater development of hospital and nursing care provided by religious may have been the frustration brought about by

Church law which had, since the twelfth century, 'prohibited religious from giving aid in childbirth and from attending women in maternity homes'.[93] Added to this was the unhelpful development contained in the new code of Canon Law, published in 1918, which forbade women with religious vows from practising medicine and surgery.[94] The latter was, in any case, thought to be an unsuitable profession even for secular women at that time. The ruling on maternity nursing came about through Rome's curious conviction that it threatened the chastity and vocations of celibate nuns. Although little evidence exists, members of the nursing congregations must have often come in contact with confinement cases. According to her biographer, Mary Potter (The Little Company of Mary Sisters), 'was almost a century in advance of her time' in her views on maternity nursing in 1877. She desired her patients to have the benefit of 'scientific treatment' and it is on record that her sisters began to provide full maternity nursing care until they were prevented from doing so by Cardinal Manning when he heard of her plans to apply to the Rome for official permission to continue with this work.[95] The lifting of these prohibitions did not come until 1936 with *Constans ac Sedula* – the publication of the instruction which allowed for dispensation under Canon Law. But change was only achieved before a long, hard battle had been fought by many different congregations to relax the rule.[96] In the end, it was Mother Mary Martin, foundress of the Irish Medical Missionaries of Mary, who argued that she had members of her congregation who had entered the community already qualified as doctors. She was thus able to negotiate from a position of some strength and challenged the Vatican ruling vigorously until she won the concession to allow religious sisters to use their medical qualifications.[97]

CONCLUSION

Even if viewed as professional providers of educational, health and welfare care specifically dedicated to serving the needs of the Roman Catholic community of England and Wales, which had grown from perhaps 750,000 in the early 1850s to about 2.5 million (or possibly up to twice this figure) in the early 1930s, then the religious congregations and orders of women were clearly very significant.[98] However, there is a great deal of evidence to suggest that their contribution to society was even more widespread than this. In almost every aspect of their work active sisters provided services which were used by Catholic and non-Catholics alike.

By far the greatest amount of convent-based work was undertaken in the provision of education. Communities of religious staffed, administered or owned free and fee-paying elementary schools, middle day and boarding schools and exclusive, high-class, convent schools and colleges. Quantification of the exact number of these schools is not possible, but their growth was at least equal to the increase in the number of convents outlined in Chapter 4. The majority of the new convents had one or more schools attached, to which were added orphanages, houses of mercy or institutions such as industrial schools, special schools for invalid children or training workshops. Several teaching congregations also set up teacher-training colleges and many also supported pupil-teachers within their schools. The provision of high-class boarding and day school education for girls became the speciality of some congregations in response to growing demands from an increasingly wealthy middle-class society.

The diversity of the work meant that many congregations engaged in overlapping services. Elementary school teaching sisters visited the poor in their local areas, provided night classes and gave shelter to women out of employment. Some Sisters of Charity expanded their social work to embrace the education and care of the physically handicapped or administered hospitals for sick children. Institutionalised care of the aged poor, the rescue of prostitutes, home nursing, hospitals and convalescent homes and care of the mentally ill also were provided by many congregations. The level and variety of these services represented a considerable contribution to voluntary charitable aid from the latter half of the nineteenth century through to the inter-war years.

These undertakings required a formidably large workforce. Without a continuing response from young women willing to embrace the professionalism and vocation that was required of those within religious life, the work of the convents could neither have been sustained nor expanded as it was. The dynamic motivating the dedicated women who took on this work might be summed up by a description of how one congregation, in 1869, strove to follow the dictates of their apostolate. Sisters were instructed to be ' . . . humble of heart, simple and modest in your dress and in your whole conduct. Love the poor and know how to understand their needs and their suffering. There are two things in life: Jesus Christ and the poor.'[99]

As we shall see in Chapter 6, the high standards expected of active sisters were demanding and there were many factors which determined the success of recruitment drives. Despite the often quoted and, according to Clear, half-jesting, self-depreciating remark made by Mary Aikenhead, foundress of the Irish Sisters of Charity, that 'we are but ignorant women and do nothing but spin and obey', the life of the active religious constituted hard work, long hours and a total dedication to serving others in whatever way, wherever and for whomsoever required their skills.[100]

CHAPTER FOUR

Networks of Convents, 1857–1937

S O SPECTACULAR WAS the proliferation of new congregations and orders throughout England and Wales in the decades after the mid-century that an element of public alarm was raised. A pamphlet in 1872 warned of 'swarms of Jesuits [attracted] to this country . . . who had got wind of a vast horde of potential recruits to Roman Catholic convents'.[1] Such fears were heightened by several unsuccessful campaigns to obtain legislation for convent inspection.[2]

It is certainly striking to examine the wide geographical distribution and impressive, spreading networks of new convent branch houses. In Chapter 2 the steady increase in the number of new arrivals or native foundations from the mid-nineteenth century onwards has been described. By the end of the third decade of the twentieth century there were at least 175 different orders and congregations. This growth is demonstrated by the following figures: by 1857 at least thirty-one orders and congregations had established 100 convents; there were sixty-eight orders and congregations with 278 convents by 1877; 105 orders and congregations with 469 convents by 1897; 161 orders and congregations with 800 convents by 1917; and 175 orders and congregations with 956 convents by 1937.

These communities' response to the increasing need for schools, nursing, hospital and social services became the driving force behind their subsequent expansion (see Table 13).

An examination of the expansion and deployment of these convent numbers and their regional locations offers a more accurate measurement and insight into the increasing volume of work nuns and sisters undertook.[3] However, we must also consider the deployment of these new convent houses in terms of type and function. It is possible to quantify the absolute numbers of convents and their rate of expansion in terms of the function and type of each house and the decades which experienced the greatest percentage of growth (see Table 14).

It has been already indicated that religious communities of women were governed by their own constitution and rules. Congregations also developed very individually in the type of work undertaken, their 'apostolate'. Some congregations and orders remained small and localised while others grew to be very large, with a network of convents spread across a number of counties in England and Wales. The work undertaken by the communities ranged from running schools to providing social services of every kind and, while some proportional fluctuation is evident, clearly the rapid rate of increase in the number of convents was generated mainly by active communities from the mid-nineteenth century onwards.[4] Convents of active nuns and sisters accounted for between two-thirds and three-quarters of all religious houses by 1877 and these establishments maintained that proportion thereafter. A smaller number – 18 per cent – of all convents were run by the mixed communities (providing the combination of an active apostolate with the contemplative life) in 1857 – a figure which, while modest, subsequently held steady in relation to the overall increase of all convent numbers, so that by 1937, there were twenty-six different congregations thus described, occupying 155 convents and making up just over 16 per cent of all convents.

By contrast, but consistent in terms of the small number of foundations of contemplative orders (see Chapter 2 and Tables 4 and 5), the number of 'houses' for this type of nun made up only a tiny proportion of all convents in England and Wales throughout the period. Contemplatives in monastic orders accounted for almost 14 per cent of the convents in 1857, but this figure had dropped to less than 6 per cent by the end of the century. A small, but noticeable upswing from 1917 onwards raised the proportion of contemplative communities to just 7 per cent by 1937.

It may be noted that the wide variance in growth rates between the active, mixed and contemplative convents can be attributed to their different modes of apostolate. Furthermore, the scope and scale of a congregation's undertakings can be related direct to the number of its branch houses or convents. Only a handful of communities operated out of a single convent house. This is demonstrated in Table 15, which indicates the growth of branch houses for some of the more widespread active congregations whose engagement in education, nursing and social care in every part of England and Wales we have already touched upon.

These active convents did not share similar administrative systems. Convents of the Irish-founded Sisters of Mercy, for example, were the most geographically widely spread and undertook by far the greatest number of all convent-based activities. Although categorised here under a single heading, the convents of the Sisters functioned autonomously.[5] They operated out of a series of small foundations, each with branch houses, and had no centralised mother house. The other sisters described in Table 15 were communities which functioned under the direction of a central mother house. For the Daughters of Charity of St. Vincent de Paul (DVDP) this was in Paris.[6] The Sisters of Charity of St. Paul the Apostle (SSP) had established a mother house in Birmingham from 1864 onwards. The Poor Sisters of Nazareth's mother house was in London and the Little Sisters' in Paris.

The increasing number and the wider distribution of convents suggests a marked expansion of new undertakings on the part of the nuns and sisters. It is not possible, however, to produce an accurate head count of women who were members of religious communities. As will be discussed later, the censuses of population are of peripheral use only. However, it is possible to surmise that the number of women entering religious life grew at an increasing rate. Except when a new convent branch house was being established, there were rarely fewer than six members of a community in each house (as dictated by Canon Law in 1918). Once settled and operational, an average of about twelve for each convent has been cited as an accepted figure, although my calculations would consider fifteen as more realistic.[7] We need to be aware that a single address listed as a convent in the *Catholic Directory* might often contain an extensive complex with, perhaps, several schools and an orphanage and a hospital attached. For example, the Mount Pleasant convent of the Sisters of Notre Dame de Namur (SND) in Liverpool housed sixty professed sisters in 1878 at this one location. Numbers rose rapidly until, by 1937, there were ninety-three sisters there, the majority of whom were engaged in teaching in local elementary schools. They undertook the running of eight elementary schools, one high school, a teachers' training college, night classes and various other activities concerned with parish work.[8] A similar example may be found near Birmingham. In 1907 four members of the SSP took charge of their newly opened St. Edward's Home for Boys in Coleshill. Subsequent expansion of the original convent at this address was extensive. Writing in 1929, George Hudson reports the complex at this time as having sixty-eight sisters distributed between 'schools, orphanages, hospitals, and a hostel for emigrant children to Canada'. Coleshill had become what he termed a 'Children's Garden City'.[9] In 1931 the Mercy Sisters in England and Wales were calculated to have had 1,837 sisters (including novices) working out of approximately 104 separate convent addresses.[10]

CONVENT LOCATIONS: REGIONAL ANALYSIS

We can now consider in more detail the regional characteristics of convent distribution within the same period. What significance can be drawn from the regional patterns? Do they suggest that there was a diversity of factors affecting where and at what rate convent numbers grew? Which of these factors might be considered the most influential? Recent research has provided clear evidence of the geographical distribution of convents in terms of percentages of the national totals (England and Wales). See Table 17; it should be borne in mind that the data presented here and in the Tables do not reflect the major changes in local government administration that took place in England and Wales in 1974 and subsequently, which saw the disappearance of many names, such as the Yorkshire Ridings and Westmorland.

A close correlation may be discerned between the growth of active convents and areas of the country with the most pronounced patterns of urbanisation. This development is more clearly demonstrated in Maps A, B and C.[11]

The pattern of convent distribution will be more clearly evident when we come to describe the sub-regional analysis in more detail. For example, many of the eight largest northern towns, especially Liverpool and Manchester, contained high concentrations of women's religious houses.[12] What is remarkable, however, is that the greatest growth in convent numbers took place in London and the South-East rather than in the North, although the last has been traditionally viewed as the Roman Catholic 'heartland'.[13]

In 1857 (see Map A) almost 50 per sent of all convent houses were found in London and Lancashire.[14] Other concentrations were in Staffordshire, which accounted for 10 per cent of the total, and Warwickshire and the West Riding of Yorkshire with 7 and 6 per cent, respectively.[15] There were few convents elsewhere and many counties had none at all.

Throughout the 1870s and 1880s the number of convent houses grew considerably and they were more widely distributed. By these decades there were already many more in London and in the surrounding counties than in Lancashire and other northern counties. This pattern was to remain so for the rest of the period. Numbers in Warwickshire and the West Riding continued to grow, and there had been substantial growth in a few other counties, but total numbers increased only marginally over most of the North and the Midlands.

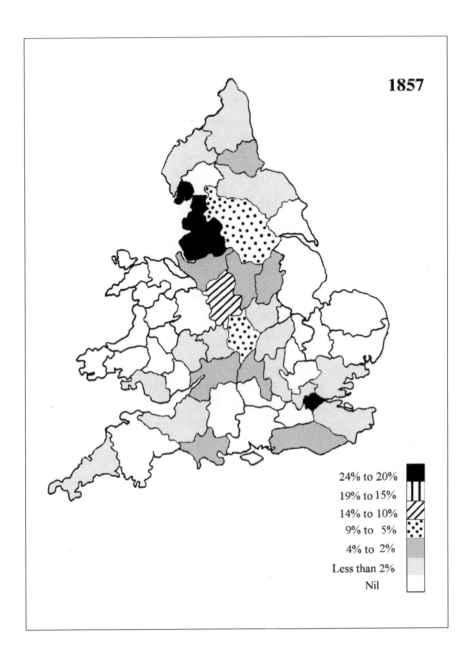

1857

24% to 20%	■
19% to 15%	⦀
14% to 10%	▨
9% to 5%	⋰
4% to 2%	▒
Less than 2%	░
Nil	□

A. The Distribution of Roman Catholic Convents in England and Wales, 1857

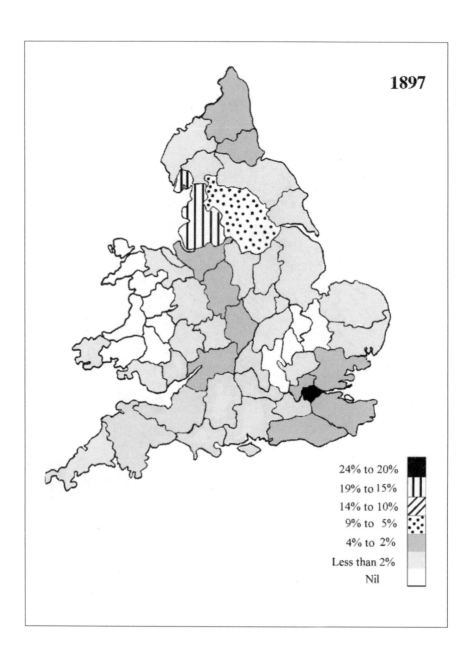

1897

24% to 20%
19% to 15%
14% to 10%
9% to 5%
4% to 2%
Less than 2%
Nil

B. The Distribution of Roman Catholic Convents in England and Wales, 1897

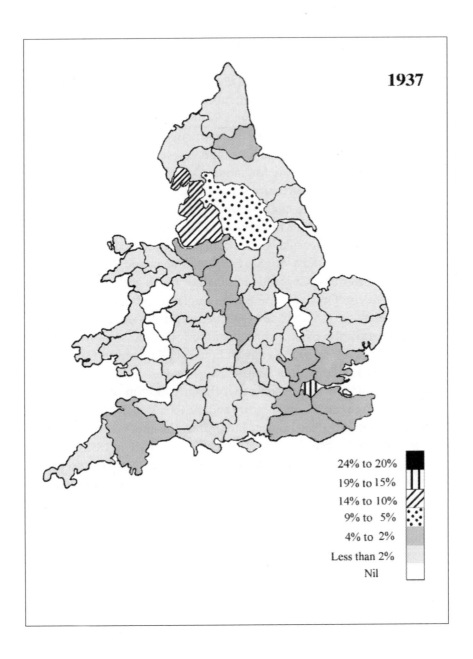

1937

24% to 20%
19% to 15%
14% to 10%
9% to 5%
4% to 2%
Less than 2%
Nil

C. The Distribution of Roman Catholic Convents in England and Wales, 1937

By 1897 (see Map B) London and Lancashire accounted for just under 21 and 16 per cent of the national total, respectively. The proportion in the West Riding, at about 6 per cent, had not altered. However, a much greater number of convents were now much more widely, albeit thinly, distributed throughout all areas of England and Wales. There had been a modest increase within the northern counties, particularly in Durham, but there is no evidence of a great surge here, and an even smaller proportional increase of movement in the Midlands. Convent numbers in southern England, however, and particularly around London, continued to grow substantially. These trends continued into the twentieth century. Between 1897 and 1917 the numbers in London and its region had nearly doubled to 351, with growth particularly evident in Sussex and Kent. Numbers also grew substantially in East Anglia, the South-West and Wales, although from much lower bases, but changes further north and in the Midlands were less evident. Only two counties in England and three in Wales had no convents by 1937. Map C, for 1937, demonstrates the continuation of a high concentration of new convents in the South-East, so that, by this time, 416 out of a total of 956 convent houses in England and Wales were to be found in London or the South-East.

This sequence of maps shows that the distribution of convents was transformed between the mid-century and the First World War and that the pattern established by then changed little during the inter-war years. London and the South-East accounted for 31 per cent of convents in 1857 but 44 per cent by 1917. Conversely, the Midlands declined from 25 to 12 per cent over the same period and the North-West from 25 to 17 per cent. The North-East marginally increased its importance in the closing decades of the century but declined relatively thereafter. Although convents had became established throughout England and Wales by the 1890s, outside the areas we have discussed they were thinly spread. By the 1930s, however, a convent of Roman Catholic nuns or sisters had been established in every county of England bar one, Huntingdonshire, and throughout Wales except Radnorshire, Brecknockshire (Breconshire) and Montgomeryshire.[16]

The regional distribution suggested above responds closely to the census figures in the late nineteenth century, which reveal that a greater proportion of women enumerated as having been members of a religious institution were located in the London area.[17] However, there are difficulties associated with the accuracy of such data and their interpretation with regard to women in religious institutions, who were defined as 'other religious' in 1871 and as 'sisters of charity and nuns' in 1891. Moreover, no distinction was made between Anglican and Roman Catholic religious, which is a factor that, albeit small, must be allowed for. Martha Vicinus relied on a figure of two to three thousand Anglican Sisters in 1900 cited by A.M. Allchin.[18] Susan Mumm's thesis made 'little use of the enumerator's reports' because she felt that the returns were not always accurate and 'not entirely appropriate for the purposes of my study'.[19] Census enumerators quite possibly listed religious under the different professional categories within which they worked, that is, as 'nurses' or 'teachers'.

Nevertheless, despite this, the census distribution mirrors that of Catholic convents. In 1871 28 per cent of women designated as 'other religious' are to be found in London, with Lancashire, Warwickshire and Gloucestershire each accounting for between 5 and 9 per cent of the national total. With the exception of Northumberland, parts of Wales, Westmorland, Lincolnshire, Rutland, Bedfordshire and Huntingdonshire, which have none, the remaining counties of England and Wales have few women firmly identified as members of a religious institute.

By 1891, 25 per cent were shown as resident in the London area. Sussex, in 1891, contained as many religious women as Lancashire, Warwickshire or the West Riding, which each had between 5 and 9 per cent. Other counties near London, especially along the south coast, now contained similar proportions to those found in Cheshire, parts of Wales, Gloucestershire, Somerset and Devon, accounting for between 2 and 4 per cent of the national total. Counties elsewhere in England and Wales had very few. The census data, therefore, despite their shortcomings and ambiguities, are consistent with the analysis of the temporal and spatial growth of convent numbers. Convent expansion in the south of England, especially around London, was more evident than in the North or the Midlands.

CONVENT LOCATION: SUB-REGIONAL ANALYSIS

If we disaggregate the figures presented in Table 16 we may obtain a clearer picture of the changes that were taking place during this period within each region and the developments which were promoting them.

London

In view of the size and complexity of the London area, it is preferable to deal first with this separately from the rest of the South-East. London inner postal districts were used as a guide in summarising the distribution of convent houses.[20]

Analysis showed that the number of convents gradually increased in many areas at about the same pace until the final decade of the nineteenth century and the early years of the new one. After the turn of the century, the establishment of new convents in London continued at a slower rate. By 1917 there were 152 convents and by 1937 a total of 169. In 1857 there had been just twenty-three. The growth of convents in the inner districts of London had achieved a rise of over 600 per cent in eighty years.

A south-west London address would seem to have been the most favoured location throughout the period 1857–1937. West of the city followed closely in popularity, especially in the period 1917–37. The East End would not seem to have been particularly targeted and the number of convents there consistently remained less than in the south-west and the west. Although growth rates in all city areas, in general, kept pace with each other, a marked parallel is evidenced in the figures for north and north-west London, which could probably be attributed to spreading suburbanisation. Increased numbers of convents in Middlesex revealed a similar pattern.

London's north-east was relatively neglected until after the First World War. Within the central areas of London (EC and WC) conventual expansion was undramatic. Early convent establishments remained *in situ*, but there were few new additions. This suggests continuity of establishments rather than any radical change. Well before 1870 the city centre had, according to Garside, become 'more compacted' with a working-class population left behind in slum communities as the middle classes 'dispersed to their own addresses'.[21] Garside comments that, 'after 1891 the population of London's central districts began to drop and even the congested East End barely retained their numbers. By contrast, the counties of Essex, Surrey and Kent had the fastest growth rates in the country'.[22] As we shall see from the evidence in the map sequence for the South-East (Maps D to F) and that in Table 17, the convents followed the middle classes out of central London and into these same counties during this period.

While there is evidence of a higher proportion of mixed convents – with about 25 per cent of the total after 1897 this was a higher proportion than in all other sub-regional analyses – it was still the case that communities of active sisters predominated in the London area. This represents the response of the nuns and sisters to Church anxiety in the 1870s over legislation on the education and welfare care of children. Both active and mixed communities in London founded large hospitals and institutions, they ran schools of all types, orphanages, refuge homes and other welfare services.

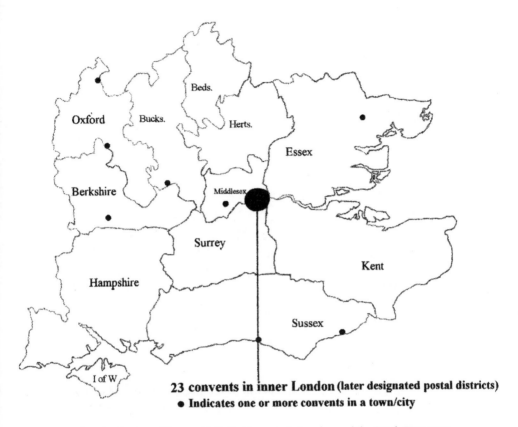

23 convents in inner London (later designated postal districts)
● **Indicates one or more convents in a town/city**

D. The Distribution of Roman Catholic Convents in London and the South-East, 1857

Convent numbers and their distribution in London therefore suggest a relationship with areas of economic growth and new settlement, especially the middle-class suburbs. This becomes more evident when the locations of London's convents are compared with those in other counties making up the rest of the South-East.

The South-East

This region outside London comprises Middlesex, Essex, Bedfordshire, Berkshire, Buckinghamshire, Hertfordshire, Surrey, Sussex, Kent, Hampshire, Oxfordshire and the Isle of Wight. Table 17 demonstrates the relationship between the metropolis and the counties in this region.[23] Absolute

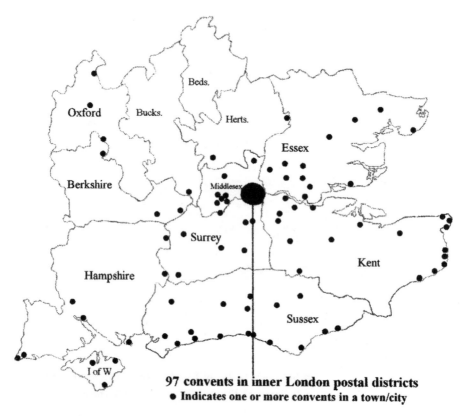

97 convents in inner London postal districts
● **Indicates one or more convents in a town/city**

E. The Distribution of Roman Catholic Convents in London and the South-East, 1897

numbers of convents expanded particularly dramatically in Essex, Kent
and Sussex, although Surrey, Hertfordshire and Hampshire also witnessed
significant increases. The concentration, Hertfordshire apart, is over-
whelmingly south of London. There were distinct clusters of convents
in coastal towns. Dover, Margate, Ramsgate and Tunbridge Wells were
popular locations in Kent; Brighton and St. Leonards in Sussex; and
Bournemouth and Southampton in Hampshire; and there were several
convents on the Isle of Wight. There are several reasons for this but most
important is the nature of the apostolate of many congregations
established there.

Middle-class affluence and the growing economic strength of the South-
East had an important impact on the characteristic of convent function. A

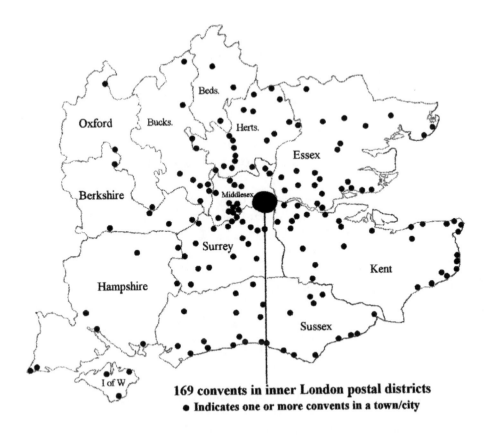

169 convents in inner London postal districts
● **Indicates one or more convents in a town/city**

F. The Distribution of Roman Catholic Convents in London and the South-East, 1937

great number of the convents in the South-East in the last quarter of the century were occupied by active congregations, who, to support themselves, set up high-class boarding schools for young women.[24] They also opened preparatory schools for very young boys – 'young gentlemen'.[25] These convents were often sited in salubrious locations on the outskirts of London. Their advertisements in the *Catholic Directories* highlighted the convenience of railway links and the advantages of healthy and bracing air.[26] Pupils could often be accommodated during the vacations – which suggests parents who lived and worked abroad in the Colonial Service. While such establishments would seem a far cry from the conditions confronted by some of the earliest communities of active sisters in the first half of the century, who were set to nurture those in need in the slum dwellings of Eastcheap or Somers Town, it would seem that the response of members of religious communities towards the end of the nineteenth century more frequently encompassed altogether different social requirements. Catholics were being suburbanised. As Mathew observed when referring to the inter-war years, the proportion of Catholics 'in this stretch of dormitory towns and urbanised countryside which grew up between the southern outskirts of London and the channel coast [was] mounting more rapidly than in any other part of the country.' There was, in his words, 'a tide of salaried Catholics [which] pressed further and further into the countryside'.[27]

The South-East also contained a considerable number of convents in coastal resorts which provided private convalescent nursing and rest homes for adults and children. Health care establishments were not always exclusively fee-paying, however, and there were several charitable undertakings. From the late 1890s onwards an increasing number of orphanages and special schools for delicate children were established in this region and there were several instances of convent-based care for the aged poor and destitute children. For example, the Sisters of Nazareth House, the Sisters of Mercy and, later, the Little Sisters were all active in large resorts such as Brighton.

East Anglia

Convent growth in East Anglia was slow and there was no presence at all up to the 1870s. This was not only because the region contained one of the lowest Catholic populations, but also for the reason that there had been little early industrial urbanisation or burgeoning middle-class conurbations.[28] Norwich saw the arrival of two active communities in the 1870s, the SND and the SSP. Between them they first provided elementary schools and some parish welfare care. Later, middle and boarding schools were established. By 1887 the Sisters of Jesus and Mary, another active congregation by then well-established in Ipswich, had responsibility for poor schools, an orphanage and a high-class boarding school for girls. By 1917 the Little Sisters of the Assumption were providing visiting and nursing care for the poor in Norwich. In 1937 there were at least thirteen convent schools for girls in the region. An order of Benedictine nuns had moved into Suffolk in 1877. By 1937, also in Suffolk, there was a convent of Carmelites. At this time there was a total of twenty-two houses in the region: ten in Suffolk, nine in Norfolk and three in Cambridgeshire.

The South-West

In the South-West a slightly more diversified pattern presents itself. Contemplative nuns particularly favoured this region to an extent not seen in the North. In 1857 there were already eight convents, six of which were evenly split between communities of contemplative and mixed nuns. By 1877 these numbers had doubled and were added to by the establishment of at least fourteen active convents. By 1897 there was a total of forty convents in the region. The following decades, from 1917 to 1937, saw a marked increase in contemplative orders. Devon alone had eight monastic convents by this time. This is not to say that the number of active sisters did not dominate in the region – especially in the urban areas. By 1937, out of a total of ninety-three convents, sixty-five were active communities.

Bristol had the greatest concentration of convents. The Sisters of Mercy were there by 1857, followed by the Little Sisters in 1877. By 1897 the provision included welfare care of the 'aged poor', an orphanage, an industrial school and a house of refuge for women. By this time, too, a Nazareth House in Cheltenham, orphanages in Woodchester, West Town and Torquay, an industrial school in Salisbury and certified Poor Law schools in Plymouth and Torquay were all run by religious communities.

After the turn of the century, however, the growth of both active and mixed congregations was dedicated to establishing new convents which catered specifically for an increasing middle-class demand for better class education for girls. In 1897 there were about ten such establishments in the South-West. By 1937 there were at least twenty-four, which included convent schools run by the SND, the Presentation Sisters, the Dominicans and the Sisters of Christian Instruction.[29]

The East and the West Midlands

Convents in the East Midlands were, for the most part, communities of active sisters. Numbers were small. By 1857 just six convents had been already established. By 1877 this number had doubled, mainly by the arrival of several active communities. In 1897 there were sixteen active convents and four mixed congregations. Two nineteenth-century English communities of sisters, one providing nursing care and the other dedicated to charitable welfare work, originated in the East Midlands. These were The Little Company of Mary, founded in 1877 and the Sisters of St. Joseph of Peace, founded in 1884. Both communities had had the support of

Bishop Bagshawe of Nottingham, whose diocesan jurisdiction encompassed Nottinghamshire, Derbyshire, Lincolnshire, Leicestershire and Rutland.

By 1937 the number of convents here had grown to thirty-four, of which twenty-six were active and mainly to be found in the region's towns. There were no contemplative communities at all up to the turn of the century. By 1937 monastic orders occupied two convents; six houses were run by mixed communities.

What is striking about the West Midlands is the early concentration of convent numbers in the urban areas of Warwickshire and Staffordshire. In 1857 nineteen convents had already been established, mainly in the Birmingham area. Throughout the period under survey Birmingham and its environs had the highest concentration of active convents. By 1937 there were seventy-four communities working in Staffordshire and Warwickshire. The sisters established here by this time were the Sisters of Mercy, the SSP and the Sisters of Providence, all communities with apostolates which focused on service for the poor and the provision of schools. In the rest of this region they were widely distributed, with one or two to be found in almost every town of substance. The SSP, whose mother house was in Birmingham, were the most strongly represented congregation. Their main function in this region at this time was the running of Poor Law and elementary schools, which was often combined with parish visiting. Convent-based welfare care of the aged poor, orphanages for boys and girls and refuges were all based in the Birmingham area. The Dominican sisters ran a hospital in Stone.

The growth in the number of convents in the Midlands, therefore, may be seen as a direct consequence of the changes in government administration of the Poor Law, and the thrust for elementary schooling in the 1860s and the 1870s. The practical encouragement of Birmingham's Bishop Bernard Ullathorne during his long episcopate (1850–88) should be noted. Ullathorne's diocese encompassed the three counties of the West Midlands (Staffordshire, Worcestershire and Warwickshire) which between them had most of the contemplative orders, and this may be seen as being a result of this prelate's particular empathy and strong support for the spiritual life of women within religious life.

By the inter-war years convent growth in both Midland regions came almost to a standstill, in contrast to the gains still being made in the South-East. The Midlands also saw notably few new foreign congregations. Out of the forty-five continental communities which arrived in England between 1901 and 1910 only three settled here, all in Staffordshire. These were the Sisters of Christian Retreat, the Sisters of Our Lady of Compassion and the Sisters of St. Joseph of Cluny. (See Table 1.)

Wales

There were few convents to be found in Wales. In 1857 there were none at all in North Wales and only one in South Wales and numbers grew slowly with no sign of any significant increase until the early decades of the twentieth century. By 1937 North Wales had a total of twelve convents, nine of which were active communities. South Wales showed a modest increase after the turn of the century, so that by 1937 there were twenty-seven here, of which twenty were run by active communities. Few contemplative orders settled in Wales. In North Wales there was one in Merionethshire by 1937; South Wales had three by this time, with two in Pembrokeshire and one in Carmarthenshire.

In 1857 the Sisters of Providence (Rosminians) were already providing poor schools in Cardiff. By 1873 they also established middle-class schools.[30] By 1859 North Wales had convent-run poor schools in Holywell. In 1870 these sisters (Charity of St. Paul the Apostle) also set up a hospice for pilgrims here. Most convents were found in Welsh towns that had ports, docks or industry – Swansea, Pembroke, Newport, Wrexham and Holyhead. These locations do suggest a particular focus on Irish immigrant workers, for these were the Welsh towns they favoured.[31] Convents of the DVDP were providing services for the poor by 1877. After 1917 active and mixed sisters moved into resorts such as Colwyn Bay, Aberystwyth and Llandudno. They provided education at every level. The Daughters of the Holy Spirit, exiled from Brittany in 1902, had opened no fewer than nine new convent schools in different resorts by 1917. Another teaching congregation, the Ursulines of Jesus (not to be confused with the Ursuline Union), were well established in Swansea by 1877, and by 1917 had also expanded to operate out of convents in several other Welsh locations. But it was the city of Cardiff that contained the greatest concentration of active communities. By 1897 Cardiff had a Nazareth Home for the care of the aged poor, separate orphanages for boys and girls and a Poor Law school for girls. Several more elementary schools, a hospital, a refuge and five convent schools for girls were in place by 1937.

Compared with regions such as the North-West and the Midlands, Wales, therefore, reveals a similar development and growth pattern.

The North-West

The region comprises Cumberland, Westmorland, Lancashire and Cheshire. The urban North-West experienced a substantial, early expansion of convent numbers before 1857, but this was not sustained in later decades and it never again equalled the expansion of religious communities in London and the South-East. In the North-West in 1857 there were twenty-five convents of active and mixed communities. Twenty years later this number had more than doubled and by 1897 the total had grown to just under a hundred. Numbers continued to increase after the turn of the century so that by 1917 there were 139 convents in the region. By 1937 there were a total of 168. As might be expected, the majority of these convents were situated in Lancashire. By the end of the period under review, Cheshire had twenty-one convents and Cumberland ten. Westmorland had never more than just one convent – established and run by the Sisters of St. Paul in Kendal since 1859.

Communities of active sisters predominated in Lancashire and Cheshire with mixed convents only accounting for about 10 per cent of all houses by 1937. Convents of strictly enclosed contemplative nuns were non-existent in this region until 1907, after which time several Carmelite convents were established in Lancashire.

The pattern of convent growth in the North-West gained momentum in the 1870s and appears to have been one of expanding clusters within neighbouring urban locations, for instance, in Lancashire, rather than a thin dispersal across new geographical areas. In Cheshire religious communities were to be found mainly in or near Birkenhead, a factor influenced by its close proximity to Liverpool. Almost half of the twenty-one convents in 1937 were clustered here. Cumberland had six convents in 1897, seven in 1917 and ten in 1937, of which two were contemplatives. The provision of schools and some care of the poor were the main convent-based activities in each of the three Cumbrian ports of Whitehaven, Maryport and Workington. The market town of Kendal contained the sole active convent in Westmorland. Arriving here in 1859, the SSP from Birmingham operated elementary and middle schools.

Most of Lancashire's convents, however, were based in and around the cities of Liverpool and Manchester (see Tables 18 and 19). Their conurbations alone covered at least three-quarters of all Lancashire convents and accounted for almost a third of the combined total for all the other counties in the north of England. In fact, not only did Manchester and Liverpool dominate Lancashire in terms of convent numbers, but

Lancashire itself, by 1937, held a higher number than the rest of the north of England.[32]

Liverpool and Manchester were the first destinations for the some of the earliest arrivals of active communities in the North in the nineteenth century. The first Sisters of Mercy convent in Liverpool had been founded from Dublin in 1843 and another early arrival were the Faithful Companions of Jesus in 1844. In the early 1850s the latter opened convents in the Manchester area, as did the Irish Loreto Sisters, who came to Manchester in 1851. In that same year the SND took over the Liverpool orphanage of the Sisters of Mercy. The apostolate of these congregations was concentrated initially on the care of the poor. Subsequently, convent-based activity proliferated in the environs of these two cities in much the same way that religious communities had in the London area, spreading into middle-class, metropolitan suburbs, suggesting similar patterns of development, albeit on a smaller scale.[33] The extent to which the ethnic communities of Liverpool-Irish and Lancashire-Irish were significant in terms of convent growth during this period has already been commented upon in Chapter 2.

Other Lancashire industrial towns such as Blackburn, Burnley, Oldham, Preston, Lancaster, Wigan and St. Helens already contained at least one established, active community by 1857. These convents were mainly those of the Sisters of Mercy or Sisters of St. Paul, but, apart from St. Helens, Wigan and Preston, few other towns had many new arrivals later. Each of these towns had a substantial Catholic population, partly indigenous, and much expanded by Irish immigrants. Highly urbanised, working-class, artisan and increasingly economically upwardly mobile, Catholic families – and Catholic women in particular – sought to improve their lot through education. These were the towns supplying a stream of much-needed vocations to the religious life.

The growth of convent distribution, for the most part, took place through the expansion of existing congregations into new undertakings, particularly the adding of new or upgraded schools and especially from 1870 onwards. Side by side with this increasing focus on education, home visiting and the nursing of the poor were also undertaken. Active religious in Liverpool and Salford were providing private home nursing services for all denominations by 1867. Their fees subsidised the free nursing of the poor.[34] In 1884 the Poor Servants of the Mother of God opened a hospital in St. Helens. It was advertised as being 'The only Free Hospital in the town. Surgical and medical cases received, of all creeds. There are also paying wards. The sisters visit the poor.'[35]

In Preston the number of convents increased from one in 1857 to seven by 1937. The Society of the Holy Child Jesus, a mixed convent established there in 1853, was already providing several levels of school by 1877; in 1872 an orphanage run by the Sisters of Charity of Our Lady of Mercy was set up with the help of lay patronage.[36] By 1877 the arrival of another mixed community, the Faithful Companions of Jesus, offered additional higher-class educational facilities for girls. By 1897 the Little Sisters of the Poor had established a convent there. By 1937 a contemplative order of Carmelite nuns were settled in a Preston suburb.

One aspect of convent development in the North-West was the growth of religious communities in seaside resorts, especially for convent boarding and day schools for 'young ladies' in Blackpool, Lytham and Southport, which were advertised regularly in the *Catholic Directory*.[37] The salubrious north-coast suburbs of Liverpool had also attracted several convent schools for middle- and upper-class pupils.

North Lancashire coastal locations saw the establishment of new hospitals and convalescent homes in the early decades of the twentieth century. For example, in 1902 the Canonesses of St. Augustine came to Liverpool and built a hospital in Waterloo. This was followed by a convalescent home in Grange-over-Sands, overlooking Morecambe Bay.[38]

In all, however, despite the similar appeal of sea air, there would seem not to have been as great a proliferation of exclusive convent boarding schools and nursing establishments as in the coastal towns of southern England. The existence of a much smaller proportion of wealthy, white-collar professional classes in the North may provide a valid explanation. But compare the earlier map sequence (D to F) with that for the North in the same years (G to I) (see also Table 17).

THE EAST AND THE WEST RIDING

Compared with the North-West, far fewer convents came to be established in the East and the West Riding of Yorkshire, although numbers in this region grew substantially in the late nineteenth century, especially in the West Riding. In 1857 just six convents were to be found there. By 1877 the total had risen to twenty-two and by 1897 to thirty-six. A further ten convents had been established by 1917, and by 1937 the total for the region came to fifty-nine, of which fifty-five were active communities. This was still considerably fewer than half the number in neighbouring Lancashire.

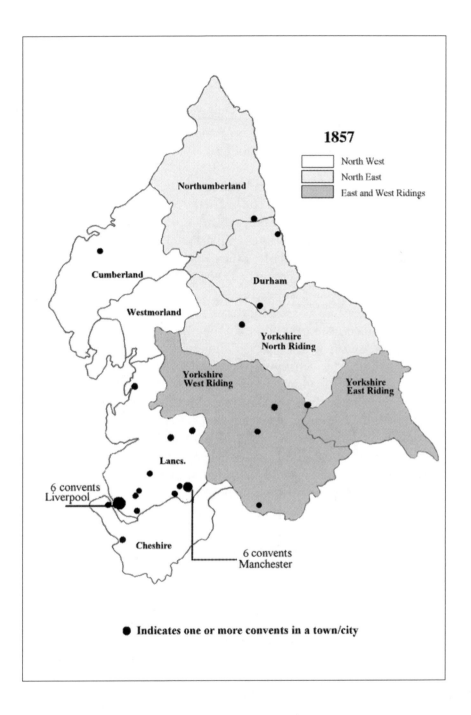

1857

North West
North East
East and West Ridings

Northumberland

Cumberland

Westmorland

Durham

Yorkshire
North Riding

Yorkshire
West Riding

Yorkshire
East Riding

Lancs.

6 convents
Liverpool

Cheshire

6 convents
Manchester

● Indicates one or more convents in a town/city

G. The Distribution of Roman Catholic Convents in the Northern Regions, 1857

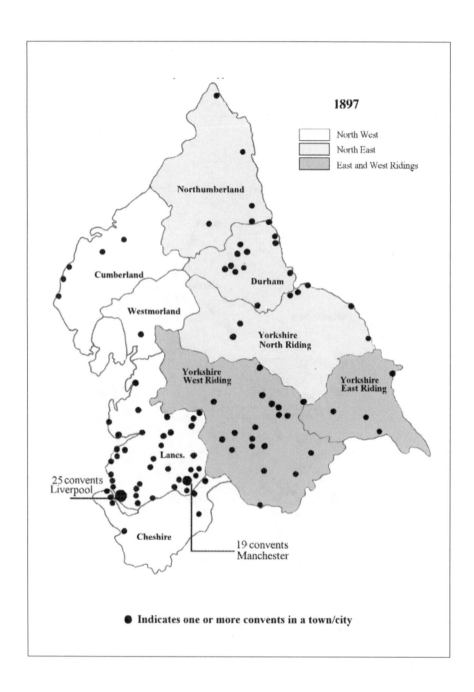

1897

North West
North East
East and West Ridings

Northumberland

Cumberland

Westmorland

Durham

Yorkshire
North Riding

Yorkshire
West Riding

Yorkshire
East Riding

Lancs.

25 convents
Liverpool

Cheshire

19 convents
Manchester

● Indicates one or more convents in a town/city

H. The Distribution of Roman Catholic Convents in the Northern Regions, 1897

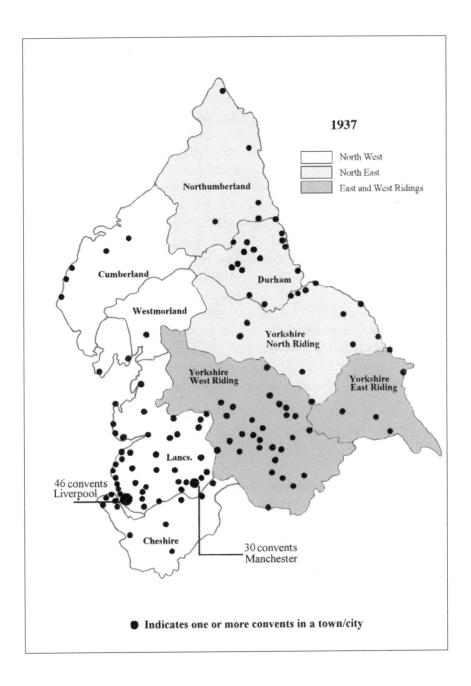

I. The Distribution of Roman Catholic Convents in the Northern Regions, 1937

Pockets of urban convent activity developed in the towns and cities of the West Riding. By 1857 Leeds and Sheffield had seen convents established by the SND and the SSP. York was notable for the Bar Convent – the Institute of the Blessed Virgin Mary – an active community based there since its foundation by the Yorkshire-born Mary Ward in the seventeenth century. There was also an early establishment of contemplatives in York well before 1857. Boston Spa, near Clifford in the West Riding, was an important convent location. A large asylum for the deaf and dumb, run by the Daughters of Charity of St. Vincent de Paul, was established there in 1870.

The East Riding had only three or four towns in which there was any sort of convent-based activity responsible for a range of activities. These included the establishment of schools for the poor in Hull, Everingham and Bridlington. The convents contained communities of Sisters of Mercy, the SSP and Daughters of St. Vincent de Paul. Soon after the turn of the century there were convent day and boarding schools for the middle classes in these towns. By 1897 Hull had an orphanage for boys and, by this time too, a convent boarding school for girls had been established in Beverley. Within a decade of the turn of the century, the seaside resort of Filey had a 'select' boarding school for women conducted by the Sisters of Notre Dame d'Evron. A second community of contemplatives, the Carmelites, had moved into the region by 1917.

THE NORTH-EAST

The North-East had even fewer convents until after 1897. A total of four convents existed before 1857. This number had risen by ten in 1877. The county of Durham had seventeen houses by 1897 and Northumberland had eleven, of which more than half were in Newcastle. By 1937 the total for the region came to fifty-one. Only two convents contained contemplative orders of nuns. Six houses were mixed communities.

A number of the North Sea fishing ports had convents of active sisters, notably the Sisters of Mercy and the SSP. These active communities provided elementary schooling, orphanages, welfare care and some nursing care for the poor. There was one long-established mixed congregation in Richmond which was already offering high-class education for young women in 1857. In addition to the religious-run parish schools in Scarborough and Whitby, convent boarding and day schools in these seaside resorts began to provide higher levels of education for girls by the 1890s. However, growth in the North East was undramatic and by 1937 there were still only fifteen convents in the whole of Northumberland. In County Durham the period 1897 to 1937 saw some increase in numbers, although by 1937 there were still only twenty-four active houses and two contemplative orders.

CONCLUSION

From the 1850s to the 1930s the number of convents established by Roman Catholic women's congregations and orders in England and Wales grew from around one hundred to nearly a thousand. The vast majority of these new convents were active or mixed communities, engaged in education, nursing and welfare services. The pressing need of the English Catholic bishops and clergy was to provide pastoral care for an increasing Catholic community and thus their anxiety to combat any 'leakage' of faith had a direct influence and was largely responsible for the growth and deployment of many convent-based undertakings. At the same time, the dynamic of the convents was generated to a great extent by their members – the young women who had taken vows as nuns and sisters – and reflects their ability to adapt their apostolate in response to the changing needs of society, whether this was influenced by legislation on Poor Law administration, the care of children or the provision of elementary and higher levels of education. The early 1870s and the period between 1897 and 1910 also witnessed the arrival of large numbers of continental congregations provoked by legislation in France and Germany which sought to secularise educational and nursing services. The effect of these European political events on educational and health care standards in England and Wales was to further bolster the numbers of new convent schools and nursing facilities.[39]

A spatial analysis of these congregations and convents clearly suggests that early arrivals of communities of active sisters had been mostly concentrated in London and the industrialised urban areas of the North-West and the West Midlands, suggesting a mission to the poor and, in particular, the Irish poor, since these regions had the highest proportions of Irish-born in 1851. However, from the 1870s onwards the most favoured location for the first arrival or foundation of a new congregation or order was the South-East and particularly around London. Although convent numbers continued to grow elsewhere in the country, this imbalance persisted through to the 1930s. This reflected the more rapid growth of this region generally during this period and the emergence of a prosperous service sector in which Roman Catholics played an increasingly prominent role. The changing distribution of convents, therefore, reflected the broader changes in the social structure of the country. In every region convent distribution followed a similar pattern. Although some new urban convents were established to deal with the social problems associated with industrial towns and ports, particularly those with large poor Catholic immigrant populations, the most dramatic growth was related to suburbanisation and to the expanding population and popularity of coastal resorts. This suggests that expansion could be attributed to the additional responsibilities undertaken by religious communities in response to the increasing middle-class, Catholic and non-Catholic population. Although significant clusters of convents were still to be found in Liverpool and Manchester, even there the movement of an upwardly mobile populace out of the city centres into middle-class suburbs and resorts had an impact, especially in relation to higher-grade schools, although not on the scale seen in the South-East.[40]

All this suggests that the ability to finance their work by tapping the income of the growing number of middle-class Catholics through fees was a major factor in the expansion of religious communities, although we should not overlook the fact that the expansion of nursing and health care facilities also increasingly involved relocation to what were perceived as less polluted environments away from city centres. One consideration which might qualify this picture of the increasing domination of the South-East is the question of whether convents were of different sizes in different regions. As shown in the previous chapter, the extensive variety of convent-based undertakings suggests that the leading congregations in the North operated, on the whole, out of a rather larger number of extensive convent building complexes than did many of those in the southern counties.

We have argued that the increase in numbers of Roman Catholic congregations and convents may not have been contingent only on Church administration and policies but that a number of economic and logistical factors also brought pressures to bear on the development of convent-based activities. In the next chapter we shall consider how convents were controlled and how they managed their finances to allow for a greater expansion of their range of activities. The growth of convent numbers and fresh undertakings also required a huge increase in the recruitment of young women willing to embrace the religious life. This, too, was linked to economic and social conditions as much as to religious motives.

CHAPTER FIVE

Control and Finance

RELIGIOUS ORDERS AND congregations of women who chose to live in community were required to manage their financial affairs as carefully as any secular institution. In this chapter we shall explore some of the means by which these women endeavoured to gain and retain their financial independence.

Convent life was regulated by Canon Law which laid down standards under which the religious life for women could be conducted. Religious life was governed by each community's written Rule or Constitution and formal recognition of a religious institute was obtained through ecclesiastical approval of this document. However, despite the necessity to have the support and assistance of male clerics in order to gain the Church's recognition of a Constitution, convent administration and day-to-day organisational decisions were the responsibility of the sisters themselves. In her outline of the development of the religious rule for the Sisters of Notre Dame de Namur (SND), Mary Linscott explains that, 'Constitutions, of their nature, are a bilateral document in which both the institute and the Church play necessary and complementary parts. The institute produces the text; the Church approves it; and both dimensions are essential . . . A constitution determines the specificity of the institute . . . [it is] the touchstone of unity, since they are what all the members have in common no matter what their culture, age, nationality or period of history.'[1]

Although Constitutions were drawn up on essentially similar lines, religious congregations and orders differed slightly in the minutiae of their individual Rule. As Linscott points out, 'no two religious institutes are identical, even when they belong to the same tradition, such as the Franciscan or Dominican, or are branches of an original, single foundation, like the sisters of St. Joseph'.[2]

Within each religious community of women a hierarchical authority governed and organised the development of their institute. Canon Law specified that members of a community elect their superiors by secret ballot. This system allowed office holders to be voted into position for varying, limited periods. For example, in the election procedures described by Clear, 'No member of a religious community could vote for herself and it was only by an overall majority that a Superior could be elected – narrow margins were not valid'.[3] Once elected, the Reverend Mother or Superior of a convent 'held total authority and had the right to appoint Mother Assistant, Mistress of Novices and Mother Bursar. Three years was the normal term of office.'[4] Evidence exists that strict observance of this rule was not always adhered to, however. Maria McClelland in her account of the Sisters of Mercy's foundation in Hull finds that these sisters had 'developed a peculiar tradition of defying Canon Law in relation to the election of their superiors' and cites terms of office which lasted twelve, twenty-seven and twenty years, respectively for the first three superiors up to 1914.[5]

It was usually deemed necessary for a congregation to appoint a superior-general for the 'sake of unity, future expansion and apostolic mobility'.[6] In most instances, the foundress of a congregation became its first superior-general and in these circumstances might be elected for life. Her successors, however, were usually voted into this position for a specific period, with the possibility of re-election into office for a second term.

Reverend Mother Superiors held the reins of each convent's day-to-day administration. Their governing responsibilities, as laid down by Canon Law, were such that 'Lawfully constituted superiors may make ordinary purchases necessary to provide food and shelter or clothing or which are needed for the ordinary upkeep of property. They may [perform] acts of ordinary administration . . . enter into contracts of buying and selling . . . gifts, loans, rents and all other acts of a similar nature.'[7] The amount of decision-making, consultation, advice and financial aid sought depended largely on the experience, skill and business acumen of individual convent superiors and the circumstances of time and place. Particularly able Superiors accepted a significantly high level of decision-making and many convent annals and obituaries contain references to individual sisters who were 'endowed with great business capacity'[8] or had 'a skill in business matters and a power of administration which astonished men of the world'.[9] Some of the more widely dispersed congregations delegated administrative responsibility by establishing self-governing provinces and, consequently, revision of a community's written Constitution might be necessary in response to changed political and economic events. After the First World War, for example, the SND expanded into five provincial administrations: Belgium, Britain, California, Eastern and Western USA, each with its own 'corporate identity with its novitiate, council, right of representation at chapters and provincial superior who, as a major superior, had canonical and constitutional rights and duties'.[10] By modifying their Constitution in 1921, they accepted 'the creation of general chapters . . . [which met every six years] to respond to the needs of this new kind of organisation'.[11]

The religious life for women, therefore, although requiring conformity with, and canonical approval of a male-dominated church, was structured in such a way as to allow women administrative control over their own organisation and functioning. As Sheridan Gilley has stated in his introduction to Maria McClelland's *The Sisters of Mercy: Popular Politics and the Growth of the Roman Catholic Community in Hull, 1855–1930*, 'despite the constraints of the religious life, women in the Victorian religious orders enjoyed a considerably autonomy from male authority in both their day-to-day work and their general strategy of deciding what work to do'.[12]

Although some research has been undertaken in respect of individual communities and the histories of individual congregations contain a wealth of incidental detail about benefactors and some of the methods of generating income that were employed by individual convents, no easily accessible, correlated data are available to present a comprehensive overview.[13] Matters concerning finance involving the Roman Catholic Church or any of its institutions were, and are, secretive and delicate and not intended to be exposed to public view.[14] The Church itself does not publish its accounts. It is only within the last few years that 'consolidated' parish and diocesan financial statements have had to conform to legislation which required that they be made available for limited scrutiny.[15] Therefore the extent to which the Church involved itself in property investment and subventions to support convents may only be surmised, although some indications drawn from primary sources have been cited as examples. Within the convents their financial records and reports were also held to be matters of great confidentiality. The exact financial status of a community was never revealed, even to their own members, and only those who served in the office of superior or bursars had any knowledge of the income and expenditure of a house.[16] It is not surprising, therefore, that in the past convent housekeeping accounts and other financial records were deemed to be either of little importance and no archival interest, or as material to be held under a moratorium. However, as more and more convent archives become organised with the purpose of assisting historical research, some understanding of the business of running a convent can begin. The records of the SND's English Province may be taken as being typical of many similar institutions, for instance, and the letters, documents and accounts relating to the purchase, building, maintenance and running of their houses, schools and teacher-training colleges provide an illuminating view of the financial skills and astute business ability of these women.[17]

Active and mixed congregations had three potential sources of income. First was their own capacity to earn money or levy fees as trained professional women in education or nursing. The vow of poverty embraced by all nuns and sisters ensured that labour costs were negligible. Second were the funds brought into a community by members as dowries or inheritances. Third was the practical support received from lay benefactors or generated by the collection of alms. The numerous commercial businesses which conducted business with convent complexes suggests that the purchasing power of the larger congregations was considerable, but also gives an indication of the sort of investment undertaken. In conjunction with all of these, consideration should be taken of the extent of the financial responsibility and level of control imposed by local bishops under whose jurisdiction the convents were allowed to operate.

By contrast with active communities, contemplative orders, with a rule and life of prayer which set them aside from society, were more reliant on funds brought in by dowries and benefactors, although they might generate some income from small ventures which they could conduct within the cloister. Such means of raising money included the making of vestments for the church, the preparation of altar breads or the operation of a small printing press. On occasions, an order of contemplatives might accommodate women for retreats or a small number of boarding pupils within their convent. Contemplatives had neither extensive networks of houses nor an expanding range of undertakings to administer and fund and this meant that the day-to-day needs of these communities were relatively modest. Quite a number of contemplatives were located in rural areas and, consequently, their small farms and gardens allowed a certain level of self-sufficiency.

BISHOPS: CONTROL AND FINANCE

The importance of the bishops in relation to convent money matters should not be dismissed lightly. When a community received permission to settle in a diocese the incumbent bishop shouldered official church responsibly not only for the spiritual well-being of the women but also for their financial upkeep. Bishops had 'visitation rights' over the convents in their diocese and would make at least one annual inspection to ensure that rules were being observed and that all activities engaged in were being run correctly and efficiently. In many instances their supervision included a watchful eye on the financial viability of the convent. The annual receipts and expenses of the Sisters of St. Paul the Apostle (SSP) in Selly Park, Birmingham, for example, show annual balances totalling several thousands of pounds meticulously calculated to account for every last farthing. In the 1880s and the 1890s these accounts were inspected and signed off by Bishop W.B. Ullathorne and his successor Bishop E. Ilsley.[18]

Bishops liked to keep, or liked the appearance of keeping, control over a community's purse-strings. However, for some congregations such financial inspections might be assessed as a token exercise especially when it came to matters of property and investments. Not all religious communities were completely powerless in having to accept a bishop's direction to the letter. The Mercy Sisters in Hull, for example, 'insisted on government inspection for their schools and on keeping the government grant themselves they were [thus] free of clerical control'.[19]

Congregations which had access to Rome through the support of a cardinal protector or similar influential churchman were in many respects far more independent of their local bishop. This was especially so if their Rule was centrally organised under a governing Mother House and internally structured hierarchy. For example, the Constitution of the SND makes it quite clear that a local bishop had no power nor authority over their administrative processes, by stating that:

> *Article 221*: In the Congregation the exercise of supreme authority is ordinarily in the hands of the Superior General assisted by her Council; extraordinarily it is exercised by the General Chapter.
> *Article 244*: If, God forbid, it should become necessary to deprive the Superior General of her charge and of her authority, the General Council, before doing anything, ought to report the case to the Holy See and submit to its decision.[20]

The SND had houses in several English dioceses and deemed it prudent to arrange for the financial affairs of each convent to be audited by outside, secular firms, from whom they also received advice and guidance. The sisters who were appointed to the post of treasurer to their English Province then submitted a summary of accounts direct to their Superior General in Belgium on a half-yearly basis, having received the detailed audited accounts from each convent bursar. An illustration of the professional support they received from outside auditors may be demonstrated in a letter from a sister appointed as convent bursar, writing to her Provincial treasurer in 1930, in which she outlines some difficulties encountered with an income tax return. She writes:

> Mr Beard audits the school's accounts, and though not a Catholic, has great sympathy with us and considers we are doing a great and generous work. He explained that if the secondary school were not connected with the convent there would be no tax at all, but since there is inter-communication it must be assessed. He says we should send in an appeal if we are assessed unduly.[21]

In matters concerning the purchase of property, negotiation of loans and mortgages and other legalities the Superior General and individual convent Superiors of this institute dealt direct with a firm of lawyers in Lincoln's Inn in London. Building programmes and maintenance work were undertaken by dealing direct with leading architects, surveyors and contractors.[22]

It was a great advantage if a religious community benefited from wealthy lay patrons or well-connected heiresses within their own membership.[23] Many a well-endowed congregation zealously guarded its 'fortune' against predatory bishops and the history of nuns is littered with the metaphorical corpses of senior churchmen who tried and failed to exert strict control over the sisters under their jurisdiction.

That said, however, one of the great worries of the English hierarchy was that of litigation involving convent matters. In times of dire trouble the bishops were loath to become financially accountable. For example, there was what became known as 'The Great Convent Case', a famous piece of litigation, *Saurin v. Starr & Another*, which came before the Queen's Bench in 1869. This involved a member of the Hull Sisters of Mercy, Susan Saurin, an eccentric but ecclesiastically well-connected, young, Irish woman who had been transferred to Hull from the Mercy Convent in Dublin. She came from 'a wealthy background and family of high reputation' and sought to sue the Mother Superior and her assistant for libel and slander for 'wrongfully and maliciously conspiring to compel [her] to leave the convent . . . '.[24] Saurin won her case and, while the damages of £500 awarded to her were affordable, the costs of £6,000 threatened to bankrupt the convent. Although several members of the hierarchy sent subscriptions to help with the costs, the sisters were in receipt of little or no support from their bishop and most of the money was eventually raised for them by a Catholic 'groundswell of support in England and Ireland'.[25] Another, less sensational, but at the time equally a *cause célèbre*, was the hearing of the case of Selly Park Convent and the Hampson Will in 1891. It involved the SSP and a disputed legacy.[26] Accounts of the case suggest that several bishops were anxious to disassociate themselves from being embroiled in the conflict and did little to help the defendants, the SSP. They lost the case and had to find costs of £4,700 from their own resources.

Such court cases caused the Catholic bishops immense embarrassment and it is understandable that they tried to avoid being over-involved in convent disputes. However it is a moot point whether their reticence extended to remaining disinterested spectators when convent property was being purchased, or when it suited their needs to persuade a community to undertake a new venture, as was the case of Bishop Vaughan and the Franciscan Sisters of St. Joseph in 1878. This was a clear case of women in religion who bowed to the dictate of a bishop, having no alternative but to do so. Alice Ingham had founded a community of women who adopted a Franciscan rule in order to care for the poor in Rochdale. O'Brien relates how, twelve years after its establishment, Ingham was still waiting for official Vatican approbation for her little body of sisters.[27] Bishop Vaughan offered to use his influence to arrange for her community to be 'placed on a formal footing' – but on condition that they gave up their work and home among the people of Rochdale and instead took over the domestic economy (the cooking, cleaning and sewing) of the Mill Hill Fathers at their Missionary Training College just outside London.[28] The sisters acceded to his wish and moved to London. Vaughan kept his side of the bargain and they subsequently received official Vatican approval of their congregation.

If a disagreement or dispute between a local priest or bishop and a community of nuns or sisters became a head-on collision, then the members of a religious institution had one weapon at their disposal. Courage was needed, however. Thwarted by an intransigent churchman, a congregation could, and often did, threaten to move out of his control altogether and into the care of a more compliant bishop. For example, in order to retain all their houses under the centralised administration of their Mother House in Birmingham, Mother Dupuis, founder of the SSP, closed many of their houses 'owing to the difference of opinion over authority'.[29] Little documentary evidence remains of these disputes, although their move out of Burnley in 1859 has been recorded as being provoked 'because the priest in charge of the mission demanded that the nuns should be independent of the Mother House'.[30] Once established as religious communities, women, therefore, could remain firm even in the face of serious official opposition from the Church. Mother Dupuis and Bishop Ullathorne of Birmingham also engaged in a prolonged period of estrangement over the 1891 case mentioned above, and while, later, she wrote formally of this time that, 'I have never disobeyed the Bishop in any matter in which he had a right of command,' she took pains to add that 'His advice, I am sorry to say, I have not always been able at all times to follow.'[31] As Scarisbrick points out, her carefully worded statement combined 'due deference with firmness'.[32]

In another similar instance, the biographer of Mary Potter, foundress of the Little Company of Mary, notes that her relationship with Bishop Bagshawe of Nottingham came under severe strain soon after the establishment of the congregation in his diocese. While careful to acknowledge that Mother Potter had 'retained the deepest gratitude' to the bishop for all that he had done for the sisters (the biography was published under the constraints of an *imprimatur*), her biographer clearly found that '[Mother Potter] . . . gradually came to realise' that her views on the future of her community and that of Bishop Bagshawe 'differed widely on vital matters'.[33] First, the Bishop tried to use his authority to usurp her position as Mother Superior by appointing another sister to this post. He then instructed the community to open many scattered branch houses 'in places where there was neither a church nor school and practically no means of subsidence . . . '. Potter objected to the imposition of this policy, and when, in due course, she was voted back into office by her colleagues she promptly defied the Bishop, closed the outlying houses and recalled the sisters back to the mother house.[34]

Citing views first aired by Mary Peckham, Maria Luddy has identified more subtle tactics used by Irish nuns and sisters in their relationships with bishops, 'Their seemingly obsequiousness to bishops or members of the clergy is often a strategy of compromise which allows them to develop their work without undue interference.'[35] An echo of this type of subterfuge is also found in Lady Cecil Kerr's *Memoir of a Sister of Charity* (1928). A superior in the Daughters of Charity of St. Vincent de Paul planned to open a new orphanage for boys in Plymouth and sought permission from the bishop. Lady Kerr relates how:

His Lordship was already weighed down by financial cares and did not welcome new suggestions kindly. However, sister had learnt how to win her point. She would go to him and describe her plan – only to be told it was utterly impossible . . . then she would gracefully retire, knowing full well that in a few days time she would certainly be sent for, and the grand idea propounded as the good Bishop's own.[36]

Peckham also provides a more strident note as to why similar conflicts required manipulation by religious superiors. Citing one Irish convent archive, she comments, 'Many bishops instead of supporting and encouraging religious women were known to harbour a serious dislike of them.'[37] What is clear, therefore, is that not all convents were entirely free to manage their affairs. Professionalism and autonomy had their limits. However, the widely held impression that the bishops' control over all religious communities of women in their dioceses was invariably despotic is also far from true.[38]

GENERATING INCOME

Evidence of how communities endured early hardships can be found in almost every congregation's history. (And telling indicators can be picked out to illustrate probabilities.) For example, the several foundations of Ursulines which later owned and maintained properties of distinction and grandeur and which were to become among the most successful of the teaching congregations, suffered considerable hardship in their early days. In 1877, the Ursulines of Upton wrote of their straitened position, 'We have often gone to bed without a halfpenny in the house.'[39] In similar difficulties some thirty years later, a group of exiled Ursulines who had settled in Plymouth in 1907, recorded that, 'At first the community was so poor that those not engaged in teaching undertook embroidery for a firm, Spooner and Company who sold their work in Plymouth and Ireland.'[40] Likewise, the Daughters of the Holy Spirit from Brittany were also beset by impecunious circumstances. They supplemented their income in the early 1900s by accepting laundry work and used a small pony and trap for the collection and delivery of washing.[41] In cases such as these, the evidence, or lack of it, suggests that there were few instances of diocesan funds being diverted to help communities which wished to retain for themselves a certain level of freedom from the agendas of local episcopal control. As a sideline, active and mixed sisters on the fringes of urban areas often sought some self-sufficiency by attaching a small farm and kitchen garden to their convents, not unlike many of the contemplative orders. It is not unusual to find references to sisters who were particularly skilled in making butter, managing the farm or supervising the employment of workmen.[42]

The capacity of a congregation to develop and expand primarily depended on their capacity to operate as professionals. This ultimately entailed ownership, administration and staffing of schools, colleges, hospitals, asylums and institutions of several kinds and undertakings such as laundries and outside nursing services. Congregations also provided the teachers, nurses and social workers who were employed in similar undertakings not directly owned by themselves. Monies earned in this way went direct into the coffers of each community. The vows of poverty taken at the time of profession did not allow a nun or sister to accept any personal payment for whatever work she was assigned to.

Any assessment of the total income on a national scale which women's religious congregations generated from staffing and running schools can only be speculative. Even the cost of the national network of elementary schools in the nineteenth century is unknown.[43] Gillian Sutherland has shown that attempts to provide a quantitative interpretation of nineteenth-century education are doomed to failure since 'we simply do not have the data'.[44] Similar deficiencies arise in relation to the scale of the involvement of nuns and sisters as teachers in convent school systems. These spanned everything from 'poor' and elementary schools to fee-paying middle- and higher-class schools. Despite the fact that the engagement of these women in education has been rather more fully studied than any other area of their work, research has tended to focus more on internal convent issues and each specific congregation's apostolate.[45] Such sources reveal little more than an occasional glimpse of financial matters, especially in relation to elementary or 'free' schools and it should be recognised that the financial strategies utilised by one religious congregation might include methods not employed by others.[46]

A sample balance sheet for one London-based convent elementary school in 1891 (Table 20) shows clear evidence of careful budget management. The education grant of just over £180 was almost equally matched by funds brought in by the scholars and one generous contributor. However, what seems curious is that the contribution of sisters from the convent as waged teachers does not appear to have been taken into consideration. Use of the term 'mistresses' salaries' itemised,

First Ursuline convent in
England 1862. Two semi-
detached houses in Upton
Lane, Upton, Forest Gate.

First community,
Upton, Forest Gate.

Ursuline Convent,
Upton, Forest Gate.
(At a later date.)

9. The Ursulines at Upton
Source: M.W. Sturman, *The Ursulines in England, 1851–1981* (1981), p. 25.

costing £145 would seem to imply the employment of trained women lay teachers.

The clearest summary relating to the earning capacity of religious-run elementary schools may be found in Hudson, writing of the early days of the SSP. He records that

> the community as a whole depended on the earning of the Sisters. Teachers' salaries were paid by the priest of the mission [parish], as manager of the schools, first out of voluntary funds, later out of the grants earned by the school . . . [that is, after negotiations arising out of the 1870 Education Act; see Chapter 2]. With the passing of the Education Act of 1902, teachers were paid direct by the Local Authority. The recognised salary for a certified teacher was £50, for an assistant teacher £35. A sum of about £18 was paid for each pupil-teacher. The earnings of a (convent) Branch House would thus be about £120. Out of this the Sisters supported themselves and made a contribution to the Mother House (in Birmingham) for the Novitiate and the sick.[47]

Hudson comments further that, 'At best, the position of a Branch House was one of poverty, at times it was one of real need.'[48] It may be added that the latter reflection should not necessarily be applied to convent life *in toto*.

Some ambiguity arises when Hudson's observations are compared with Wall's research on Catholic certified elementary school teachers in Liverpool, which found that wages paid to the sisters as teachers were smaller than the subventions received by women lay teachers. Wall, for example, found that the annual salaries of nuns in 1852 were '£40 for two' at a time when it was usual for a women teacher to earn £30 a year and that infant school teachers who were nuns or sisters were also paid about half the going rate and possibly even less than this.[49] A similar conclusion was reached by Fahey whose research on nuns staffing the national schools of Ireland found that 'by the 1870s [nuns employed as teachers] cost the State . . . on average about one-third that of lay-teachers in ordinary schools'.[50] Why the sisters should have been taken advantage of in this way may have been due to the straightened circumstances experienced by what were termed 'the voluntary' denominational schools, often managed by the local priest, and it may reflect the difficult bargaining power of some religious congregations in their dealings with schools that were not under their direct control.[51] The Education Act of 1870 (which did not apply in Ireland) had created a dual system of 'newer undenominational schools,

entirely provided and maintained out of public funds, and older denominational schools, provided by voluntary subscriptions and helped only by
Privy Council grants'.[52] No change in this system took place until the
Education Act of 1902, which put the voluntary schools on the rates. It
is understandable, therefore, why almost all of the teaching congregations
expanded into the 'private' fee-paying sector and used this source of
income to supplement the meagre pay provided by elementary school
management boards. Teaching in Sunday school and night schools would
have been mostly voluntary, although there is evidence that the 'pennies
of the poor' were gathered to defray some costs. In one recorded instance,
Hamer notes, the Notre Dame sisters in Blackburn held 'Two night classes
of 80 and 180 pupils [working-class poor, who paid] . . . 2d or 3d a week.'[53]

More significant was the level of income generated by fee-paying,
secondary-level convent schools, of which there were many. The advertisement sections of the *Catholic Directories* from 1857 to 1937 contain patchy,
but illuminating information as to the scale of school fees charged by
convent schools, an indication of the scale of income that convents derived
from their services to education. In 1857 the SSP in Banbury advertised
their terms in the *Catholic Directory*. Clearly, they were aiming at providing
secondary schooling for the middle classes:

> For board and education, for young ladies under fourteen years of
> age, 20 guineas per annum; above that age 22 guineas. To be paid
> quarterly in advance. French 10s per quarter. Music, Drawing &c. on
> the usual terms. Each young lady to bring two pairs of sheets, six
> napkins, and knife, fork and spoon which will be returned on her
> leaving the school.[54]

The sisters in the Banbury convent also conducted a free school for local
poor children.[55] In nearby Oxford in that same year a community of
Ursuline sisters charged similar terms for their boarders; the fee for day
scholars was one guinea quarterly.[56] It would appear that the scales of fees
increased over time, although in respect of the boarding schools especially,
a wide variation gradually crept in which reflected the standard of convent
school facilities and the type of pupil catered for. For example, on the one
hand the Convent of Mercy in Dighton Street, Bristol in 1897 advertised:
'a Higher Grade Boarding and Day school. Besides a careful religious
training, the course of education comprises tuition in all branches of
English, plain and fancy needlework, drawing, French, singing and music.
Pupils prepared for the College of Preceptors, South Kensington, and other

Local Examinations. Pension £20 per annum . . .'[57] On the other hand, in the more salubrious suburb of Birkdale near Southport in Lancashire, the SND sought twice this amount by offering: 'a Boarding School for a limited number of young ladies, whose parents wish to send them to the seaside for their education. Pension 45 guineas.'[58]

The religious communities almost invariably ran a two-tier system of fees for their schools, in addition to segregating pupils by social class.[59] Not only were free schools for the poor run on the income derived from more exclusive establishments, but scholarships and pupil-teacher schemes were set in place so that brighter girls could be assisted to aspire to a career in education. Charitable undertakings were thus indirectly financed by the wealthy. For example, with annual running costs well over £8,000, the accounts of one London convent in 1930 clearly illustrate how fees generated by their boarding and day school heavily subsidised the outgoings, including the cost of running two elementary schools. Although government grants for their elementary schools came to almost £1,300, this amount would probably not have provided sufficient funding for their operation.[60] In a similar way, communities dedicated to overseas missionary work used money generated by providing exclusive education for 'young ladies' to fund work in Africa, India, China and elsewhere.

The same two-tier systems operated in the work of hospital and nursing services, with the care of needy patients being heavily subsidised by those who could afford to pay. Advertisements in the *Catholic Directories* assured patients that they would be cared for 'without distinction of creed or class', and, if necessary, 'gratuitous'.[61] Many of the hospital and nursing congregations sought and received assistance through advertising for subscriptions and contributions to assist in the work of caring for the sick poor. (Lay patrons and benefactors are discussed below.)

It would be wrong not to acknowledge that, on many occasions, individual members of the clergy and superiors of male religious orders, in addition to bishops and other senior churchmen, often made substantial contributions to convent-run schools and hospitals from their personal financial resources. Donations from clerics with private means are usually mentioned only with great reticence and with deliberately vague detail in the histories of religious institutions. What is certain is that such payments usually came in times of crisis or when capital was needed in start-up situations, or as charitable bequests and legacies. For example, Bishop Ullathorne is credited as having shared part of his stipend to support the establishment of Margaret Hallahan's Dominican Sisters of St. Catherine of Sienna, and the SSP record that the 'considerable personal property' of their chaplain the Revd Dr Tandy helped to support the sisters in their early days.[62] Clerkin writes of the 'considerable private means' of the parish priest of Carlisle and implies the use of his money in helping to set up the Sisters of the Sacred Hearts of Jesus and Mary there in the 1900s.[63] The archives of the SND hold a small ledger account dated 1847–50 recording 'monies received for the purpose of purchasing ground and erecting a convent and church for the Catholics of Northampton'. The entries in it acknowledging donations from lay people include a number of small amounts given anonymously by well-wishers each signing himself as 'a priest'.[64]

On the whole, however, only a calculated guess can be made from reading the histories of many different communities as to the extent of such personal gifts from clerics and it would be difficult to quantify the importance of these sources of finance in the absence of any accessible, correlated data.

DOWRIES

The second source of finance for a congregation was the dowries brought in by new members. Canon Law dictated that income thus derived was deemed 'frozen' and could not be spent during the member's lifetime. In some respects, the dowry might be regarded as providing a pension underwriting the care and upkeep of a community member throughout the time of her working service and into old age. Dowry funds could and were, however, carefully invested and the interest thus earned could be used to contribute to the day-to-day running of the community.

Explaining the function of dowries to his Protestant readers in 1873, John Murphy suggested that 'a lady is required to bring in with her a dower of about £600, yielding, at five per cent interest, £30 a year, which is deemed sufficient for her food, clothing and all other requisites'.[65] In fact, the amount of dowry that girls were expected to bring with them varied very considerably. In many instances a large, fixed sum was not necessary for girls who chose to join an active congregation. Dowries might consist of a nominal amount or be reduced or dispensed with entirely if aspirants came with a qualification as a teacher or nurse. Consideration was given to family circumstances and the ability to pay a dowry.[66] While a definitive generalisation cannot be made, on the whole the lower scales of dowry were mostly applicable to the more active congregations.

Examination of the condition of entry in 116 orders and congregations by Hohn, *Vocations: Conditions of Admission to Convents* (1912), reveals that twenty-one stipulated a specific figure for the amount to be brought in, either on entry or at profession of vows. Sums for choir nuns ranged from £1,000 to as little as £12.[67] A further twenty-one religious institutions indicated that a large or a small dowry was necessary, without stating a figure, and girls seeking entry to these communities as lay sisters were almost always accepted without a dowry. The remaining seventy-four institutions, while not stating what figure was preferred, gave assurances that dowries could be fixed according to means or circumstances, especially if an aspirant were particularly suitable or had training or qualification as a teacher or nurse. Because members of active congregations were able to contribute earnings to their community in these roles, the lack of a dowry was no drawback to admission. In some cases merely the defrayment of postulant and novitiate expenses might be sought. Certainly, the system operated very flexibly and much depended on the circumstances and potential earning power of each candidate.

Those congregations and orders that sought the most substantial dowries did so for different reasons. For some, the interest that could be generated on these sums might form an essential source of regular finance. This was particularly so in respect of those communities which were not active. For others, however, quite large sums were sought even though such institutions administered operations that were able to earn substantial income for themselves. This was particularly so in respect of teaching orders that made a speciality of educating high-class pupils. It would seem that they did so to ensure that applications for entry came only from girls with a financially comfortable background and were therefore perceived to be 'ladies'. Dowries for choir nuns in this type of community ranged between about £400 and £600 – a not inconsiderable amount at the turn of the century. The dowries for lay sisters in these instances were always considerably smaller, being below about £120.

Comparison may be made with the dowries accepted by convents in Ireland, since many were recruiting branches for English or French mother houses. In nineteenth-century Ireland rates for convent dowries were roughly comparable to marriage dowries. K.H. Connell has cited Cork tenant farmers in Ireland in the 1880s paying rents of £30 or £40 a year who provided their daughters with marriage dowries of £300 to £400, and research carried out by Clear suggests that similar sums were made available to dower a girl's entry into a convent.[68] Clear gives evidence of sums ranging from £200 up to £2,000 and there were exceptions such as a 'wealthy Limerick business family heiress [who] entered Loreto at Rathfarnham with a dowry of £35,000, freeing this convent's funds to build a Pugin-designed chapel . . . '[69] The Loreto nuns, it must be said, were not only prominent, high-class educationalists in Ireland and England but engaged much of their efforts in an extensive – and expensive – apostolate in the missions fields of India, Africa and elsewhere overseas.

Evidence of dowry payments made by entrants in the registers of the Sisters of the Sacred Hearts of Jesus and Mary (SSHJM) at the turn of the century record some sums as high as £300 but more usually they were around £120.[70] Some suitable candidates were accepted with only a nominal amount of dowry so that they could be subsequently trained as nurses or teachers within the community.

The role of the dowry system might be seen, therefore, as a filter to select the most promising aspirants in addition to making provision for their future within the community.

COLLECTING ALMS

While the activities of most communities designated as 'Sisters of Charity' included the collecting of alms from time to time, the rules and constitutions of at least three well-known congregations did not allow them to accept any form of payment for work and they had to rely on public soliciting and the collecting of alms as their sole methods of raising funds.[71] The Little Sisters of the Poor, the Little Sisters of the Assumption and the Poor Sisters of Nazareth were entirely dependent on charity and alms collection. There were strict rules laid down by the Holy See under Canon Law which dictated in great detail how these sisters were to conduct themselves while collecting alms: 'There must always be two sent out, they must always conduct themselves humbly and modestly, be neat in appearance, avoid places not suitable to their religious profession . . .'.[72] They regularly made rounds, not only to collect money but also to gather food, money or cast-off clothing and goods for the poor in their care.[73] On many occasions in slum areas, the pennies of the poor in one street went to help the unfortunate in the next. Only rarely were they subjected to abuse or adverse publicity. In Derby, in 1875, the wide publicity which ensued from the 'wrongful arrest' of two members of the SSHJM who came before the local magistrate for collecting alms in the town served merely to assist a 'gaining an increase of support'.[74]

It is worth considering whether the practice of alms gathering pursued by many congregations of Sisters of Charity, which, on the whole, had remained strongly influenced by the ethos of their egalitarian origins in Republican France, was driven in part by their traditional French distrust of the English Poor Laws.[75] The French regarded the Poor Laws as as much of an affront to the dignity of the recipient as to those who felt it their duty to give generously. Recent comment on the debates over rights of assistance which raged in France suggests that 'Liberal economists, social Catholics and republicans of all shades used the same evidence, drew the same analogy and reached the same conclusion about the inherent dangers of the Poor Law', and that '[These] critics of legal charity charged that public assistance was too cold, impersonal and bureaucratic . . . The French believed that charitable impulse must remain just that – an impulse, and not a legally mandated responsibility.'[76] It is possible that because Sisters of Charity felt no loss of dignity, other than self-abnegation, in either begging for or dispensing help, neither they, nor those that benefited, underwent any dehumanisation by exposure to officialdom.

HEIRESSES AND FORTUNES

There were many instances of heiresses or young women who were wealthy in their own right entering convents. In such cases these women were entirely free to dispose of substantial fortunes for the benefit of their congregation, if they so desired. Two notable examples were aristocratic heiresses who entered the English Province of the SND in the nineteenth century. Their financial contribution enabled this congregation to prosper and expand to become one of the leading educational institutions in England and Wales. The first heiress was the widow of Sir Edward Petre, nephew of the Duke of Norfolk, who entered the community in 1850 on the death of her husband. This lady (Sr. Mary of St. Francis) devoted her large fortune and her talents to the establishment of the teacher-training college in Mount Pleasant, Liverpool and many other new convent foundations. An account of her life has calculated that 'when she entered the community in 1850 there was one convent of the Institute existing in England. When she died in 1866 there were twenty.'[77]

In 1872 another well-connected heiress entered the same community: the Hon. Mary Elizabeth Townley, of Townley Hall, Burnley in Lancashire. Her fortune was largely responsible for the foundation of eight more convents and at least four overseas missions in Africa.[78] Sr. Marie des Saints

Anges, as she was known in religion, subsequently governed the English Province of the SND sisters for thirty-six years (1886–1922). During this time the congregation administered convent schools in nineteen locations and, in addition, provided free education for the poor in sixty-eight elementary schools.[79] A rich source of information in regard to the 'hands-on' entrepreneurial skills exercised by these two exceptional women exists within the archives of this institution. Letters, legal documentation and accounts show clear evidence of their foresight and drive to achieve excellence in the provision of schools and training colleges. The copious correspondence which was exchanged between the 'Very Reverend and Dear Sister Superior' and their legal advisers, architects, surveyors and building contractors reveals these women's close personal supervision of all purchases, building and renovation work in the English province.[80] Furthermore, their astute management skills are displayed in the way they delegated of much of the direct supervisory work to the local Sister Superiors, while expecting to be kept informed by detailed and regular reports.[81] A letter dated 16 February 1897 acknowledges their reliance on the local superior during building work in one of their London convents: 'Sister Catherine of Sienna has spared herself no trouble or fatigue. She has really done the office of Clerk of the Works and I am sure must have saved thus more than £100. There would have been many mistakes without her supervision.'[82]

Something of the scale of the enterprises entered into can be demonstrated by an illustration of the gradual acquisition, refurbishment and rebuilding of property around the original Mount Pleasant convent to accommodate the expansion of the associated training college (see Plate 10).

The Sisters of Notre Dame de Namur were not unique in enjoying the contribution of well-connected and wealthy members of their community. Convent finances of other congregations also benefited from the financial astuteness of Mother Superiors who had moneyed family backgrounds or connections with landowning families, the professions or successful dynasties in business and trade. These upper- and middle-class women who had chosen the religious life were likely to have relatives and advisers with commercial experience to guide them. Backed by timely investments, land and property could be purchased, buildings renovated or built and many Superiors proved themselves women of assertiveness, skill and foresight. For example, in 1889 the Sisters of St. Joseph of Peace were able to raise money from the sale of railway shares in order to purchase a property for a new convent in Grimsby.[83] The shares had been donated to the congregation by the astute, if controversial, Sr. Margaret Anna Cusack.[84]

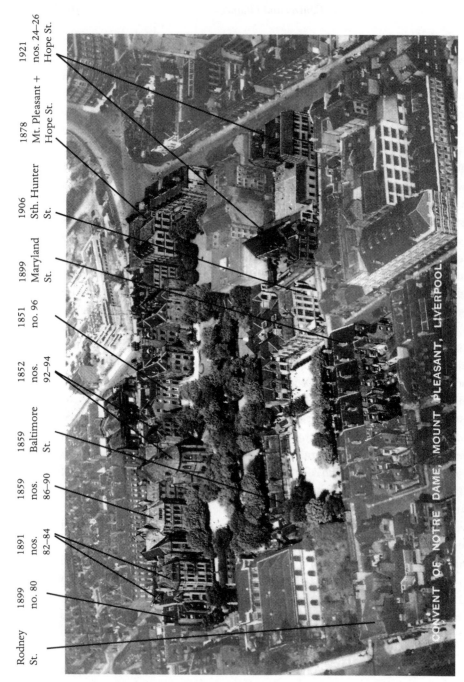

Rodney St.	1899 no. 80	1891 nos. 82–84	1859 nos. 86–90	1859 Baltimore St.	1852 nos. 92–94	1851 no. 96	1899 Maryland St.	1906 Sth. Hunter St.	1878 Mt. Pleasant + Hope St.	1921 nos. 24–26 Hope St.

CONVENT OF NOTRE DAME, MOUNT PLEASANT, LIVERPOOL

10. Growth and development, 1851–1921: Convent and Teacher Training College, Mount Pleasant, Liverpool
Source: Sisters of Notre Dame de Namur Provincial Archives, Liverpool.

LAY PATRONS AND BENEFACTORS

Another important source of income for religious congregations emanated from the aid of lay patrons who provided moral and practical support, especially through donations of money, gifts or loans of property. There were many influential advisers on financial and other matters among the ranks of Catholic society to whom women's religious communities could turn for help. The records of congregations and orders are full of accounts of such lay involvement and the scale of their contribution deserves a separate study. Not to be forgotten, either, is the fact that many of the bishops within the English hierarchy had kinship ties with the close-knit upper echelons of recusant 'Old Catholic' families which had retained the Faith since the Reformation. Moreover, there were many daughters, sisters, aunts and nieces who had entered religious communities and well-connected families networked untiringly in their offers of help. The volume of support for convent-based activities, which included the building of schools, chapels and other institutional complexes, was often reliant on the subscriptions, endowments and fund-raising efforts of the Catholic laity, despite a lingering hierarchical distrust of their enthusiasm. Monsignor Talbot's famous advice to Pope Leo IX, that all that should be required of the leading members of England's Catholic society was 'to hunt, to shoot, to entertain. These matters they understand, but to meddle with ecclesiastical matters they have no right at all', might be seen as a concept that was soon outdated and probably taken rather more seriously in Rome than it was in many English dioceses.[85] The laity, however, did indeed 'meddle', especially in providing practical support for the response of nuns and sisters to the needs of social care.

The histories of religious congregations contain many examples of lay patronage. A few illustrations of the range and nature of the assistance offered may be given to provide some idea of their significance. The Servants of the Sacred Heart in Stratford, East London benefited from the patronage of the Marquis of Lothian and the Marquis of Londonderry in the 1870s.[86] A charity sale in aid of an orphanage run by the Daughters of St. Vincent de Paul, advertised in the London press in 1875, lists no fewer than twelve patronesses with noble titles among the 'ladies of distinction' appealing for support.[87] There are other examples such as the assistance given by Throckmorton family to the SSP when they took over parish schools in Studley in 1881. When the Poor Servants of the Mother of God founded their Providence Free Hospital in St. Helens in 1882, further extensions were accomplished with the help of a strong lay committee supported by the Duchess of Norfolk, Lord and Lady Gerrard and other local notables, including members of the local glass-making firm of Pilkingtons. Such patrons were described as 'supplying initiative and suggestions that were of untold assistance, and not only suggesting but supplying the means of carrying out many plans for the benefit of the work'.[88] Instances of less significance include the first establishment of the Presentation Sisters in Manchester in 1836, which was funded by the gift of £2,000 for their convent and school by a retired silk merchant, an immigrant from County Cavan in Ireland.[89]

Apart from the fortunes of their two famous heiresses, the SND also received several legacies and bequests by way of gifts of money, shares and property which were duly accounted for in their audits. An insight into the reason for one small bequest can be gleaned from a letter written by a former pupil of the Mount Pleasant Teacher Training College, in the 1920s, advising that her father had left the sisters £100 in his will, with the intention that it be 'in memory of the kindness shown to my daughter during her stay at the said College'.[90]

Support for the convents was by no means reliant on the recusant Catholic nobility and wealthy Irish immigrants. Converts to the Roman Catholic faith were particularly prominent and increased lay involvement from this direction might be seen as having been one of the consequences of the wave of conversion to Catholicism in fashionable society in the latter half of the nineteenth century in the wake of the Oxford Movement. Arnstein cites the recording of 'twenty-seven peers and 417 members of the nobility' who became 'Roman Catholic converts during the Victorian era', adding that 'most significant nineteenth-century Englishmen had either a close friend or relative who became a convert . . .'.[91] Biographical listings reveal that among the well-connected converts were three of the sons of William Wilberforce, the daughter and son-in-law of Sir Walter Scott and a sister of Mr Gladstone.[92] The newly converted were invariably enthusiastic and eager to assist in every type of charitable activity. Church histories include many mentions of the encouragement and financial aid given by Lady Georgina Fullerton, the novelist, who was 'for the last twenty years of her life, the very pattern of the great lady wholly given over to works of charity'.[93] Not only has she been credited with inviting the Daughters of Charity of St. Vincent de Paul to England in 1859, but the establishment of the Poor Servants of the Mother of God in 1868 has been attributed to her patronage of their founder, Fanny Taylor, another convert and a former nurse in the Crimea.[94]

Another aristocrat who became a leading benefactor following conversion to Catholicism was the third Earl of Bute who, with his wife, a daughter of Lord Howard of Glossop, 'committed themselves to alleviating many of the uncared for social needs of the day'.[95] Their support for the SSHJM, for example, was immense. Apart from all their other good works, the Butes built hospitals, schools and orphanages to accommodate the expanding apostolate of these sisters.[96] But not all lay support came from wealthy aristocratic circles and 'new' converts. There were other 'old Catholics' of more modest middle-class backgrounds who engaged in charitable endeavours by supporting the work of the convents. Many entertained a distrust of newly introduced Ultramontane church rituals and practices, and it was often the case that, in supporting the independence of women' religious congregations, they created and maintained a bulwark against what was sometimes seen as the overzealous encroachment of authority imposed by post-1850 diocesan control systems. An excellent example can be found in the philanthropic work of a Preston woman, Maria Holland. In 1871 she had 'personally funded the erection of an orphanage for Roman Catholic girls' at a cost of £5,454.[97] In 1877 she 'financed the building of St. Joseph's Institute for the Sick Poor in Preston'.[98] In both instances she arranged to have these institutions supervised by the Sisters of Charity of Our Lady Mother of Mercy, while control of the charities was to be overseen by their chaplains, the Jesuit Fathers.[99] At the same time she also 'provided an Endowment Fund of £2,200 for the upkeep of the orphanage with instructions that any surplus should be applied to the maintenance of the Institute'.[100] This fund was 'increased by a further £10,600 at the time of her death in 1879.[101] Maria Holland's distrust of Bishop Goss of Liverpool is transparent in her specific instructions as to how her beneficiaries were to manage and run her foundations: 'The Bishop of Liverpool shall not, nor shall any other Bishop or Priest or lay Commissioner, society, order, body or corporation . . . interfere or be entitled under any circumstances to interfere in the management or supervision or have any control . . . over the funds thereof or the property belonging thereto.'[102]

Clearly, while trusting the sisters and the Jesuits to carry out her instructions, she was determined to keep this bishop safely at arm's length. An interesting hidden agenda lurks behind the story of this reliance on and trust of Preston's Jesuit Fathers. The Society of Jesus had always been the target of the English hierarchy's immense distrust and suspicion and in 1875 their English Province was described in a letter written by Manning to Bishop Vaughan of Manchester as 'altogether abnormal, dangerous to themselves, mischievous to the Church in England'.[103] The comment was occasioned in the aftermath of a clash resulting from Vaughan's refusal to allow the Jesuits to open a school in his diocese.[104] In Preston they were more firmly entrenched and did their best to ensure that the Bishop of Liverpool was given little occasion to hold too much sway. Nothing so dramatic occurred regarding another Lancastrian lady benefactor. The elderly Miss Margaret Coulston was 'a member of a wealthy family of bankers, carriers and tanners in Skerton [Lancaster]. In 1890 she provided the lands and funds to erect a Catholic church in Skerton', this was followed by her provision of additional financial assistance in the building of a school which opened in 1896.[105] The Catholic elementary schools in Lancaster at this time were under the supervision of the Sisters of Mercy in a branch house of the sisters' foundation in Liverpool. Unlike the situation in Preston some twenty years earlier, in this instance the Bishop of Liverpool would have enjoyed considerable control over the Mercy convent's financial affairs because of their being constituted as an autonomous religious community of women in his diocese.

There are also many instances of lay people assisting the SSP, and there is evidence of at least twenty individuals or families who provided this congregation with practical and financial aid.[106] The SSP, although constituted into a separate English foundation within a few years of their arrival, were originally partly supported by funds from their original Mother House in Chartres. They also received financial support from the personal income of their own chaplain and the backing of the Bishop of Birmingham. One typical example of support in their early days of expansion came from a Mrs Kate Bishop in Leamington, who generously provided them with a house in which to establish a new convent in 1852.[107] She also paid the sisters' salaries and built and endowed their schools.[108]

With an apostolate in many ways similar to that of the SSP, the Sisters of Mercy also record that over twenty of their early convent foundations received financial or practical help from lay benefactors.[109]

It is striking how many instances of gifts of property or money were provided by women who were anxious to show their solidarity and practical support of communities of nuns and sisters without actually becoming members themselves. In most cases of this type, the arrangements were privately conducted by single ladies or widows. Quite often, this practical assistance was rewarded in due course, and especially in old age by their receiving the attention and perhaps nursing care of the

11. Mother House of the Sisters of St. Paul the Apostle, Selly Park, Birmingham
Source: G. Hudson, Mother Genevieve Dupuis (London, 1919), p. 228.

sisters. In Birmingham, for example, the Sisters of Mercy received an endowment of £5,000 from the Earl of Shrewsbury on their arrival in 1849, but were helped also by 'a local resident, Mr John Hardman, the distinguished promoter of ecclesiastical art who pledged himself to build and furnish a convent'.[110] His two daughters and a granddaughter became members of this community and his widow, who continued to support and help the sisters financially, subsequently took up residence in rooms attached to the convent, where she lived until her own death. To find similar instances of mutual rewards of charity, given and returned, is not uncommon in convent histories and is consistent with the ideals of socio-economic interdependence practised by the Catholic community.

The number of women who involved themselves in nineteenth-century philanthropic and charitable endeavours is now recognised as having been a feature of all the religious denominations. The key role played by these women has been identified by Prochaska, who presents a strong case for arguing that the number actively involved in such work belies the popularised ideal of the 'idle' Victorian female.[111] He claims that 'nineteenth-century women exploited the belief in their superior morality to increase their power in a society dominated by men.'[112] Basing his findings on research during the 1890s, Prochaska concludes that 'about 500,000 women laboured continuously and professionally in philanthropy; another 20,000 supported themselves as paid officials in charitable societies', and he notes that these figures 'did not include some 20,000 trained nurses or the 5,000 women in sisterhoods and nunneries who took on work which was essentially philanthropic'.[113] His sources, while clearly underestimating the number of sisters and nuns, would possibly have also been unaware of the number of lay women who supported the work of the convents.

The amount of financial support offered to women's religious institutions from the Catholic community in England seems not to have been overly affected by the residue of anti-Catholic legislation which still existed on the statute book. This imposed certain constraints on bequests to religious communities and it was a continuing problem that Catholic trusts were by law liable to confiscation or reapplication – being perceived as supportive of what was termed 'superstitious' practices.[114] Those who wished to support women's religious orders and congregations financially had recourse to several methods by which these legal difficulties could be overcome. These complexities need not be addressed here. However, what is interesting is a controversy which arose over the Act of 1853 which set up a permanent body of commissioners to register and administer all charitable trusts.[115] What has been called a 'genuine cleavage [within the Catholic hierarchy] on the point as to whether Catholic Trusts should be registered or not' split the Catholic bishops into two camps.[116] The chief concern of the bishops was the fear of losing authority and control over how such financial matters were arranged, and while most of the bishops agreed with the concept of registration, others, including Cardinal Wiseman, claimed it was 'hazardous'. It was not until 1862 that the differences of opinion between Cardinal Wiseman and the bishops were settled by a decision from Rome 'which ruled that to have Catholic Trusts registered would jeopardise Catholic bequests'.[117] In due course, the matter was eventually resolved. By 1880 a number changes to the law regulating property bequests to religious institutions had been implemented and Baldwin's Catholic Relief Act of 1927 finally abolished what remained of these obsolete pieces of legislation.[118]

THE BUSINESS OF RUNNING A CONVENT

To remain financially viable, the typical convent was required the balance its books and, if at all possible, to provide a small annual surplus of income over expenditure. As has been shown, income for active communities was derived from running schools, hospitals, nursing services and institutions or from the collection of alms. The wherewithal of ordinary household expenses, food, heat, light, rent and rates also had to be met. There were also extraordinary expenses to be covered, loan and mortgage repayments and the building and repairing of property. Communities with schools to run had to provide wages for pupil-teachers and any other lay staff members employed. School supplies had to be purchased. The sister superior and her assistant, the convent bursar, were accountable for every penny spent, either to their institute's Superior General or to the local bishop. Many expanding congregations acquired large, old buildings which required substantial repairs or refurbishment and, thereafter, regular maintenance. Building and repair programmes feature frequently in convent archives.[119] In taking responsibility for the supervision of construction work, local Superiors had direct dealings with surveyors, architects and building tradesmen, plumbers, carpenters, painters and decorators. In 1891 one convent superior writes to her Mother General to ask whether it would be the possible to transfer to new premises because the present house was 'in such a tumbledown condition that, last winter, we spent over £40 in repairs there, pipes being burst, ceilings falling down, drains given way . . .'.[120] Five years later, the same correspondent is writing to convey the contents of a surveyor's reports and quotations from architects and builders for a proposed new convent: 'there is a difference of £1,000 between the highest and lowest estimate [for the] same specification . . . and five quotations. Mr Blackmore guarantees that there should be not more than one penny extra beyond the quotation'.[121]

Occasionally, convent property included other premises which were already occupied by tenants. In such instances, rents had to be collected and the maintenance of the properties undertaken. Boundaries on convent grounds, because of the desirability of privacy, had to be secured and, if the archives of the Notre Dame sisters are typical examples of some of the problems experienced, references to disputes over walls, abutting buildings, rights of way and similar encroachments were not uncommon.[122]

The business of running a religious community required that, at times of extraordinary expense, loans and mortgages had to be arranged and bank overdrafts negotiated. Ownership of convent property and lands provided collateral for communities requiring mortgages and loans. The summarised accounts for the SND's English Province in 1905, for example, show that the greatest element of income in that year was raised by way of a mortgage on one of their convents, possible for a building programme. (Mortgage documents utilising this congregation's property as collateral were usually signed by the sisters who had been appointed to positions of authority within the community.[123]) With a surplus of income over expenditure which amounted to almost 20 per cent in that year, the accounts list interest received from six investments in overseas shares and funds available from two bequests under the heading of 'investment and bequests'. In the 'miscellaneous sources' column, a total of over £1,000 came from four personal legacies. In addition, the province benefited from rents received, the income of the sisters, payments channelled from their Mother House in Namur and amounts earned from other interest-bearing investments. Outgoing expenditure included money given to each of the English convents, charitable donations and pensions, a sum put aside for new investments, payments to Namur and a number of miscellaneous costs which included fees for lawyers and bank charges.[124]

Each convent's house accounting system had to make provision for the cost of insurance cover in much the same way as any household or business venture. Apart from the usual type of cover for water, fire or storm damage, there were occasions when unusual additional insurance was incurred. In August 1915 one large convent in the south of England obtained special insurance against aircraft raids. Lloyds of London charged an annual premium of £35.16s.6d (£35.82^1/$_2$p) for convent premises valued at £14,320.[125] How the sisters came to be so alert of the potential danger from 'flying machines' in wartime is an intriguing question, for they were still a novelty and it was hardly a common worry at that time. Just over two decades later this fear would become much more of a reality.[126]

By the turn of the century, the larger congregations' purchasing power was formidable and the extent to which business conducted by members of women's religious institutions with local traders was recognised as being of substantial value may be indicated by an incident in Hull in 1906. A controversy had raged for some time over the reluctance of the Council to grant bursaries for local Catholic schoolchildren. The matter was settled when, arguing successfully to reverse this decision, a member of the local education committee pointed out to fellow councillors that, not only had the Catholic population contributed to rate aid for education for more than thirty years, but that a considerable amount of money had been spent by the Sisters of Mercy in the city amounting to: '£65,000 in buildings alone since their arrival [in addition to] their personal rate payments of £177.10s a year and considerable sums paid to local tradesmen. Any private trader who spends that amount of money in the city as the Catholic nuns did, would be welcome with open arms.'[127]

Clearly, the financial purchasing power of individual convents made them part of the expanding service economy of the late nineteenth century. The advertising section of the *Catholic Directories* is replete with building suppliers and wholesalers offering plumbing and heating systems, laundry machinery, desks and school supplies of every description, in addition to day-to-day catering requirements. The partisan appeal of the tea merchants, Alexander and Co., may be noted in particular (see Plates 12 to 14).

Support for the convent from local Catholic business people in return for patronage might be seen as being an interdependent, quid pro quo relationship, although there were occasions when a community might receive undue pressure to support local tradesmen in preference to their own choice of supplier for goods and services. The archives of the SND provide an example of an unsuccessful attempt to intimidate them in this way.[128] In the early decades of the twentieth century, during negotiations for a substantial contract to build a new convent in Sheffield, the Sisters had agreed with their non-Catholic architect to employ his choice of builder in preference to accepting one of several quotations from local contractors. With a budget in excess of £20,000, the amount of money involved was substantial and there was a great deal of talk in the city's business circles which culminated in the Sisters receiving strongly-worded letters of protest, not only from a member of the local clergy, but also from a Sheffield bank manager who wrote on behalf of local building contractors and tradesmen. Hinting that the chosen builder might possible be connected to a Masonic lodge (a strongly effective argument, if proved true) the manager threatened that:

> The feeling in Catholic business circles in this city is becoming very bitter . . . I have to inform you that this matter will certainly be brought to the notice of His Eminence the Cardinal and the Bishops . . . and may have very serious effects . . . I have always been a friend of the Order and should very much regret anything to arise that would interfere with the present feeling.[129]

Having first reaffirmed and satisfied themselves as to the worthiness of their selected contractor, the response of the sisters was to stand their

12. *The Catholic Directory*, 1897: advertisement for laundry machinery and heating boilers

13. *The Catholic Directory*, 1920: advertisement for desks and school supplies and equipment

ground. The warning of 'serious effects' if they incurred the supposed displeasure of the Cardinal and bishops did not perturb them (they had no direct control over the way the sisters conducted their business, in any case). So they ignored the threats, let the building project commence as planned and reported the incident to their London-based lawyer. He replied : 'I am very glad you have decided to take no notice of these letters . . . the whole affair is certainly very unpleasant but I am convinced that it is all caused by petty jealousies and the Institute of Notre Dame is quite strong enough to ignore such things.' He added, 'I do not know if Mr. M is the manager of your bank at Sheffield, but if he is I should be inclined, after his letter, to transfer your account.'[130] It is not recorded whether the sisters followed this last piece of advice.

While professionals and experts advised and guided women's religious institutions on every aspect of legal and investment policies, the sisters themselves often used their own connections and experience in decision-making. Members of a community who came from well-connected families were adept at networking. A typical instance is evidenced in a letter from a cleric to Sr. Mary of St. Francis, SND (Mrs Petre) in 1869, in which the architect Charles A. Buckler and his associate builder are being strongly recommended for the contract to build a new convent in Battersea.[131] The writer of the letter had just completed a successful church and school building project and was putting in a good word for the architect although obviously unaware that Buckler would have been, in fact, no stranger to Mrs Petre. Her father, Lord Stafford, had some years previously employed Buckler's father as architect for the work on the family home in Costessey. On this occasion it would seem that the connection, plus this clerical recommendation, ensured that the junior Buckler was duly appointed.[132]

At a more mundane level, it can be illustrated that individual convents conducted their household expenditure and day-to-day outgoings with the same thrifty management as was required of any ordinary Victorian middle-class home. Good value and savings were sought in the purchase of all necessities. In the 1880s Mother Dupuis, Superior of the SSP in Birmingham, held a pass book account with a London-based firm, The Civil Service Supply Association, for the regular delivery of groceries and other goods.[133] This type of 'middle-class pseudo-Co-operative' store offered customers several benefits arising out of their membership which included credit facilities and discount prices resulting from the policy of bulk buying.[134] Even so, Mother Dupuis's pass book records that the quality and exactitude of their supplies were carefully monitored. A discovered overcharge of 4d for coffee, later itemised as a credit refund, shows how carefully she or, more probably, the sister appointed as convent bursar, checked all balances.

Overall indications, supported by case studies and random examples, suggest that the methods used by convents to remain economically viable involved three main means of raising funds. These were: income from work; dowries; and subscriptions, donations and gifts of property or endowments received from benefactors, which included their own members, the laity, individual contributions by the clergy and the underlying responsibility and support of the English hierarchy. Active and mixed communities in particular were increasingly able to generate income by owning, administering or charging fees for their services in schools, hospitals and a range of nursing and institutional work which included the administration of laundries.

Such fees in many instances subsidised the free provision of the same services for those who could not afford to pay and for the many areas of unpaid social care they undertook. Most congregations and orders drew in funds from dowry payments which their members brought into their communities on entry. Under Canon Law, safeguards were in place to ensure that these funds were never spent during a member's lifetime, but money could be invested to provide an income for the benefit of the community. Over time, the cumulative growth of such capital funds would have been considerable. Women who chose the religious life who were wealthy in their own right had the discretion to use their personal fortunes and inheritances for the benefit of their community and there are instances of such funds being used for investment in property and expansion of convent-based undertakings.

There is also evidence of significant support forthcoming from the Catholic laity. Gifts or loans of property, direct financial assistance and engagement in fund-raising on behalf of congregations was commonplace. Members of the nobility were prominent among the 'old Catholic' families who traditionally offered financial aid to communities of nuns and sisters. Catholics who were members of the professions, landowners and families with connections in business and trade provided useful networks of support. A wave of new converts to the Catholic faith was eager to give levels of funding in amounts which ranged from the relatively modest to the dispersal of great fortunes. Communities particularly designated as Sisters of Charity, and possibly influenced by French-inspired disdain of the Poor Law, created and sustained many practical channels for dispensing charity through the collecting of alms and goods for redistribution to the poor. Donations and subscriptions were solicited from all walks of society.

Finance was inextricably linked to issues of control. Officially, the English bishops had responsibility for the welfare of women's religious communities under their diocesan care. This responsibility could (but not always did) include a certain level of control over financial matters and, on occasion, caused convents and bishops to become embroiled in controversies which required delicate negotiation to resolve. Evidence suggests that the Victorian social climate was not the easiest one within which women's religious communities could be perceived as retaining their total financial independence. Public appeals almost always cited the support of a male member of the clergy or lay patron. However, the fact that so many of the congregations that expanded in England and Wales in the nineteenth and the early twentieth century rose from very poor and simple beginnings to become the custodians and administrators of vast wealthy and efficient corporate institutions – many operating an international scale – suggests that the women who governed the finances of these convents, while at the same time dedicating their whole selves to the religious life, were also highly exceptional, innovative and courageous entrepreneurs. Mothers superior were required to be financially astute managers of funds and property and the convents were veritable hives of industry. The sisters were fanatically thrifty, hardworking and, having been trained by rigorous rules to seek perfection in all their endeavours, it is not altogether surprising that their struggles to gain and retain the convents' financial stability would appear to have been enviably successful.

Religious communities wielded considerable financial purchasing power which made them part of the expanding service economy of the late nineteenth and the early twentieth century. As the communities grew in number and size, convent superiors were required to undertake responsibility for numerous construction projects. The sisters supervised the building of convents, schools, colleges, hospitals and other institutions and they attended to the repair or renewal of old premises. In this work they dealt direct with architects, surveyors, contractors and tradesmen. In addition, religious communities generated a considerable volume of business for the suppliers and purveyors of goods and services catering for the day-to-day running of convents.

The growth in the number of convents and the wealth of the property maintained by them reflect their financial strength. Sustained investment in the building and maintenance of convent property provided subsequent collateral for mortgages, loans and bank overdrafts when expansion was needed. Careful investment of monies received from legacies and bequests ensured additional stability and convents grew larger along with the increase of their own membership and the growing number of pupils, patients and people in their institutionalised care. The income from these expanding undertakings would have risen accordingly.

As Clear in her study of nuns in nineteenth-century Ireland concludes, quoting Fahey, that because the work of nuns and sisters was 'positively valued and their status perceived as distinctively feminine, [albeit] as defined by men and regulated by man-made rules . . . they won a vital beach-head in women's liberation in Ireland'.[135] In England and Wales, women's communities have been rarely considered as having been large groups of self-governed, powerful women who had freed themselves from day-to-day male-dominated society and who enjoyed financial and managerial responsibilities far beyond the experience of the average women of their day. Their lifestyle was reliant on their ability to earn a living selling services and, for many congregations, their 'market' was not confined to the expanding middle-class, Catholic community but embraced all comers. Communities especially dedicated to the care of the poor generated their own methods of supplying the needs of their own specialised markets. All were driven by the fervour of their faith and ideals.

Previous chapters have already shown how the demand for improved education of the young was growing, how the value of good nursing care was appreciated and how a plethora of social needs awaited attention. The key to providing a response to all this endeavour was the expansion of convent networks and the recruitment of enough suitable candidates. Many hundreds of young women were to answer the call.

CHAPTER SIX

The Call: A Plentiful Supply of Aspirants

The growth in the number of Roman Catholic religious congregations in England and Wales and the expansion and development of their convent-based undertakings could not have taken place without a plentiful supply of girls able and willing to embrace the religious life. This chapter will consider from whence and how the convents recruited new members. Was recruitment dependent on push or pull factors? What other forces, other than that of religious fervour, were at work?

It is important to recognise the existence of a deeply religious and spiritual sincerity motivating much of the impetus driving young women to take the choice of entering a convent. However, such motivation can be difficult to quantify. When viewed from a purely secular angle, convent life might be seen as having provided educated, single women with the dignity and security of a professional status for life, as teachers, nurses or social workers. Studies by Susan O'Brien, Caitriona Clear, Mary Peckham, Hope Stone and Susan Mumm have already identified much of the social contribution made by this level of professionalism within religious communities of Roman Catholic and Anglican women in nineteenth-century Britain.[1] In terms of the personal development of women within the religious life, research so far has helped to show that, although still largely unrecognised and unacknowledged in terms of general social history, the sisters who managed and controlled convents had unique opportunities to achieve positions of managerial and financial authority and power not usually possible for women in secular society at that time. By the same token, however, the life of many women in convents did not rise above a lowly status, especially for girls who entered communities which maintained internal class divisions as lay sisters (most usually working as domestic servants).[2]

Whence and how the convents drew women was dependent on many complex and interlocking factors, and not until we have additional data can the exact levels of diversity in respect of motivation be definitively identified. However, recent studies, and my own findings, can add further confirmation. For example, O'Brien's early research found that 20 per cent of the mainly middle-class girls educated by one of the three congregations she studied, the Society of the Holy Child Jesus, subsequently entered the religious life, 'with many of them going on to hold positions of responsibility and leadership'.[3]

At another level, sisters who were engaged in elementary education and social work were often, but not solely, drawn from working-class or artisan backgrounds. O'Brien comments that the Cross and Passion Sisters postulants 'remained predominantly urban lower class', while at the same time citing three entrants who had come from exceptional backgrounds.[4] Her examination of an English foundation, the Poor Servants of the Mother of God, concludes that, in their case, 'young women from rural Ireland and the Irish communities in England made up almost the entire membership of the congregation during the nineteenth century'. She held that this was 'a far higher proportion than in the other two congregations' she had researched.[5] In her most recently published study, she found that the Manchester-founded Cross and Passion Sisters had 50 per cent Irish-born members in the 1850s and 80 per cent in the 1870s.[6] She also usefully provides a closer look at 'eight francophone congregations, in particular the Faithful Companions of Jesus and the Society of the Sacred Heart'.[7] In referring to the latter's drawing in of vocations, she quotes from their founder Sophia Barat, who wrote in 1842 that an establishment in Ireland would be 'the road into England'.[8] O'Brien's work confirms that Ireland was a rich source of supply for vocations, although detailed recruitment figures to substantiate this are neither provided nor perhaps necessary in her commentary since this is focused on the influence of French convents on Roman Catholic life in England.

What we need to know now is how typical this high intake of Irish women was when compared with that of entrants to other English religious communities. From which regions of Ireland were they drawn? And for what reasons? The absence of information defining their socio-economic backgrounds has hitherto been a drawback, especially so in constructing some assessment of the sorts of Irish farming family whose daughters were so readily drawn into English convents. At the same time, we should be aware of the hidden Irish diaspora. When closer examination is made of the entrants' registers for the Sisters of St. Paul and the Sisters of Notre Dame de Namur, for example, it may be posited that a high proportion of their English-born entrants were, in actuality, drawn from second- or third-generation Irish immigrant family backgrounds.[9] O'Brien has indicated that she suspected this may have been so in regard to the congregations chosen for her studies.[10] Commenting some years ago that 'more extensive research is required before we can be sure what was typical either of the English foundations or of the English branches of "imported" congregations', she was conscious of gaps in the definitive data.[11] She was then unequivocal in noting the need 'to tease out the differences and similarities.'[12]

The links between English and Irish convents uncovered by O'Brien may be supplemented and compared with Clear's study of nuns in Ireland which, although confining itself to the nineteenth century, provides clear statistical evidence of patterns of recruitment to Irish convents.[13] Data drawn from my own studies reveal a considerable volume of inter-convent movement, linking recruitment in Ireland to the expansion in England. At least one of the communities Clear studied was a branch house of a congregation with European origins but with bases in England and Wales, so her statistics can provide useful comparisons. Peckham's study of Irish female congregations and Stone's examination of Victorian England also offer clues, although less clearly.[14] The latter concentrates on the difficulties encountered by foundresses of both Roman Catholic and Anglican English orders and congregations, while Peckham's study ends in 1870 and deals only with early Irish foundations. Nevertheless, Peckham has identified areas of continuity, for example, in the percentage of siblings who entered congregations together, and her findings have helped to link patterns of early recruitment to those existing later in the century.[15] Much, too, may be gleaned from studies which, at first, would seem to have little to offer. Mumm's thesis sheds light on the recruitment, socio-economic backgrounds and regional origins of entrants to the Victorian Anglican communities, which is useful as a comparative gauge.[16] Hoy's investigation of the recruitment of Irish girls for religious communities in the United States offers a transatlantic comparison with the similar methods used to encourage entrants for English convents.[17]

These studies suggest that convent life in England and Wales escapes simple generalisations. We need a greater concentration on identifying patterns of recruitment in regard to the socio-economic backgrounds and regional origins of girls who embraced the religious life in England and Wales. This chapter offers a first attempt at this. It includes an analysis of data drawn from four congregations, looking at the girls' average age and educational standards on entry, former employment and longevity. Why they joined convents and why they were rejected by, or left the convents, are also important factors to consider.[18]

The methods of recruitment that were employed also need to be considered in relation to changing social and economic pressures in England and Ireland from the mid-nineteenth century to the early decades of the twentieth. What was the extent of these pressures and how important were they? How can we explain surges in recruitment to convent life, for example in the 1870s or the post-1917 period? It is worth considering whether Irish recruitment trends were comparable to those in Europe during the same period.[19] The late Ralph Gibson's work on French religious houses suggests that, despite the high levels of anti-clericalism that existed in Europe, there were quite extraordinary levels of intake to the religious life for women. His figures reveal upwards of 155,000 women *religieux* in France and Belgium alone by the early 1880s.[20]

The four active congregations reviewed here had constitutional rules that did not allow, at least officially, any internal class distinctions.[21] In this, these four were typical of many active congregations that had similar rules during this period. By concentrating on the registers of postulants, novices and professed sisters, it is possible to construct a detailed picture of recruitment since the registers were, of necessity, compiled with care and meticulously maintained by each of the congregations. Of the four case studies, the records of the Sisters of Charity of St. Paul the Apostle (SSP), held in their mother house in Birmingham and contained in several original, bound volumes, proved to be the most useful and concise. The details of each entrant's name address, family, age on entry and other information were given, as was her subsequent progress up to the date of her death or of leaving the community. The Sisters of Notre Dame de Namur (SND) in Liverpool also afforded me access to records of their English province. While the original early registers are maintained in Namur, data relating to the intake and careers of professed sisters from England, Ireland, Scotland and Wales are held in their Provincial archive office and are now available on a database. This archive holds a wealth of useful additional material which includes the original records of their postulant intake from 1915 onwards, for the reason that the First World War had disrupted travel to Belgium and a separate novitiate was established in Liverpool to accommodate the intake at that time. The original registers of the Sisters of the Sacred Hearts of Jesus and Mary (SSHJM) are contained in bound volumes in their Chigwell mother house.

Here again, access was obtained to these volumes. These list the details for postulants, novices and professed sisters. The records have also been sorted and tabulated by their archivist. The English Province of the Daughters of Charity of St. Vincent de Paul (DVDP), which covers the intake from Ireland and England, provided access to a volume, recently drawn up, which, although excluding the intake of postulants and novices who did not persevere, none the less contains much useful information such as the names, addresses and subsequent placements of professed sisters from Ireland. This is held in their Irish Provincial archives in Blackrock, Dublin.

Each of the case studies has some directly comparable records, such as the birthplace and year of age at entry, longevity and incidence of kith and kin within congregations. Other details are sporadic, however, and allow some comparisons only over a few decades. Much can also be gleaned from the occupations of entrants' fathers given in the records of the SSP and the educational qualification or previous work experience of entrants to the SND.

Each of these communities has roots in France. However, they differ from each other in their development, size and structural organisation. Within the first decades of arrival in England in 1847 the SSP gradually detached themselves from their French origins. By 1867 they had reorganised themselves into a separate English foundation with a mother house in Birmingham. As we saw in Chapter 3, their early development and expansion began with the provision of elementary schooling and parish work. This soon extended into orphanage and child care. Middle schools and teacher training followed.

By contrast, the SND, having arrived in England in 1845, continued to function as a province of their Belgian mother house. Novitiate training of English-speaking recruits was maintained in Namur until it was disrupted by the onset of the First World War, after which time recruits remained in England. The SND apostolate began by providing schools and night schools for the poor and progressed to providing schools for girls at all levels, from elementary to university entrance. With the establishment of their Liverpool College at Mount Pleasant in 1855, they became leaders in the field of Catholic teacher training.

The third congregation examined here is the DVDP, another of the congregations discussed in Chapter 3. These sisters maintained a hierarchical organisational structure with a mother house in Paris from where several provincial branches throughout the world were governed. These Sisters' first arrival in these islands was made at Drogheda in Ireland in

1855. By 1858 they had sent a contingent of sisters to England to open a convent in Sheffield. We concentrate here, however, on the records of women who were recruited from Ireland.[22] The DVDP established hospital and institutional establishments in England and Ireland in addition to visiting and caring for the sick and poor in their own homes. One of their fields of specialisation was the provision of institutional care for blind children and adults and for the deaf and dumb. The Sisters of the Sacred Hearts of Jesus and Mary (SSHJM) are the smallest of the congregations selected here for review. This congregation was a much later arrival from Europe (1870) and also one which chose to become detached from its French foundations in 1903. With this separation, the reformed community changed their name from the Servants of the Sacred Heart and established a mother house in Essex. The work of the SSHJM quickly became focused on the needs of handicapped children and mother and baby homes.

The apostolate of each of these active congregations evolved and widened in scope as both needs and opportunities arose for engaging in new undertakings.[23] For reasons of confidentiality and to avoid including details relevant to many sisters who may still be living, 1926 has been fixed as the concluding entry date.

THE NATURE AND CHARACTERISTICS OF RECRUITMENT

Numbers

The registers of the four congregations reveal that the growth in the number of successful entrants from 1847 to 1926 clearly parallels the expansion of convent numbers and convent-based educational and social services. Each decade from 1847 to 1926 saw an appreciable, sustained rise in the annual intake of new aspirants to the SSP and the SND (see Table 21). All of these congregations experienced a marked upswing in the late 1860s and the 1870s, and, while the SSP figures levelled off after the late 1890s, the SND figures continue to show a steady annual increase.

Girls entering the SSHJM also grew steadily in number following the arrival of this congregation in England. Applicant numbers peaked between the late 1890s and the First World War. The high intakes into the SSP and the SND between 1867 and 1886 reflect, first, their response to the 1870 Education Act, and, secondly, the substantial improvement in the provision of higher education for girls. The same decades also saw the SSP's work expand as a result of changes to the administration of the Poor Law.

Growth of entry to the SSHJM, particularly in the 1890s, reflects this congregation's response to the 1889 legislation for the provision of special schools for mentally-defective children, and also assisted their expansion of the education and care of sick children after the turn of the century.

The data for the DVDP (see Table 22) were calculated separately, being confined to records of Irish-born members of the English-speaking province. The full intake to this English province from mid-nineteenth century to 1937 has been calculated by Sr. Judith Greville as about 2,000, of whom about 1,139 were Irish.[24] Again, a similar surge of new aspirants to this congregation is evidenced from the late 1880s onwards and this may be seen also as a response to the growing need for social services for the poor, a particular focus for these sisters.

Entry regulations for all the women's orders and congregations were stringent. Baptism and confirmation certificates and evidence of legitimate birth had to be accompanied by references of irreproachable character and a clean bill of health.[25] The number of entrants who achieved final profession as sisters fell far below the level of the total applications. The life of an active sister working in social services for the poor, in schools or in hospitals was highly disciplined and rigorous. Not all entrants who aspired to this 'vocation' had the personal attributes, the physical strength or the deep religious faith and fervour necessary to succeed. Maria Luddy comments that, 'nuns describe, and have described their motivation for entering convents as a "vocation" but this rhetoric, which conjures up images of otherworldly ideals, should not blind us to the expectations which nuns, as women, had for convent life'.[26]

Cecil Kerr reveals the clinical efficiency of the novice mistress's task in the DVDP. Sr. Mary Howard describes the training period in Paris for novices as 'like a great manufactory of sisters, in which characters are formed and reformed, wills broken and worldliness planed down . . . everyone is passed through the same mould, just as a piece of clay is made into a china cup'.[27]

The registers of the SSP between 1877 and 1926 show that 37 per cent of their applicants failed to persevere, either within the six to nine months as a postulant or during the three training years spent as a novice (see Table 23). An examination of the numbers that persevered reveals that, while the number of applicants to the SSP and the proportion of final professions both dropped back slightly in 1887–96, this trend was reversed during the period 1897–1906. Intake and successful outcome dropped once more after 1907 and levelled off to remain steady throughout the following two decades. It may be noted that the earlier nineteenth-century failure rates were substantially lower than the twentieth-century figures. By 1917–26 the failure rate had risen to 45 per cent of all aspirants.

Did the standard of entrants slip – or had the weeding out process become even more rigorous? Both explanations may be valid. It could be that the extreme urgency to find enough sisters to staff schools had passed. Membership records show that the number of sisters levelled off during the years of the First World War and the size of this congregation did not begin to grow once more until after 1924. The peak was reached in 1937–38.[28]

How typical are the examples taken from the SSP? Some indication can be obtained by constructing a comparison of the levels of non-perseverance for all three congregations across a shorter sample period for which comparable details are available. For example, between 1914 and 1926 the SSP records show a failure rate of 46 per cent of the intake; SSHJM registers reveal that 30 per cent did not persevere, while the SND did demonstrably better with 20 per cent of entrants not progressing past postulancy or novitiate (see Table 24).

The lower level of failure for applicants for the SND is quite possibly due to the fact that their work was almost exclusively in education and many aspirants were already qualified teachers, unlike the other two congregations which preferred to consider untrained applicants who could be later assessed and either dismissed as unsuitable candidates or assigned for dedicated training for the posts within their more diverse apostolate.

How do these findings compare with those from congregations examined by other historians? Little research has been done on religious communities in England and Wales. However, work that focused on nineteenth-century Irish convents has revealed similar levels of unsuccessful vocation. Luddy claims that almost 40 per cent left or were dismissed out of the 1,348 applications to the Religious Sisters of Charity in Ireland between 1812 and 1900.[29] Clear found that Galway's Mercy Convent had a 32 per cent failure rate between 1840 and 1900, while the Good Shepherd sisters lost 18 per cent of their aspirants between 1861 and 1900.[30]

Thus the high levels of non-perseverance would indicate that, while the choice of a life-style as a religious sister would seem to have been a popular and desirable one at a time when there were few or no opportunities for girls to gain professional status as single women, the congregations were rigorous in weeding out candidates. It was, indeed, the case of many being called, but few being chosen. Examination of the SSP and the SSHJM registers reveals that the majority of those who were sent home as 'unsuitable' or who left at their own request did so within the first year, mainly because of what was described as a 'lack of vocation'. In the SSP almost as many had to be declared unfit for the religious life due to a 'lack of health' or 'delicate health'.[31] Nervous or mental weaknesses were quickly detected. Overscrupulous or unstable candidates were summarily despatched. On rare occasions a novice mistress might expand her notes on the deficiencies of an unsuccessful recruit with a scathing honesty: 'not a worker, distinctly sluggish . . . too delicate for housework . . . legs bad . . . weak eyes . . . untruthful . . . useless . . . no loss!'[32] The process of slow and careful selection for acceptance as a member of a community ensured that only the fittest and most dedicated of girls made the grade to final profession as a nun or sister.

The registers of SSHJM entrants relate to postulants who entered subsequent to their English foundation in 1903. Although these records are not as comprehensive as those of the SSP, they clearly display a similar, rigorous vetting of recruits, with many rejections on health grounds: 'Found to be delicate'; 'suffering varicose veins'; 'sent home owing to heart trouble'.[33] In both congregations it is highly probable that the frequently termed 'delicate' health of the girls as a reason for rejection was a euphemism for indications of incipient tuberculosis.

The number of sisters who left a congregation after their time in the novitiate and the taking of their final vows was extremely low. To leave a community at this stage was taken as a very serious step and departure was strictly governed by Canon Law (Canons 637–45), according to whether the vows taken were simple or solemn, temporary, renewable or perpetual. Departure without permission was deemed either 'Flight or Apostacy' and could automatically incur excommunication (Canon 2385). In respect of diocesan institutions which functioned under the control of a local bishop, official release from vows required his permission in addition to the assent of the congregation's superior. Members of papal institutions were required to apply to the Holy See in Rome for the necessary dispensations.[34] In all instances, therefore, a member making the decision to leave a community was subjected to a series of slow and cumbersome procedures.

The DVDP, whose rule allowed members to renew their simple vows annually, were, for this reason perhaps, more free to leave than was the case for many others. Yet evidence indicates that out of the 907 Irish women who were accepted into this congregation between 1847 and 1926 only seventy-nine left, or just over 8 per cent of the intake. This percentage of lost members after profession of vows is congruent with the level of loss from the SND and the SSP, which also had figures of around 8 per cent when those who departed just before taking profession are included. From the data that are available, it would appear that the proportion of sisters who made the difficult decision to leave after a number of years as a member of a congregation came to only about 5 per cent.

Demographic Factors

Young women who applied to be accepted by the SSHJM and the SND had an average entry age of 23, with the SSP only a shade below at 22.8.[35] The DVDP's average entry age was 24. By the time entrants were trained and fully professed they were usually between 25 and 28. It was rare for postulants to be over 30 or under 17. Those who became teaching sisters often entered after they had achieved qualification and experience as lay-teachers.

These average entry ages are congruent with other research findings. For example, Luddy found 24 to be the average age of entry to the Religious Sisters of Charity in Milltown, Dublin in the period 1840–1900, with peak entry numbers during the decade 1880–90.[36] Clear found that the average entry age of entry to four Irish-based convents, comprising the Sisters of Mercy in Galway and Limerick, the Good Shepherd Sisters and the Dominicans, never rose above 26 nor fell below 20 across five decades, 1851–1900. Peckham, although she concentrated rather more on the earlier decades of the nineteenth century, found entry ages only slightly younger at between 22 and 24.[37] O'Brien did not discuss the implications to be drawn from the entry age.[38]

Two preconceptions existing in the popular understanding of convent life, based on false assumptions, may now be challenged. First, the idea that girls who became nuns entered that state while still extremely young, inexperienced and impressionable cannot be sustained. As we have seen from the evidence of the numbers of rejected aspirants and the reasons for their unsuitability, the immature and those with illusions or lack of dedication soon dropped out or were asked to leave. Furthermore, it is significant that the average age for failed entrants varied little from successful aspirants in at least one of the congregations studied. The second popular misconception is that life in a convent was chosen when a girl reached an age when it was to late for her to find a suitable husband. This is patently not true. However, the likelihood of marriage differed between the English, the Scots and the Welsh and the Irish entrants and it should be recognised that social and economic pressures in Ireland made for a completely different attitude in regard to marriage.[39]

The same may be said of the choice of the religious life.[40] The evidence derived from the average age of entry suggests that, to a great extent, the choice of the religious life was made by mature young women who were not yet past the marriageable age. Between 1851 and the First World War the average age of marriage showed virtually no change at just over 25 in the United Kingdom.[41] Timothy Guinnane, in a more recent study of Ireland, estimates the marriage age of female cohorts born in 1821 at 26.2, rising to 27.5 for those born in 1861.[42]

The debate over 'surplus' single women, estimated to have risen from 3 per cent in 1821 to 8 in 1931, has recently been revised by demographers.[43] What was perceived as a 'problem' in the mid-nineteenth century is now thought to have been 'inaccurately diagnosed . . . [and single women] gave an enormous impetus to the early growth of the social services and nursing professions'.[44] This being said, however, the choice of the religious life might indeed have been *preferred* to that of marriage or the expectation of life-long spinsterhood.[45] Single women were expected to remain within the family home or household of a close male relative. A striking note with regard to aspirants from English households is the number of girls who gave the address of a widowed mother, a brother or a sister as their home address on entry. In 1857, a contemporary writer had noted, 'Happier by far is a sister of Charity or Mercy than a young lady at home without work or a lover.'[46] As to Irish-born entrants, another contemporary account has an extremely bleak view of the prospect of marriage in post-famine rural Ireland, 'young girls had nothing to look forward to but a loveless marriage, hard work, poverty, a large family and often a husband who drank'.[47] Life in a convent would seem, by comparison, considerably more acceptable.

The number of professed sisters who lived to enjoy old age in each of the congregations examined was remarkably high, suggesting that convent life was relatively healthy. In the period 1847–1917 the average age of death for members of the SSP, the SND and the DVDP was 67. The SSHJM lived on average to 71 (records for 1869–1918). Not inconsistent with these findings, Mumm's analysis of her Anglican sisters produces average ages of 70 to 73.[48] She comments that this compares 'very favourably' with Hollingworth's research on longevity within female members of the Victorian aristocracy, which set life expectancy at 66.[49] O'Brien found, too, that over 50 per cent of the Society of the Holy Child Jesus lived to be over 70.[50] Citing Wrigley and Scofield and 'projecting their data', she concludes that 'fewer than 10 per cent of the general female population lived beyond the age of eighty, while 25 per cent of the Holy Child nuns did so'.[51] Such figures indicate a lifestyle that was contented and healthy.[52]

A striking number of blood relatives are found in the registers in these case studies, particularly in respect of Irish families. There are many instances of two, three or four sisters and cousins following each another into the religious life. (Not always with a successful outcome, it must be said.) Some examples of close family ties are noteworthy, such as the six sisters and two cousins from a farming family in Co. Meath who entered the DVDP between 1890 and around 1907.[53] Excluding other relatives within the congregation, identifiable siblings in the ranks of the SSP made up almost 15 per cent of the intake for the period studied; for the SSHJM this figure stood at 11 per cent and, for the DVDP, at 20 per cent. These figures are probably underestimates. Congregation registers contain clues that suggest many other blood relatives over and above the easily traced siblings, but it is not possible to identify cousins, aunts and nieces with sufficient accuracy.

This networking influence of kith and kin in convent recruitment has been noted by others. Referring to several examples among Irish-born entrants to the Mercy, Presentation and Good Shepherd congregations in Ireland, Clear identified 'The incidence of blood relations entering the same congregations . . . to have been high.'[54] On the other hand, Peckham, while noting the trend in the earlier decades, makes the unproven assumption that family ties within convents lessened off in the latter part of the century.[55] Evidence here suggests quite the opposite.

With one or two exceptions, it was rare to find the same level of close kith and kin among the English, Scots and Welsh-born entrants. On the one hand, this may be interpreted as evidence of the absence of extended family unit networking, very much a feature of Irish families. On the other, it may have been indicative of less pressure in terms of a girl's parents concern with status or economic considerations. There were more alternative employment opportunities for young women in England than in Ireland. Was there, in addition, a greater reluctance on the part of parents to see their girls take the veil? Oral evidence suggests the latter, especially in families with a parent who was a convert or, as happened frequently, a non-Catholic. An elderly member of the Daughters of the Holy Spirit, recently interviewed, recalls how her mother feared that her daughter was embracing 'a selfish way of life' and the family were 'not at all too keen' about her choice.[56] Another interview, collected twenty years ago from a Sister of the Holy Child born in 1879, relates that her father had been in favour of girls benefiting from higher education, and, wanting his daughter to become a doctor, had initially sent her to

Cambridge. The man in question was an agnostic, originally from a Reform Jewish family. His daughter's experience at Cambridge was not successful and she went, instead, into teaching and became a Catholic. This sister recalled that, 'My darling mother was upset . . . he [father] didn't say much.' She admitted that her decision to enter religion was taken with some reluctance. She was 33 years of age, which was much older than the average, before she finally made up her mind. 'I thought I probably would be a nun, but I wasn't too keen . . . I admired the nuns tremendously.'[57]

There is a darker side to the many instances of members of the same family or close friends who had, with shared aspirations, entered a congregation 'together' at the same time or within a year or two of each other. The practice of the French-run congregations, it would seem, was to place such friends and close relatives in houses far apart from each other after novitiate.[58] Most were never ever again to be together in the same convent. This harsh rule was designed not only to assist the formation of the total denial of self expected of girls who chose the religious life, but to avoid possible occasions of scandal. What were termed 'particular friendships' between members in a community were stringently guarded against.

Geographical Origins

A breakdown of the regional birth origins of members recruited to the congregations casts light on several factors which have a bearing on how we might consider the growth of the religious life for women in the nineteenth century. Analysis of the country of birth for entrants in respect of three case studies reveals that the growth in the number of aspirants was largely reliant on a large intake of Irish-born girls (see Tables 25 to 27). The number of Irish entrants is particularly noticeable within the professed sisters in the SSP and the SSHJM. Fifty-eight per cent of the subsequently professed sisters in the SSP and 78 per cent of the SSHJM were Irish. The SND, despite having more English and Scottish entrants, were also heavily reliant on Ireland, almost a quarter of their members coming from there. Although the DVDP figures have the drawback of providing only estimates for the English, Welsh or Scots-born professed sisters recruited into their English Province, it is feasible that more than half of their intake was Irish-born. The considerable growth of DVDP recruitment from Ireland can be usefully compared with the levels of Irish entrants in the other three congregations.

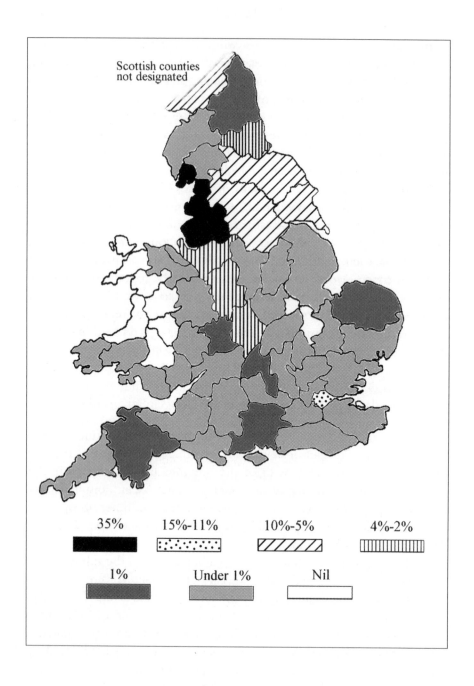

Scottish counties
not designated

| 35% | 15%-11% | 10%-5% | 4%-2% |
| | | | |

| 1% | Under 1% | Nil |
| | | |

J. Intake of Recruits from England and Wales for Three Congregations, 1845–1926;
Place of Birth of Professed Sisters

If the figures for all the studied congregations are combined, a geo-graphical overview of the birth origin of total recruitment can be mapped (see Map J). It is possible to demonstrate that, for three of the four studied, between 1847 and 1926, intake of their successfully professed sisters born in England, Scotland and Wales was reliant on girls living in what were urban and industrialised regions – Lancashire and the Greater London area. (See also the detailed analyses of the birth origins of professed sisters in each congregation set out in Table 28 for England, Scotland and Wales and Table 29 for Ireland.)

It is striking that the number of English members recruited to the SSP and the SND born in Lancashire far outweighed those from any other county in England, Scotland or Wales. While Yorkshire, Scotland and London also had significant numbers of entrants, the proportion was at a relatively lower level. The two important Notre Dame teacher-training colleges in Liverpool and Dowanhill, Scotland were undoubtedly contributed influential factors in relation to recruitment from these locations, as did the entry of girls educated at their own boarding schools. In respect of the SSP intake, their teacher-training facilities in Birmingham would have also contributed to some extent to the number of aspirants from the Midlands towards end of the period under study. Analysis shows that the SSHJM drew far fewer entrants from England than either the SSP or the SND, and, unlike either of these, new recruits born in London and Scotland outnumbered those from Lancashire.[59]

When the figures for Irish recruits to all the congregations studied are combined (see Map K) it is clear that recruitment from Ireland was dependent on the intake from the rich farming provinces which lie below the line from Louth on the east coast and Limerick to the west. Detailed analysis has demonstrated (set out in Tables 29 and 30) that the Irish-born members of each congregation came mainly from the 'strong-farmer' cattle and dairy-farming areas of Munster and south Leinster, most especially the counties of Cork, Limerick and Tipperary. The intake from County Dublin and Cork was affected to some extent by the number of entrants drawn from city conurbations, although none of these cities was very large. Dublin's population hovered only around the 200,000 mark, while Cork remained half that size. There were several interlocking social and economic factors which encouraged large numbers of Irish-born girls to join English convents. However, it is necessary to recognise here that the high levels of Irish kith and kin present within the congregations must necessarily be linked to localised concentrations of recruitment.

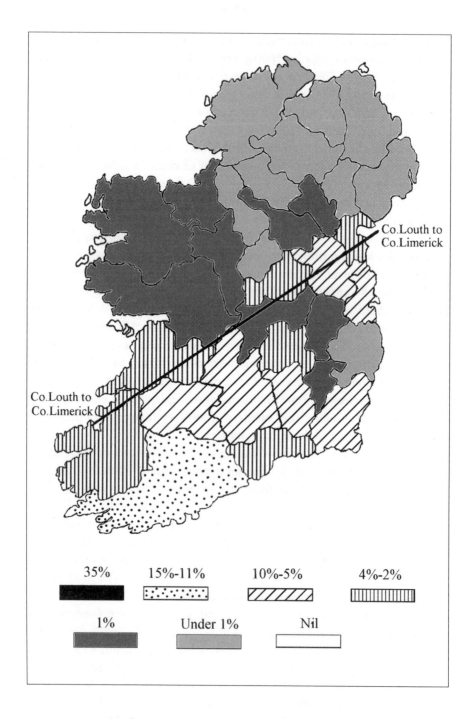

Co.Louth to
Co.Limerick

Co.Louth to
Co.Limerick

| 35% | 15%-11% | 10%-5% | 4%-2% |

| 1% | Under 1% | Nil |

K. Intake of Recruits from Ireland for Four Congregations, 1845–1926;
Place of Birth of Professed Sisters

The early presence of the DVDP in Ireland, mentioned earlier, which, unlike the other congregations, had maintained houses in Drogheda, Dublin, Cork and Belfast, enabled them to draw in a rather wider geographical spread of entrants. The greatest number of professed sisters, almost 15 per cent, were born in County Cork. This mirrors more general patterns of emigration from Ireland for 1851–1921, which also shows that emigrants were drawn mainly from the province of Munster and particularly Cork city and county, accounting for over 16 per cent of all emigrants from Ireland between 1851 and 1910, and 12 per cent between 1911 and 1921.[60] The provinces of Munster and Leinster combined, accounted for between 55 and 65 per cent. of the emigration for the period 1851–1921.[61]

These findings suggest very different patterns of migration: short distances for young women born in England and long distances for Irish-born girls. The predominance of Lancashire and the other northern counties may be attributed to the high Catholic population and the Irish diaspora. English entrants were drawn, in the main, from their local environment, especially through convent-run schools. The short, localised migration undertaken by English recruits may be seen as consistent with attitudes which did not accept long-distant migration as the norm, even though it was clearly apparent that a commitment to the religious life involved parting from family and friends. These patterns of short-distance migration for English girls are congruent with the findings of Pooley and Turnbull whose largest single category for women leaving home consisted of those moving 'less than five kilometres, with those going further afield mostly remaining within fifty kilometres of their home'.[62] Girls from Ireland, on the other hand, were prepared to travel to England to begin their novitiate. For the most part, they were never again to return to Ireland.

While the evidence based on only four congregations is not sufficient to offer a definitive conclusion, the data nevertheless strongly suggest that Irish women, and especially those from Munster and Leinster, dominated within the rank and file of Roman Catholic convent life in England and Wales by the end of the century. This is congruent with general emigration records, which place these two provinces as the major source for all Irish emigrants at this time.

A Hidden Irish Diaspora?

There is little question that Lancashire accounted for many of the English-born members of the SSP and the SND. This raises a serious question about the ethnic backgrounds of non-Irish-born entrants. Were these entrants mainly drawn from the ranks of English Roman Catholic families or is there evidence of a hidden Irish diaspora?

From the registers it was apparent that a significant proportion of entrants bore Irish surnames although they had been born in England, Scotland and Wales.[63] When a comparative sample segment for 1911–26 is compiled (see Table 31), this shows that girls born in England, Scotland or Wales with Irish surnames made up 45 per cent of the professed sisters who entered the SSP; 33 per cent of the membership of the SND; and 16 per cent of the membership of the SSHJM. It is highly likely that these recruits were drawn from first-, second- or third-generation immigrant Irish families. A similar exercise was applied to the SSP for the full eighty-year period 1847–1926. (Table 32). The incidence of Irish surnames over this longer timescale is shown to have been somewhat less (28 per cent) than for the period 1911–26, calculated to be 40 per cent. This outcome is not altogether surprising. This decade would be more likely to contain a proportionally higher number of second- or third-generation Irish immigrant families than would be evidenced in the earlier decades.

A hidden Irish diaspora of some considerable influence and strength therefore certainly existed in each of these congregations. Can evidence be found to suggest that, once recruited, there were subtle levels of prejudice against the Irish within conventual life in England?

A letter from the superior of the SND training college in Dowanhill, dated 1896, in response to the possibility of her accepting postulants from Ireland, states unequivocally that, 'We were glad of sisters able to work', adding the warning that 'everyone could not teach.' Her letter goes on to regret that 'some Irish girls were so perfectly useless . . .'[64] The writer left unspecified whether she meant either in terms of their work or spirituality. Examination of the SND records shows that this congregation relegated many of their Irish members to relatively humble roles as portresses, infirmarians (nurses within the community) and kitchen staff, although towards the turn of the century rather more of their Irish entrants came in as trained elementary teachers. Between 37 and 38 per cent of all the Irish sisters had teaching, music or similar qualifications. However, it is evident that few subsequently went on to hold high office within the congregation.

This would appear to suggest a degree of ethnic discrimination since the SND had rules which excluded formal internal class divisions.[65] O'Brien refers to such communities as having 'a single common status for all members'.[66] But this is not to say there was not a hierarchical system and class consciousness within the SND's English Province. It may have been brought about, albeit unwittingly, by the influence and powerful patronage generated by the two titled English heiresses who had entered the congregation in the mid-nineteenth century and who subsequently rose through the ranks to gain authority, respectively, as assistant Mother General and English Mother Provincial.[67]

The memoirs of one SND sister recruited from Ireland, compiled when she retired some twenty years ago, reveals how she came to be aware of these distinctions in rank. 'It isn't easy to explain the divisions. It showed in queer little ways . . . the snobbishness was there from the beginning.' She recalls how a superior corrected a house sister for addressing a boarding school pupil by her Christian name. 'She is Miss Twomey to you, sister.' After a Christmas sale 'the superior gave each sister some money . . . the boarding school sisters always got a piece of silver. The rest of us got twopence. I think most of us were just amused.'[68]

O'Brien's research also noted these divisions in the SND. Moreover, she has attributed the attitude shown towards Irish members of all types of community, whether divided or not, as being a class issue: 'all English congregations readily accepted Irish-born women as lay-sisters.' She saw the function of these sisters as 'essentially being that of domestic servants'.[69] Referring to attitudes shown to Irish entrants within the Society of the Sacred Heart, for example, she comments that 'the brogue was not always felt to be suitable in a choir nun'.[70]

French congregations such as the SND, the Society of the Sacred Heart and many others who were subject to direct government from France had little appreciation of the subtlety of social structures in Ireland. This may be true, even, for those who maintained houses there. When seeking Irish recruits for their English convents they were influenced by the existing popular prejudices against the Irish in nineteenth-century Britain. However, it would be unexpected indeed to find evidence of this type of class prejudice against Irish sisters within the SSP and the SSHJM. 'We didn't have a two-tier structure of choir nuns and lay sisters. There are no privileges. We're all the same.'[71] Not only did Irish women predominate within the ranks of these congregations but they rose to hold positions of great authority in their mother houses in Birmingham and London. (There may have been some rivalry and favouritism on a provincial level, but this cannot rate as ethnic prejudice.) As will now be shown, the middle-class socio-economic background from which the majority of members of the SSP were drawn was one of relative superiority and high educational standard within Irish society.[72]

The Socio-economic Backgrounds of Entrants

The registers of the SSP have the rare distinction of listing brief details of the occupation of each entrant's father. Table 33 provides a breakdown and comparison of English, Scottish and Welsh-born sisters with those from Ireland. (Tables 34 and 35 show the named occupations.) Entrants drawn from the families of Irish farmers make up the highest category, followed by the daughters of English, Scots and Welsh artisans and tradesmen. Daughters of professionals, shopkeepers and other commercial occupations were twice as common among British recruits, but there was a slightly greater proportion of those with fathers who were teachers or in the police, the army or seafaring occupations among those from Ireland. The major differences, however, are to be found in the percentages from artisan and farming classes. Over 60 per cent of Irish sisters came from an agricultural background, as contrasted with just 8 per cent from elsewhere in Britain. Artisan families accounted for less than 10 per cent of Irish sisters but nearly 40 per cent from elsewhere in the kingdom.

As will be shown, similar economic and social circumstances affected the majority of the intake of girls from rural Ireland – the daughters of 'farmers'. Less easy to identify are those factors which might have affected the decision of, say, a miner's daughter from the North-East or Scotland to enter a convent, in contrast to a girl whose father worked as a clerk in London or as a commercial traveller in Liverpool.

Records held by the SND, although not noting the occupations of fathers, can provide further clues which reflect entrants' backgrounds. Much can be gleaned from an examination of their educational standards or former employment. A sample of entrants for the decade 1915–24 reveals that over 54 per cent of aspirants had already gained a qualification as a teacher, 15 per cent had worked in domestic service, 13 per cent in shops or mills, 9 per cent came from home or farm duties, 5 per cent worked as typists or in similar commercial employment, and just over 2 per cent had been employed in laundries. This emphasises the point already made that girls who made this choice of life within a religious community were experienced and mature. Particularly noteworthy is that over half of the aspirants were already trained teachers at the time of entry.

MOTIVES AND METHODS

Were there push or pull factors at work? So far, evidence suggests that for each of the congregations studied there was a great reliance on the recruitment of vocations from Ireland. This suggests that close-knit community and family links were therefore likely to have been important and, when regional patterns are examined, the tight geographical concentrations that emerge can be seen to emanate from the strata of 'strong farmer' communities in the rich cattle and dairy counties of Munster and south-east Leinster, particularly Cork, Limerick and Tipperary (see Map K). Why was this so?

Motivation and Opportunity

The construction of socio-economic patterns based only on Irish farm land valuations is not without danger. Hughes points out that 'the condition of his [a farmer's] dwelling house and his farmstead [is] no sure guide to the quality of a substantial farmer's lifestyle in the Tipperary of the nineteenth century'.[73] In the registers of the SSP, a simple descriptive listing of a father's occupation as 'farmer' ranged in actuality from gentleman farmers, cattle dealers and landowners, to more modest, if solid farming households engaged in dairying and calf- and pig-rearing. However, manuscript census returns for 1901 and 1911 can reveal a wealth of additional useful data.[74] For example, analysis of households in the county of Limerick from which girls entered this congregation clearly confirms that three-quarters of the intake were girls from comfortable, farming backgrounds[75] (see Table 36). The data also provide information on other aspects of their life, such as levels of off-farm employment for farmers' daughters, the size of the families and the numbers of adult siblings in the household. Out of eighty-eight households traced only eight relied on a father who was engaged in a non-agricultural livelihood.[76]

In the earlier part of the century, entrants to the SSP from County Limerick were the daughters of large tenant farmers ensconced in strong family clusters in localised areas.[77] These substantial family clusters had held on to their land over one or two generations as tenant farmers or as land agents for absentee landlords. After the turn of the century these and all the other farmers with daughters recruited to the SSP were enumerated in the census as land-owning farmers, having bought out their land and houses under the land acts of the 1880s, the 1890s and the 1900s. These girls all came from sturdy homesteads reliant on cattle and calf-, pig- and fowl-rearing. Manuscript census returns for forty-six households in 1901 and 1911 reveal that a third of the farms with five to seven out-offices had a dairy. Almost half of these households had domestic and farm servants.

Thirty-seven had from three to five adult siblings still living at home. Spot-checks on entrants drawn from the counties of Tipperary and Wexford show a similar picture of farming household backgrounds and a lack of other occupations for women.[78]

This social structure represents the consolidation of farm landholdings in parts of post-famine, rural Ireland which has been well documented by historians as regards inheritance, marriage patterns and emigration.[79] To an increasing extent, migration for non-inheriting siblings was a fact of life. Hickey quotes a Cork land agent's advice in the 1850s exhorting farmers to 'keep more cattle and grow more crops to feed them . . . send your sons and daughters out into the world and retain your farms unbroken'.[80] In the decades that followed, the emigration of the young was the sacrifice demanded of such landholding farming families.

The migration of a farmer's daughters was not brought about only by the need to make way for a brother to inherit the homestead, however. There were other economic considerations. In the sample for County Limerick, a severe lack of alternative, respectable employment for un-married daughters is evident. Out of the eighty-eight farming families examined, only two households indicated any form of occupation for the adult daughters. In one instance, three worked as seamstresses, in another one daughter was a teacher. Such findings are typical for much of the Munster area for 1901 and 1911, and it would seem that the only favoured alternatives suitable for educated daughters were marriage, entry into the religious life or emigration.[81] In reality, the last two options were many times one and the same. The bourgeois standards of such households would not be likely to allow a single girl to leave home except under the strictest of chaperoned circumstances and, moreover, for parents to give sons and daughters to the church was considered one of the greatest blessings and of high social approbation. It was said, 'A priest in the family is the mark of big people.'[82]

Fahey termed the nuns in his study as 'solid examples of middle-class respectability'.[83] Such families were of substance, as evidenced by the amount of dowry that accompanied many young women to convents.[84] Whelan reinforces this conclusion by drawing from Smyth's research of a Tipperary parish to point up the unlikelihood of nuns or priests coming from the households of cottiers, labourers or farms with under 30 acres, 'the small farm was barren ground for vocations'.[85] However, some of the entrants to the SSP and the SSHJM might well have come from relatively modest farming holdings. There are instances in the records of these congregations of dowries being forgone or reduced for families, perhaps those with several daughters to settle, or with kinship links within the community, the reason for this reduction being that a girl would be making a lifelong contribution to the community by her earnings as a teacher or nurse.[86]

The 1870s had marked the beginning of a series of agricultural depressions with economic consequences which reduced opportunities for women within farming families.[87] Even after the 1880s and the 1890s, when farming fortunes improved, there were still few employment opportunities for women in Ireland. Curtis comments that 'even educated and reasonably affluent women found it hard to enter, let alone ascend to positions of rank in institutions, other than convents, elementary schools and the professions of nursing and midwifery'.[88] To which may be added that entry to the last two professions was quite often controlled by the religious-run communities.

This lack of alternative employment for the daughters of the comfortable 'strong farmers' is a major explanation of the high intake of Irish women into the religious life. In the Munster area, in particular, studies of changes in farming practice have suggested that the establishment of more and more male-run creameries and co-operatives eroded women's work in the dairy industry from the late 1880s onwards.[89] Butter-making, pig- and poultry-keeping and egg production had all been traditional areas of work for rural women.[90] With the decline of their involvement in day-to-day husbandry and the introduction of new farming technology, much of the farm-based employment for women had all but disappeared by the first decades of the twentieth century, and attempts to introduce alternative cottage industries had proved to be dismal failures.[91] Joanna Bourke has argued that the fortunes of the respectable, bourgeois farmers improved as the century progressed. Farmers' daughters were sent off to be convent-educated in the local town where they were instructed in French, music and the domestic skills of housewifery and child care.

Farm work or employment in domestic service for this class of girl was never envisaged and Bourke identifies these changes in living standards and expectations with the decline in the availability of servants. Only the daughters of the poorest farmers were willing to seek work in domestic service.[92] A further point she did not address was the fast disappearing 'great houses' of Ireland, whose estates had created employment for respectable local girls of good background in the higher echelons of service – dairymaids, cooks, nursemaids, ladies' maids, governesses or companions. The decline of the ascendancy class, especially in the first decades of the new century, may well have created a decline in work outlets for young women.

Yet another point to reiterate is the high standard of education in nineteenth-century Ireland. Rossiter cites David Fitzpatrick, who argued there were 'higher literacy and numeracy rates and greater diligence in the schoolroom among women emigrants to the USA', brought about by 'the culture of emigration which recognised the merits of education built into the life-cycle of women'.[93] Kiberd asserts that, 'As far back as the 1830s . . . Ireland was given a streamlined national school system . . . by the 1880s and 1890s Ireland was, in certain respects, clearly advanced by contrast with England . . . '[94] The daughters of strong farmers, suitably instructed by the refined convent schools of rural Ireland, can be considered as well prepared to become the schoolteachers, nurses and social care workers who formed the backbone of many congregations working in English towns and cities.

How this sample of Limerick farmers' daughters leaving home to join convents in England fits into the broader picture of female emigration from Ireland may now be considered. It may be noted, for example, that the average age for entry to the four sample congregations, shown to be 23 to 24 years, is congruent with the average age of the majority of female emigrants to all destinations outside Ireland between 1852 and 1921. Eighty-nine per cent of female emigrants to all destinations were single.[95]

Statistical evidence relating to the emigration of women from Ireland to England and Wales in the nineteenth century, however, is at best blurred when compared with the data gathered on 'overseas' emigration from Irish and English ports.[96] In respect of net emigration statistics for 1871–1901, it is usually accepted that the number of women who emigrated to *all* destinations was about equal to that of men and, from 1902 onwards, only marginally higher.[97] Women leaving Ireland between 1871 and 1921 averaged at about 20,000 a year, with the majority travelling to North America. Despite misgivings on the part of the compilers of the reports in the Commission on Emigration in regard to the accuracy of figures for emigrants from Ireland to 'Great Britain', some indication of the scale may be gleaned from at least one table in which an average of just over 5,000 female emigrants per annum to Great Britain from the thirty-two counties is cited.[98] It has been impossible to say how many of these women were short-term migrants, whether they subsequently settled, or whether they moved on further afield. As to what proportion of the 5,000 to Britain may have been postulants destined for a novitiate in an English convent this is, as yet, an even more indefinable figure and must remain only speculative until research on other convent archives is undertaken. However, it is certainly worth considering here that in the third quarter of the nineteenth century there were already more than a hundred congregations in England and Wales very possibly engaged in the recruitment of large numbers of girls from Ireland, and, leaving aside the fact that perhaps maybe a third more recruits did not persevere, this sampling of successful applicants suggests that a 'vocation' to the religious life may have been responsible for a considerable proportion of the female emigration to England and Wales from the late 1870s onwards. This is especially so in areas of high recruitment, which also provided most of the female emigrants, at least until the early twentieth century.

Methods of Recruitment in Ireland

It is seen as significant that, for three out of the four congregations we have looked at, the recruitment of Irish girls cannot be attributed to these communities having had branch houses in Ireland. The SSP recruited large numbers of Irish women before establishing their (for many years sole) convent in Limerick, but it was 1903 before it did so, and this actually post-dates the considerable numbers of entrants already drawn from Munster. The SND had no convent in Ireland at all, despite efforts to get permission from several Irish bishops. In correspondence relating to one of their unsuccessful attempts, the Bishop of Galway wrote of them, that there would be 'no room for them as we have nuns (even in small centres) conducting primary and secondary schools', adding, waspishly, that 'Perhaps they would like a recruiting station!'[99] Even the SSHJM had no Irish convent until 1922, despite the fact that three-quarters of their numbers were from Ireland. They established a house in Cork, not for recruitment, but as a mother and baby home at the invitation of the newly-formed Department of Health.[100]

The DVDP by contrast, did have the benefit of a house in Ireland, having arrived in Drogheda from Paris in 1855. By 1857 they had also set up in Dublin. The impact of their presence in this part of Ireland in respect of regional patterns of recruitment can be seen in the relatively high number of entrants from Louth, Dublin and Meath (see Table 29). After the foundation of their first house in Cork in 1867, there was a steady supply of recruits from the province of Munster.

For the other three congregations, having no house in Ireland until the twentieth century was not an insurmountable problem. Apart from the strong family networking of kith and kin already demonstrated in the congregations, there were a number of other ways by which congregations could draw aspirants from Ireland. The assistance and recommendation of the clergy was one route. For example, the SND could draw on their close connections with the Redemptorist Fathers working in Ireland. One of the SND sisters wrote in 1896:

> The head of the Seminary at Wexford, the Rev. Fr. Sheridan, was here last month . . . He said he often sent girls into religion but not knowing whether we would take those not capable of teaching, he had never thought of offering them to us. He has sent many to the Good Shepherd and to the Sacred Heart Servants at Homerton. He assured me we could depend upon him and that he would never send anyone unadvisable.[101]

These findings confirm O'Brien's research on some active congregations in England which also relied on recruits from Ireland.[102] The fact that Irish convent schools actively encouraged their pupils to consider the religious life is found well documented in examples of fiction and biography.[103]

Suellen Hoy's investigation of recruitment methods to the United States points out the rich source of vocations from Child of Mary Sodalities in convent-run schools throughout Ireland.[104] She demonstrates the success of this method by citing one Sister of Charity in Dublin who, between 1868 and 1905, 'had found places for approximately seven hundred women'.[105] Hoy also draws attention to the travelling 'recruiting nuns', whom she describes as having 'regularly launched major drives to acquire new members'.[106] These sisters, usually chosen by their congregations for their ability to communicate and for their personable liveliness, made the rounds of Irish convent schools in the spring and the autumn to give instructive talks to the senior girls on the benefits, opportunities and value of 'becoming a nun', and thus hoped to encourage entrants to their own congregations. Similar recruitment drives were made seeking aspirants to English convents.

Methods of Recruitment in England, Scotland and Wales

Convent-run schools in England, Scotland and Wales also played a large part in the encouragement of aspirants to the religious life. The registers of the SND, in particular, reveal that many members had been former pupils of their high schools and teacher-training colleges. O'Brien's study of a teaching congregation discovered similar high levels of intake from convent-school pupils.[107] Children of Mary Sodalities, organised by schools and parishes, provided another source for the steady stream of aspirants, as in Ireland. A high proportion of postulants were already trained teachers on entry. Recruitment generated through family links to Ireland within the Irish diaspora would have been strong. Recent research has provided impressive evidence that immigrants to Lancashire tenaciously held on to family links in Ireland in the first half of the twentieth century – a tradition, it is suggested, that was inherited from the previous fifty years. 'Rather than escaping from increasing religious and family ties, southern Irish women in Lancashire were motivated to uphold their religion and keep in close contact with their original homes in Ireland.'[108]

A considerable contribution to the drive for vocations was made through the production of pious reading materials in cheap pamphlet form which were published under the auspices of the Catholic Truth Societies of England and Ireland.[109] Sold for a few pence, the earliest little booklets produced by the Societies in the mid-1880s mainly concentrated on refuting the wilder fantasies about nuns and convents which were being circulated, not only by anti-Catholic factions, but also by the purveyors of popular and profitable penny-dreadful pulp fiction.[110] With a growing range of titles covering religious topics, the Societies went on to organise displays of pamphlets and booklets in the porches of churches and arranged for their distribution to Catholic schools. Aimed at young people, the titles included the potted histories of religious congregations, information and encouragement to consider life within religious orders and congregations. Proof of their popularity is enforced by the hundreds of reprinted editions that continued to be run off for many years.

At a higher level of scholarship, there was an enormous amount of other printed support for vocations. On a practical level, were several books produced specifically for consultation. Girls who were considering entering a religious community could gain information not only about the history, rule and apostolate of each but all the conditions necessary for entry and where to apply.[111] Some guides included a description of the design, colour and cloth used by congregations for habits and veils, with illustrations. This rather curious focus on the cut of habits and veils strikes a worldly tone which may have misled some aspirants. One wonders how many failed entrants were influenced by this kind of persuasive information?

There were, too, innumerable publications of spiritual reading available, ranging from the lives of the saints to texts specifically designed to encourage the attainment of religious fervour. The power of the printed word in the drive for vocations in the nineteenth century and later can be only faintly sketched in here.

The Attraction of the Religious Life

One of the most important of the 'pull' factors, as we have already seen, was the increasing need for the religious congregations to recruit and find enough members to staff the growing number of their schools and nursing, health care and social services being set up in England and Wales. In this chapter we have considered two more factors: first, the status and opportunity afforded to idealistic and educated young women who chose to become professionals within religious life, and secondly, the attractive arguments put forward by the Church which promised each woman who took the veil a guarantee of gaining higher spirituality through sacrifice and prayer.[112] However, in regard to the latter, any assessment of the driving power of the search for spiritual fulfilment, although important, is a topic that is neither possible nor appropriate to study here and must be left to others with more familiarity with this field. But there were also significant 'push' factors which can be identified in familial, social and economic constraints relevant to recruitment from Ireland. Under pressure to leave farming homesteads, there were no other career or employment alternatives in Ireland for respectable educated girls from rural areas. Similarly, in England and Wales, employment opportunities for women in middle-class society had undergone many changes, not all for the better. Thompson has written of the 'amorphous anomie' of the Victorian, urban, lower middle class, from which were drawn many of the English, Scottish and Welsh entrants.[113] Thompson views the lower middle class as being atomised and fragmented with notions of respectability and 'obsequious deference' which had created a 'class without cohesion, isolated in their family units'.[114] The data presented here have shown this class of society to have been the second largest socio-economic grouping from which the sisters in our four congregations were drawn.[115] Such families were obliged to shelter adult single women, and, if not settled into a suitable marriage, provide a role for them within the family household, as unpaid housekeepers, childminders or carers for elderly parents. For some young Catholic woman it may not have been too difficult a decision to exchange the claustrophobic confines of lower-middle-class family life for the companionship, activity and fulfilment of a convent community.

The choice of entry to a community may be seen as being influenced by the continued importance of religious and spiritual values for women and the security that convent life offered, or, on the other hand, as a reaction to the 'respectable' secular alternatives available – high status as a married woman or low as a spinster. However, the proposition that life as a nun was a popular alternative for a woman when she failed to gain a husband cannot be sustained. The evidence shows that women entered before their opportunities to marry had slipped by.

Finally, it may be worth observing that, although based on relatively few case studies covering the mid to late nineteenth century and the early decades of the twentieth, we can construct a fairly clear indication of the size and the characteristics of the recruitment of Irish girls for English convents. This enormous drain should not be seen as being unique in the context of what was then happening elsewhere in Europe.[116] It suggests that, when Ireland is seen as part of Europe, further force is added to the argument that the dynamic of convent-based engagement in social services is due to the response of nuns and sisters to changing economic conditions, and to the pressures and demands generated by society itself.

CONCLUSION

The expanding religious congregations and orders which provided convent-based undertakings in educational, nursing and social services throughout England and Wales clearly experienced little difficulty in recruiting substantial numbers willing to embrace the religious life. Social and economic factors as much as religious motives were major influences on the supply of women and hopeful aspirants who were drawn from an increasingly prosperous and educated Catholic middle class in England, Wales, Scotland and Ireland The considerable involvement in education in England and Ireland of active congregations created a 'chain' of migration through their convent schools.

In selecting suitable aspirants, the expectations of the congregations were high and this may be seen as having been subsequently reflected in the improvement of standards in many of their schools, hospitals and social services. The numbers of young women embracing the religious life who went on to become successful professed members, far from slackening off, increased substantially throughout the late nineteenth century and into the early decades of the twentieth. This matches the Continental experience at this time. Many more offered themselves than were accepted. Unsuitable recruits, especially those with poor health or 'no vocation' were rigorously weeded out.

The average age of all aspirants, whether subsequently successfully professed or not, was between 23 and 24. Those who were accepted underwent up to three years of novitiate before profession. A choice to embrace this life, therefore, cannot be seen as the decision of immature or inexperienced girls. The lifespan for those within the convents was considerably higher than the average for most women in the nineteenth century, which suggests a serene and fulfilling or at least healthy lifestyle.

Accepting the life of a religious sister in preference to marriage or as a solution to the lack of marriage prospects was shown to be an issue affected differently by the social and economic pressures and family aspirations of Irish and English families. The large intake from rural Ireland reflects the popularity and practical solution convent life offered to young women who had little other choice. It was concluded that Irish-born members were drawn to a great extent from bourgeois farming families, with a distinctive predominance of the daughters of 'strong farmers' from Munster and south Leinster. The patterns of intake showed Munster to be the most common place of birth. There was a high percentages of Irish-born siblings and blood relatives in each of the congregations.

By contrast, the intake of young women born in England, Scotland or Wales was drawn mainly from urban backgrounds and the artisan or middle classes. Disappointingly, analysis of the socio-economic back-grounds of these girls does not provide as clear-cut a picture as can be drawn with regard to the majority of the Irish entrants who were influenced by a similar set of social conditions in rural areas throughout the period. There was a far greater regional diversity of lower-middle-class households in England, Wales and Scotland. The occupations of the fathers of these girls varied widely, from skilled tradesmen or clerks, to those in managerial or professional positions. No common socio-economic factor thus can be shown as having a striking influence on girls born in England, Scotland and Wales, bar the social constraints common to all single women of the time, being expected to remain at home under the protection of their parents or siblings, whether nor not engaged in suitable employment. It may be that English girls from urban backgrounds were not as inclined to accept the need to move far from home. However, it is noticeable that girls employed in the teaching profession often subsequently entered the religious life. One congregation's records showed that a high number of their entrants were girls who had earlier been educated or trained as teachers.

Among those registered as of 'English, Welsh or Scottish' birth were many girls who bore Irish surnames. This evidence of the second- or third-generation Irish reveals an Irish diaspora of considerable size within English convents. In none of the case studies were there formal class divisions between choir and lay sisters, but one of the French-governed congregations produced evidence pointing to levels of prejudice or class distinction, and possibly preconceived attitudes towards members who were Irish. It was suggested that this attitude was due to a lack of knowledge or appreciation of rural middle-class social status in Ireland whence recruits were drawn.

There is evidence of effective recruitment resulting from strong Irish kith and kin links within the membership of each of the congregations. However, the policy of the two French-governed congregations, the DVDP and the SND, with regard to friends and siblings who entered together was never to place these girls subsequently in the same location. Intended in part to avoid what were perceived as the dangers of 'particular friendships', such strategies might be viewed as harsh, but were not uncommon within large religious congregations. The strict organisation and control of time and space within the congregations, of which this is an example, may be seen as being typical of the nineteenth-century 'disciplinary' mechanisms which came to be applied to the structured routine of all large insti-tutions.[117] Foucault sees society as using such institutions to generate 'recurrent emphasis on control, domination and punishment as the only mediating qualities possible in personal and social relationships'.[118] It is not possible here to establish whether or not the SSP and the SSHJS, both of which grew away from their French roots to be controlled by Irish women, continued to embrace such bleak and clinically cold regimes of internal authority.

Apart from the Irish kith and kin links which encouraged and approved of vocations, recruitment methods for the congregations studied included intakes from convent schools in Ireland, England, Scotland and Wales, where girls had been exposed to nuns as role models; sorties by recruiting nuns who regularly visited schools in Ireland; the encouragement and advice of the clergy; and a copious amount of material in book and pamphlet form on the desirability of choosing the religious life produced by the Catholic press. Having a branch house in Ireland, specifically for recruitment purposes, was not seen as being crucial for the successful intake of large numbers of Irish aspirants, although there is evidence that the influence of DVDP houses in Ireland generated a somewhat wider geographical spread of entrants for this congregation.

There were a number of interlocking 'push' and 'pull' factors which promoted the appeal of the religious life for young women. Pull from the congregations, who needed recruits to function their expansionary programmes; and pull from the opportunities of gaining status and professionalisation that 'becoming a nun' offered single women; pull, too, from the arguments of the Church which presented the religious life as being a choice which carried superior spiritual benefits. 'Push' factors, however, included the social and economic pressures placed on young, single women to make this choice, albeit for different reasons in Ireland than in England.

The number of young women who emigrated from Ireland to work as a nun or sister in English convents needs to be considered in the wider context of how we interpret the shadowy statistics for emigrant, single women. These case studies, while typical of active congregations of their type, do not provide enough evidence to decide how many single Irish women were, in fact, destined to life as members of communities in England, Wales and Scotland. More work needs to be done to pare away broad generalisations which have categorised the majority of young female emigrants as having come to take up work as domestic servants.

It is worth considering that the year 1937 saw the peak in the membership of one of these congregations, with 702 sisters actively engaged as teachers, nurses and social care workers.[119] If the intake to this sample congregation is taken as representative of many of the larger communities of active sisters, it would seem that the number of women who chose to be members of Roman Catholic women's religious institutions in England and Wales by the mid-twentieth century may be measured, not in their hundreds, but in their thousands, or even tens of thousands.

Conclusion

THE AIM OF THIS BOOK has been to consider the significance of Roman Catholic women's religious communities in relation to our understanding of a variety of interlocking historical areas. One of the major themes has been the extent to which the study can add to our knowledge of the history of women in Victorian and early twentieth-century England and Wales, especially in terms of how the choice of this lifestyle provided many young women with high professional status as teachers, nurses or social workers. The study has shown that community life as a professed member of a religious institution offered single young women an acceptable career alternative to marriage at a time when suitable employment for middle-class women was at best limited, or even (in the case of rural Ireland) non-existent. The role of educated women within Irish 'strong farmer' households was particularly under pressure in this respect.

Analysis of the recruitment needs and standards of the English-based convents selected as case studies has provided material which can add to our knowledge and understanding of the emigration patterns of young Irish women. Likewise, the records scrutinised have provided data on the educational levels and socio-economic backgrounds of English-born entrants, who were drawn mainly, but not solely, from the middle-class artisan and commercial classes. Many aspirants had links to the Irish diaspora, already a generation or two settled in England. Averaging about 23 years on entry, the girls were somewhat younger than the usual marriageable age. All were rigorously tested for personal suitability and good health before being accepted into a congregation's novitiate.

It has not been possible to explore the interesting strand of inter-pretation of the religious life for women put forward by Mumm in her assessment of Anglican sisterhoods. She suggests that women in religious communities might be seen as a proto-feminist movement undermining a patriarchal society. She indicates that Victorian public opinion was disturbed by what was seen to have been 'their [the sisters'] willingness to

157

discard the normal social and moral markers'.[1] Clear gives this argument some credence too, asking whether convents were not 'islands of female self-determination in a male-determined and male-defined society?'[2] More recently, Gilly has added commentary in this vein in his introduction to Maria McClelland's story of the Sisters of Mercy in Hull: 'It is an odd paradox that the nuns, apparently at the remotest pole from nineteenth-century feminism, were its most successful proponents and practitioners.'[3] Certainly, this argument carries weight when viewed through the lens of to-day's feminists' value systems and there has been a significant amount of attention given to it by others who are more closely engaged in discussion of the mechanics of internal structures and organisational systems within religious communities.[4]

Lifting the veil on the dynamic which brought about the profession-alisation of women who chose the religious life has exposed the hitherto hidden nature of their work and lifestyles which were subject to regimes which demanded stringent training, high standards of discipline and strict adherence to the individual rule which governed each community. It may be recognised that these formally constituted communities of single women were symptomatic of most strictly regimented, Victorian, secular institutions of their time, and not, therefore, as might be thought of now, often over-disciplined and harshly run regimes. The professional attitude of nuns and sisters was dictated by vows of obedience, poverty, chastity, and, in many cases, an additional dedication to care for the poor. Management and organisational skills were required of these women for the operation of institutions, schools, hospitals and other convent-based complexes. They voraciously sought, and achieved, official secular qualification in the skills of their professions, often with earlier successes than those experienced by lay women. Teaching congregations led the way in opening up opportunities for girls to attain the highest degree of education. Innovative teaching methods were introduced into convent schools and standards of excellence were set in teacher training. At least one English nursing congregation was almost a century ahead of Victorian medical professional standards in seeking, although not being granted, the scientific training and professional medical accreditation of their sisters. The expansion of their services and the economic viability of the convents, albeit well supported by patrons and sponsors, was reliant on the financial acumen and hard work of their members. Often viewed by Church authorities as mere 'foot-soldiery' or malleable, willing helpers, the early manifestation of their professionalism was rarely recognised and acknowledged, and, indeed, there were attempts to curtail their activities significantly by stringencies imposed by the recodification of the Canon Law governing convents in 1918.

Ecclesiastical history is the second historical area to which this study contributes. Attention has been drawn to the fact that, in their provision of supportive social services, the involvement of active religious congregations and orders played a crucial, but often unrecognised and unacknowledged role in assisting the development and growth of the English Roman Catholic Church in England and Wales. The importance of their contribution is indicated by the demonstrable growth in scale and scope of convent-based undertakings. The work of women's religious communities encompassed a wide range of activities which extended to the provision of education at all levels, the staffing and operation of hospital, nursing and health care services, the operation of the institutionalised care of the young, the aged, those with special needs and those requiring rehabilitation or reformatory care, and the operation of localised nursing and welfare care services. For the less well-off, their services were usually offered free of charge, having been subsidised by wealthier clients in a two-tier system of funding. Convent-run undertakings and services were not confined to those of the Catholic faith, but advertised as being available to all.

An area of investigation relating to Church history which remains still relatively inaccessible because of the lack of easily available, corroborative research, is the economic viability and financial structures of convent life. However, from evidence relating to one community, it has been possible to provide some indication as to how a large religious institution might undertake the business of running a convent. Elected into office by members of their community, superior generals and convent superiors undertook the responsibilities for all day-to-day needs. These women also took on the personal supervision of building projects and the management of complex financial affairs. Active religious congregations had con- siderable purchasing power in the growing service industry of the nineteenth and the early twentieth century. The many and varied under- takings entered into by active communities suggest there were tactics employed that modified the constraints of much strict episcopal control and that the impetus and financial independence of many institutions was self-generated and self-regulated. The role of the Catholic laity in their practical support of women's religious communities was an important and significant contributory factor to their success.

The potential significance of this study for our understanding of a third and overlapping area is concerned with expanding our awareness of the regional development of Victorian and early twentieth-century secular society *vis-à-vis* charitable and philanthropic endeavour, much of which manifested itself in the services and institutions operated by religious orders and congregations. The undertakings engaged in by active sisters were predominately urban-based and we have seen the distribution of convents displaying distinctive regional patterns of development. By the last decades of the nineteenth century, the Catholic population of England and Wales had becoming wealthier and more suburbanised and was quite possibly of greater size and rather more dispersed and defused than demographic calculations have recognised. In monitoring the scale of the growth and development of convent numbers from the late 1870s into the first three decades of the next century, the emphasis clearly shows an increasing shift of convent growth and expansion from the North to a greater concentration in London and the South-East. This emphasis indicates, not so much a lessening of religious-run care for the poor and needy, which indeed continued, but a greater middle-class demand for higher education and the specialised nursing care which religious congregations increasingly responded to. Poverty remained widespread in industrial centres and it is not yet possible to say whether or not the most highly used convent-based services were used by Irish immigration stock, 'Old' Catholics, 'lapsed' Catholics, those of a different denomination, or of no faith at all. Convent-based undertakings provided a range of services which cut across every class division. Soup kitchens, workrooms, crèches, free schools, hospital and home care continued to be provided for the poor throughout the nineteenth century and later, while, at the same time, the English middle classes sought out convent-based services to improve their children's education, to nurse their sick and to provide nurturing care for social sand medical problems that required institutionalisation.

The study has indicated that these convent-generated social services in England and Wales which, while quite unprecedented in their scale, were not altogether unique for their time. England and Wales, and Ireland, too, can be viewed as witnessing an extension of the much wider European phenomenon which had seen the emergence of foundations of many large, highly disciplined and institutionalised communities of active sisters in the late eighteenth and the early nineteenth century. They dedicated themselves to the organisation and supervision of charitable undertakings for the poor, to supplying nursing and welfare care structures and to providing formalised, improved education for women. These European congregations and institutions were inundated with applications from young women, particularly in France, who wished to embrace an active religious life as a means of engaging in a respectable, worthwhile and spiritually self-fulfilling vocation outside the structure of a family household.

The expansionary growth of religious foundations peaked in mid-nineteenth-century Europe. By this time, there had been a similar flurry of enthusiasm for the viability of community religious life for single women in England, and Ireland, too, which witnessed the foundation of several new English and Irish congregations. In the latter quarter of the nineteenth century, however, there was increasing anti-clerical, political pressure imposed on the activities of religious institutions in France and Prussia, which continued sporadically into the first decade of the new century and which brought about a dispersal and movement of religious communities to seek exile in England and Wales.

It is hoped that this book will open up a number of possible avenues for further research. There is much relating to the nineteenth-century religious life for women that remains shadowy until more individual communities are scrutinised. While the congregations and orders which flourished in nineteenth-century England and Wales operated under similar conditions and rules, many different characteristics and variations of apostolate are to be found. There is a need for further analysis of recruitment records and the family backgrounds to widen and confirm the findings here. Further exploration of the level of recruitment of Irish girls to English-based convents would add significantly to our understanding of female emigration patterns. Localised studies covering the work of religious congregations would be useful in filling in detail as to the size of individual convent complexes and to gauge their specific contributions to the development of social services in parishes, villages and towns.

Statistical evidence relating to adoption, fostering and child care services conducted by communities of nuns and sisters should rank as important as secular sources in research studies. Improved access to and the opening of diocesan archives (especially in Ireland) would allow for a greater understanding of episcopal attitudes; for example, in regard to the setting up of foreign recruitment or novitiate training houses in Ireland. There is an enormous need for additional data relating to the viability of convent finances, how fees were administered, funds raised and expansion expenses covered. While, clearly, communities of women contributed to the expanding service economy of the nineteenth century, it would be interesting to discover the extent to which secular, commercial firms were affected by expanding convent-created 'markets' for buildings, maintenance services and the day-to-day supply of goods.

The growth and development of religious congregations and orders in these islands lasted, perhaps, only about 150 years. Their decline was that of an accelerating free-fall that took place within a mere decade or two in the mid-twentieth century. The gathering of oral history from the remaining sisters and nuns is now of crucial importance in order to provide material for our understanding of the changes that affected community religious life for women since 1960.

This study has uncovered many more questions than it has been possible to answer. However, it has been shown that the scale and influence of Roman Catholic women's congregations and orders was not as marginal as social historians may have perceived. The distribution of convent networks was widespread and the activities undertook by the congregations and orders multifaceted in scope. The contribution of active sisters to the social fabric of Victorian and twentieth-century England and Wales has been, therefore, of quite considerable influence, although never widely publicised. It can be hoped that the recognition of the work of these dedicated women, long neglected, will receive some greater measure of acknowledgement and understanding in the future.

Glossary

Common usage has designated all women who entered the religious life as 'nuns' and their communities as 'orders'. Correct terminology for the period covered by this book may divide women's religious communities into three main, distinctive types: contemplatives, active sisters and communities that were 'mixed'.

Contemplative orders
The members are correctly called nuns. They took solemn perpetual vows and remain strictly enclosed (cloistered) within their convent cloisters. The majority of contemplative orders date back to the early history of the Church and had rules based on monastic traditions. Their time was spent in prayer. Some contemplatives worked inside the cloister making vestments, altar breads or, traditionally, occasionally accepted the education of a few pupils within the convent.

Communities/congregations/institutions of active sisters
The members are correctly called sisters. They took simple vows which had rules which varied from one congregation to another. Simple vows might be renewed annually or at intervals, or for life. The work of active sisters usually took them out and about within their local community, in schools, in nursing services and welfare care. Some active communities, however, chose to stay enclosed, or semi-enclosed within their convents.

'Mixed' communities/congregations/institutions/orders
These sisters and nuns contrived to combined the active with the contemplative life. There were some communities which had active work, such as running homes of refuge, that allowed them to keep rules of enclosure. Other 'mixed' congregations did not keep such strict rules until after the recodification of Canon Law in 1918, at which time rules of enclosure were reimposed on many women's communities. Functioning in much the same way as the active sisters, mixed communities are found to have engaged in education, nursing and welfare work.

Third orders
These were active branches of the older type of monastic nun. This category was created to engage in more active work which cloistered nuns could not undertake.

Enclosed
This was the term used to refer to communities which did not leave the confines of their convents at any time excepting very rare occasions.

Semi-enclosed
This was the term used for communities which relaxed the former rule more frequently.

Lay sisters
They took simple vows and undertook the domestic duties in those communities that retained social class divisions of choir and lay religious members.

Professed nuns or sisters
These terms refer to those members of a community who had taken final vows. Depending on the community rule, they might be either solemn or simple, for life or renewable at intervals. Postulants and novices were entrants who engaged in periods of training of about two to three years before taking their vows.

Tables

Table 1. Post-Reformation Orders and Congregations: Location of Return, First Arrival or New Foundation

A: active; M: mixed; C: contemplatives. Not all mixed congregations could be clearly identified owing to lack of information. Communities marked with * see notes at end.

Name	Origins	New Foundation		
		Type	Date	First Location
Institute of Blessed Virgin Mary (IBVM)*	English	A	1639	London/Yorks.
Benedictines**	English	C	1794	Hants.
[Canonesses of Lateran]***	English	M	1794	Suffolk
Canonesses St. Augustine. Perpetual Adoration	English	C	1794	Wilts.
Carmelites (Primitive Observance)	Spanish	C	1794	Cornwall
Dominicans 2nd Order	English	C	1794	Warwicks.
Franciscans (Taunton/Woodchester)	English	C	1794	Somerset
Poor Clares	Italian	C	1795	Yorks., WR
Canonesses of Holy Sepulchre	Belgian	C	1799	Essex
Cistercians	English	C	1801	Dorset
Visitation Nuns Order of the BVM	French	C	1804	Gloucs./Bristol
Faithful Companions Jesus	French	M	1830	London, NW
Presentation Order of BVM	Irish	A	1836	Lancs./Manchester
Sisters of Mercy	Irish	A	1839	London, SE
Good Shepherd	French	A	1841	London, W
Sacred Heart (Sacre Coeur), Society of	French	M	1842	London, SW
Providence (Rosminians Institute of.Charity)	Italian	A	1843	Leics.
Notre Dame de Namur	French/Belgian	A	1845	Cornwall
Holy Child Jesus, Society of	English	A	1846	Sussex
Sisters of Charity of St. Paul the Apostle	French/English	A	1847	Oxon.
Filles de Marie (Daughters of Mary)	French	A	1847	London, SW
Faithful Virgin	French	A	1848	London, SE
Assumption Srs. Bless. Lady Perpet. Adore	French	A	1850	Yorks., NR
Poor Clare Colletines	French	C	1850	Warwicks.

→

Table 1. *(cont.)* Name	Origins	New Foundation		
		Type	Date	First Location
Irish Instit.Blessed Virgin Mary (Loreto)	Irish	A	1851	Lancs./ Manchester
Nazareth, Poor Sisters of	English	A	1851	London, W
Servites, 3rd Order (Mantellate)	Italian	M	1851	London, N
Ursulines (later Roman Union and others)	Italian/ French	M	1851	London, E
Dominicans, 3rd Order (Rose of Lima)	English	M	1855	Gloucs.
Daughters of Charity of St. Vincent de Paul	French	A	1857	Yorks., WR
Franciscans (Braintree)	English	A	1857	Essex
Immaculate Conception, Holy Family Bordeaux	French	A	1857	Yorks., WR
Dominicans, 3rd Order (Stone)	English	M	1859	Staffs.
Sainte Union	French	A	1859	London, N
Sisters of Jesus and Mary	French	A	1860	Suffolk
Misericordie, Soeurs (Sees)	French	A	1860	London, W
Sisters of the Finding of Jesus in the Temple	French	A	1860	London, W
Brigittine Nuns (Syon Abbey)	Sweden/ Portugal	C	1861	Dorset
Charity of Our Lady of Mercy	Dutch	M	1861	Flints.
Little Sisters of the Poor	French	A	1861	London, SW
Ursulines of Jesus	French	A	1861	Glamorgan
Blessed Sacrament of Perpet. Adore. (Taunton)	French	C	1863	Somerset
Holy Cross and Passion	English	A	1863	Lancs./ Manchester
Cross, Daughters of the (Liege)	French	M	1863	London, SW
Marie Reparatrice	French	M	1863	London, NW
Our Lady of Charity and Refuge	French	A	1863	Herefords.
Notre Dame School Sisters.	Bavarian	A	1864	Essex
St. Joseph of Annecy	French	A	1864	Wilts.
St. Andrew/Andre, Religious of /Dames of	French	M	1865	London, NW
Carmelites (Cardinal Berulle Reform)	Spanish	C	1866	London, SW
Bon Secours (Troyes)	French	A	1867	Lancs./ Liverpool
Franciscans of the Five Wounds (Mill Hill)	English	A	1868	London, NW
Poor Servants of the Mother of God	English	M	1869	London, W
Daughters of Mary and Joseph (Ladies of Mary)	Belgian	A	1870	Surrey
Augustinians (Bruges)	Belgian	A	1870	Sussex
Providence (Immaculate Conception)	Belgian	A	1870	London, NW
Bon Secours (Paris)	French	A	1870	London, W
Servants of the Sacred Heart	French	A	1871	London, E
Cross, Religious of/Dames of	French	A	1871	Hants.
Marists	French	A	1871	London, SE

→

Table 1. *(cont.) Name*	*Origins*		*New Foundation*	
		Type	*Date*	*First Location*
Notre Dame, Co. of Mary (Notre Dame Nuns)	French	A	1871	London, N
Poor Child Jesus	German	A	1872	Warwicks.
Sacred Heart of Mary	French	A	1872	Lancs./ Liverpool
Helpers of Holy Souls	French	A	1873	London, NW
Notre Dame des Missions	French	A	1874	Kent
Blessed Sacrament (Most Holy Sacrament)	French	M	1876	London, SW
Little Schools, Sisters of	French	A	1876	Guernsey
Poor Handmaids of Jesus Christ	German	A	1876	London, E
Little Company of Mary	English	A	1877	Notts.
Hope, Sisters of	French	A	1878	London, N
Assumption, Little Sisters of	French	A	1880	London, E
Dames de Nazareth (Order of Nuns)	French	A	1880	London, W
Retreat of the Sacred Heart (Dames Retrait)	French	A	1880	London, SW
Notre Dame de Sion	French	A	1882	London, W
Franciscan Missionaries St. Joseph	English	A	1883	Lancs./ Manchester
St. Joseph of Peace	English	M	1884	Notts.
Franciscan Missionaries/St. Mary of Angels	French	A	1886	Hants.
Most Holy Trinity (Trinitarians)	Spanish	A	1886	Kent
Canonesses of Lateran (Haywards Heath) ***	Belgian	M	1887	Sussex
Franciscan Missionaries of Mary	India	M	1887	Somerset
Cenacle, Religious of Our Lady of the Retreat	French	A	1888	Lancs./ Manchester
Institute Perpet. Adoration Blessed Sacrament	Belgian	M	1888	London, SW
Jesus and Mary, Sisters of Charity (Ghent)	Belgian	M	1888	Lancs.
Marie Auxiliatrice	French	M	1888	London, E
Mere de Dieu, Dames of	French	A	1888	Gloucs./Bristol
Servites, 2nd Order	Italian	C	1888	Sussex
Franciscan Minoresses	English	A	1888	Leics.
Augustines St. Cœur Marie, Dames of	French	A	1889	Sussex
Christian Education, Institution of	French	A	1889	Hants.
Visitation Sisters of Ghent	Belgian	A	1889	Devon
Irish Sisters of Charity	Irish	A	1890	Cheshire
St. Ursula, Company of	French	A	1890	Oxon.
Christian Education, Dames Chretienne (Ghent)	Belgian	M	1891	Dorset
La Sagesse (Daughters of Wisdom)	French	A	1892	Hants.
Dames of St. Maur (Cong. Holy Child Jesus)	French	A	1892	London, SE
Nativity of Our Lord, Ladies of	French	A	1894	Kent
Franciscan Sisters (Littlehampton)	English	A	1895	Sussex
Holy Family of Nazareth	Italian/Polish	A	1896	London, E

→

Table 1. *(cont.)* Name	Origins	Type	Date	First Location
			New Foundation	
Mary of Namur (Soeurs St.Marie)	Belgian	A	1896	Herts.
Bernadines, Dames	French	M	1897	Bucks.
Franciscan Sisters of the Holy Ghost	English	A	1897	Lancs./ Manchester
Immaculate Heart of Mary	French	A	1897	Sussex
Most Holy Redeemer (Redemptoristines)	Italian	C	1897	London, SW
Sacred Hearts and Perpet. Adore (Picpus Sisters)	French	M	1897	Dorset
St. Catharine VM (Polish)	German	A	1897	Lancs./ Liverpool
St. Louis (Sisters of Charity)	French	A	1897	Somerset
Adoration Reparatrice	French	C	1898	London, SW
Adorers of Sacred Heart (Tyburn)	French	C	1901	London, W
Our Lady of Immaculate Conception	French	A	1901	Kent
Augustine Hospitallers, Canonesses	French	M	1902	Lancs./ Liverpool
Holy Ghost, Daughters of (White Sisters)	French	M	1902	Bucks.
Providence (Sisters of Charity Ruille sur Loire)	French	A	1902	Kent
Annonciades, Order of Our Lady	French	C	1903	Kent
Assumptionists (Oblates)	French	A	1903	Kent
Charity under Protection of V. de Paul	French	A	1903	London, SW
Christian Instruction (St. Gildas)	French	A	1903	Somerset
Christian Instruction of Nevers	French	A	1903	Sussex
Christian Retreat	French	A	1903	Staffs.
Christian Schools	French	A	1903	Berks.
Cross, Daughters of (Torquay)	French	A	1903	Devon
Immaculate Conception, Holy Family St. Meen	French	A	1903	Devon
Marie, Congregation de (Paris)	French	A	1903	Beds.
Our Lady of Consolation (Nurses)	English	A	1903	London, SE
Sacred Heart of Jesus Missionary Sisters	French	M	1903	London, SE
Sacred Hearts of Jesus and Mary (Chigwell)	English	A	1903	Essex
Salesians (Our Lady Help of Christians)	Italian	A	1903	Hants.
Saviour and the Blessed Virgin	French	A	1903	Somerset
St. Clotilde, Dames of	French	A	1903	London, SE
St. Joseph of Bordeaux (Tamworth)	French	A	1903	Lancs./ Manchester
St. Martha	French	A	1904	Herts.
St. Martin of Tours	French	A	1904	London, N
Nativity of the Blessed Virgin	French	A	1904	Leics.
Our Lady of Compassion	French	A	1904	Staffs.
Presentation of Bourge St. Andeol	French	A	1904	Devon
Providence (Rouen)	French	A	1904	Sussex
Sacred Heart Sisters of Saint-Aubin	French	A	1904	London, SW

→

Table 1. *(cont.)* Name	Origins	*New Foundation*		
		Type	Date	First Location
St. Joseph of Cluny	French	A	1904	Staffs.
St. Paul of Chartres	French	A	1905	London, N
Holy Cross, Teaching Sisters of	Swiss	A	1905	London, SW
Immaculate Conception, Our Lady of Lourdes	French	M	1905	Middlesex
Jesus, Daughters of (Filles de Jesus)	French	M	1905	Kent
Presentation Sisters (Broons)	French	A	1905	Guernsey
Sacred Heart Sisters of Saint-Jacut (Morbihan)	French	A	1905	Herts.
St. Cheretienne (Infancy Jesus and Mary)	French	A	1905	Kent
St. Joseph of the Apparition	French	M	1905	Worcs.
Charity of Notre Dame d'Evron	French	A	1905	Yorks., ER
Providence (St. Brieuc)	French	A	1906	London, N
Good Saviour, Daughters of	French	A	1907	Anglesey
St. Thomas Villanova	French	A	1907	Cumberland
Augustinians of Precious Blood	French	A	1909	Kent
Mary and Joseph	French	A	1909	Herts.
Oblates of St. Benedict	English	A	1909	London, SE
Dominican Sisters of Charity of Presentation	French	A	1910	Berks.
Pallotine Missionary Sisters	German	A	1910	Lancs.
Sacred Heart of Jesus, Handmaids of	Spanish	A	1910	London, SW
Canon. St. Augustine Perpet. Adore. (of Paris)	French	M	1911	Yorks., ER
St. Anne	English	A	1911	London, SW
Augustinian Sisters of Meaux	French	A	1913	London, N
Handmaids of Mary (Spanish)	Spanish	A	1913	London, NW
St. Dorothy	Italian	A	1914	Leics.
Divine Charity, Sisters of	Austrian	A	1915	Norfolk
St. Louis	Irish	A	1920	Norfolk
Canonessian Daughters of Charity (Verona)	Italian	A	1923	Herts.
Holy Family (Villefranche)	French	A	1926	London, SW
St. John of God	Irish	A	1926	Devon
Grail, Ladies of (Lay-Women of Nazareth)	Dutch	A	1929	London, SW
Missionary Sisters of Our Lady of Africa	Algerian	A	1929	Middlesex
Divine Saviour, Sisters (Salvatorians)	Italian	A	1930	Herts.
Brigittine Sisters (Iver Heath)	Italian	C	1931	Bucks.
Holy Ghost, Missionary Servants of	Dutch	A	1933	Staffs.
Mary Immaculate, Daughters of	Spanish	A	1933	London, W
Medical Missionaries, Catholic	USA	A	1933	Middlesex
Notre Dame, Sisters (Mulhausen)	German	A	1934	Herts.
Our Lady of Good and Perpetual Succour	Belgian	A	1934	Durham
Oblates of St. Francis de la Sales	French	A	1936	Herts.
Missionary Sisters of Our Lady of the Apostles	French	A	1937	Sussex
Total	176			

Compiled from: *Catholic Directories* for relevant years, Steele (1902), Hohn (1912) and Anson (1949). Note that the origins of older orders had often several different branch roots. In some instances foundations from abroad later became separate English communities. Allowance may be made for a date of arrival or foundation to be up to twelve months earlier or later due to a transition period or print error. A few English foundations were active for several years before their official recognition date. Not included (change of name): Franciscan Missionaries of Divine Motherhood, listed here as Franciscans (Littlehampton). Not found in *Catholic Directories*: Sacred Heart Hospitallers; Spanish; 1926; London, SW. Although the total listed here is 176, the figure of 175 has been used in subsequent Tables (see the third note below).

Notes
* Briefly in London before main establishment in York (Anson, p. 319).
** Several different foundations of Benedictines returned c.1795 (this was the first).
*** This congregation returned to Bruges in 1802 and came back to England in 1887 (Anson, p. 192).
Yorkshire was formerly split into three administrative areas: ER: East Riding; NR: North Riding; WR: West Riding.

Table 2. Women's Religious Orders and Congregations, England and Wales, 1800–57: First Regional Location/Arrival/Foundation

Region*	1800	1820	1830	1840	1850	1857
London + South-East	2	2	3	4	10	14
East Anglia	1					
South-West	3	5	5	5	6	7
Wales	–	–	–	–	–	–
Midlands	1	1	1	1	3	3
North-West				1	1	2
Yorkshire	2	2	2	2	3	5
North-East	–	–	–	–	–	–
Totals	**9**	**10**	**11**	**13**	**23**	**31**

Compiled from Table 1.
* Regions as designated by R. Floud and D. McCloskey (eds), *The Economic History of Britain since 1700*, Vol.2, *1860–1939* (London, 2nd edn, 1994), pp. 465–6.

Table 3. Women's Religious Orders and Congregations, England and Wales, 1857–1937: First Regional Location/Arrival/Foundation

Region*	In situ 1857	1877	1897	1917	1937
London + South-East	14	39	62	98	109
East Anglia	–	1	1	2	3
South-West	7	10	16	21	22
Wales	–	2	2	3	3
Midlands	3	7	9	15	16
North-West	2	4	10	14	14
Yorkshire	5	5	5	7	7
North-East	–	–	–	–	1
Totals	**31**	**68**	**105**	**160**	**175**

Compiled from Table 1.
* Regions as designated by R. Floud and D. McCloskey (eds), *The Economic History of Britain since 1700*, Vol.2, *1860–1939* (London, 2nd edn, 1994), pp. 465–6.

Table 4. Active, Mixed and Contemplative Orders and Congregations, 1800–57

	1800	1820	1830	1840	1850	1857
Active Sisters	1	1	1	3	11	16
Mixed	1	–	1	1	2	5
Contemplatives*	7	9	9	9	10	10
Totals	**9**	**10**	**11**	**13**	**23**	**31**

* Some contemplatives might accept a small number of girls for private education but this has not been taken as constituting an active apostolate.
Compiled from Table 1.

Table 5. Active, Mixed and Contemplative Orders and Congregations, 1857–1937

	1857		1877		1897		1917		1937	
	No.	%	No.	%	No.	%	No.	%	No.	%
Active Sisters	16	51.6	43	63.2	69	65.7	114	71.3	128	73.1
Mixed	5	16.1	12	17.7	21	20.0	28	17.5	28	16.0
Contemplatives	10	32.3	13	19.1	15	14.3	18	11.2	19	10.9
Totals	**31**	**100**	**68**	**100**	**105**	**100**	**160**	**100**	**175**	**100**

Compiled from Table 1. Calculations based on: Murphy (1873), Steele (1902), Hohn (1912), Anson (1949) and *Catholic Directories* for 1857–1937.

Table 6. Congregations and Orders, 1857–1937: Approximate Nature of Primary Activity/Apostolate in England and Wales

Year	Education (including those with nursing and social care services)	Social Work (combined with some education and nursing)	Nursing and Hospital	Contemplatives (non-active but occasional education*)	Total
1857	16	5	–	10	31
1877	43	7	5	13	68
1897	74	8	8	15	105
1917	122	8	12	18	160
1937	133	8	15	19	175

Compiled from: *The Catholic Directories* for 1857–1937, J. Murphy (1873), F. Steele, (1902), H. Hohn, (1912), P. Anson (1949).
* The parameters of the research for this study do not allow for detailed discussion of the activities of contemplative orders

Table 7. Sisters of Notre Dame de Namur, Mount Pleasant, Liverpool: Schools and Pupils, 1878–1938*

Approximate Decadal Intervals	Number of Sisters	Poor Schools/ Later Government Elementary Schools	Pupils	Pupil Teachers	Practice School Pupils	High School Pupils	Training College Students
1878	60	8	5,557	110	295	174	103
1889 **	66	8	7,202	136	477	219	103
1898	68	10	6,413	92	n/a	178	107
1908	87	8	5,030	27	n/a	326	173
1916 **	76†	8	5,061	n/a	n/a	327	182
1929 **	93	8	6,086	n/a	n/a	438	187
1938	89	8	5,293	n/a	n/a	442	151

Source: Notre Dame de Namur Provincial Archives, Liverpool. Ref. MP sector C.
* Excludes three or four night schools during 1880–1900 with c.700 pupils
** No figures available for 1888, 1918 or 1928
† Plus 43 novices and 16 postulants following opening of English novitiate brought about by travel restrictions after 1914

Table 8. Roman Catholic Town and Rural Schools with Successfully Prepared Pupil Teachers for Training Colleges: Lancashire and Cheshire, 1863–70

School Location and Name	Locality	Estimated Number of Children	Pupil Teachers Prepared	Teachers
Lancashire Towns				
Liverpool				
St. Mary	Ray St.	472	14	Srs. Notre Dame
St. Peter	Seel St.	325	10	Srs. Notre Dame
St. Anthony	Newsham St.	497	8	Srs. Notre Dame
St. Nicholas	Hawke St.	254	8	Srs. Notre Dame
St. Helen	Eldon St.	393	5	Srs. Notre Dame
SS. Thomas and William	Edgar St.	419	5	Srs. Notre Dame
St. Thomas	Elm St.	224	5	Srs of Mercy
Practising School	Mount Pleasant	142	4	Srs. Notre Dame
St. Anne	Goulden St.	299	4	Srs. Notre Dame
Holy Cross	Fontenoy St.	334	3	Srs. of Mercy
St. Oswald	Old Swan	188	2	Srs. of Mercy
St. Francis Xavier	Haigh St.	556	1	Srs. of Mercy
Manchester				
St. Chad	Stork St.	411	9	Srs Notre Dame
St. Patrick	Livesey St.	475	7	Presentation Nuns
St. Wilfred	Bedford St.	405	6	Loreto Nuns
St. Alphonsus	Clarendon St.	204	3	Loreto Nuns
St. Alban	John St.	143	1	Secular
St. Mary	Tonman St.	135	1	Secular
Preston				
St. Austin	Lark Hill	263	5	Faithful Companions
St. Ignatius	Ignatius Sq.	415	4	Faithful Companions
The Talbot	Maudlands	503	3	Srs. Holy Child
St. Wilfrid	Fox St.	281	1	Srs. Holy Child
St. Joseph	Ribbleton Lane	184	1	Secular
Salford				
St. John	Cleminson St.	312	3	Faithful Companions
St. Peter	Greengate	220	1	Faithful Companions
St. Helens	Cowley Hill	238	4	Srs Notre Dame
Greenbank	Liverpool road	146	3	Srs Notre Dame
St. Joseph	Parr	228	3	Srs Notre Dame
Wigan				
St. John	Dickinson St.	279	3	Srs Notre Dame
St. Patrick	Scholes	303	4	Srs Notre Dame
Blackburn				
St. Anne	Paradise St.	291	5	Srs Notre Dame
St. Alban	Penny St.	412	3	Srs Notre Dame

Table 8. *(cont.)* School Location and Name	Locality	Estimated Number of Children	Pupil Teachers Prepared	Teachers
Lancashire Towns (cont.)				
Bolton	Pilkington St.	194	3	Srs. Holy Family
Chorley	St. Mary	262	6	Secular
Oldham	Cardinal St.	244	4	Srs. of Mercy
Accrington	St. Oswald	172	2	Secular
Warrington	King St.	200	1	Secular
Sub-total		11,023	155	
Lancashire Rural Schools				
Ashton-le-Willows	–	146	4	Secular
Hurst Green	–	113	2	Secular
Hindley	–	275	1	Secular
Blundell *(endowed)*	–	82	1	Secular
Townley	–	151	1	Secular
Sutton	St. Anne	121	1	Secular
Prescot	–	122	1	Srs. St. Paul
Lea	–	34	1	Secular
Sub-totals	1,044	12		
Cheshire and North Wales				
Birkenhead				
St. Wedburgh and St. Patrick	–	206	10	Faithful Companions and Secular
Macclesfield	–	118	2	Secular
Edgeley, Stockport	–	146	1	Secular
Hyde	–	137	1	Secular
Holywell	–	101	1	Srs. St. Paul
Sub-total	708	15		
Summary				
Lancashire:	towns	11,023	155	number of religious-run schools: 33
	rural	1,044	12	
Cheshire and North Wales:	–	708	15	number of secular schools: 16 combined: 1
Grand Totals		12,775	182	

Source: compiled from J. Murphy, *Terra Incognita* (1873), Tables I, II and III, pp. 485–6

Table 9. Charitable and Other Institutions Supervised or Staffed by Nuns Listed within Roman Catholic Dioceses, 1857–1937

Type	1857	1877	1897	1917	1937
Orphanages	5	26	39	57	48
Reform schools	1	5	4	3	*
Industrial schools	5	8	13	13	2*
Homes for children (various)		1	6	8	10
Homes for women/girls		1	2	8	14
Homes for servants	4	6	5	5	6
Homes for mothers and babies				1	3
Home for girls in business			4	9	15
Night homes for girls			1	3	4
Houses of refuge (penitents)	2	8	15	21	25
Night refuges for homeless		1	1	1	1
Home for aged poor	1	9	25	28	28
Crèches		1	*	*	*
Hospices for pilgrims		1	1	1	1
Hospitals/nursing homes	1	6	10	22	29 *
Asylums for blind	1	1	1	1	1
Deaf and dumb institutions		1	1	1	1
School mistress training	1	2	4	4	4

Source: Catholic Directories 1857–1937
* Approximated numbers, possibly understated; institutions changed/merged or not clearly designated

Table 10. Women's Religious Communities Engaged in Charitable Undertakings in England and Wales, 1912

*Charitable Undertakings Generalised**	*Managed or Staffed by Nuns and Sisters*
Homes/orphanages/certified and non-certified for boys	25
Homes/orphanages/certified and non-certified for girls	80
Homes/industrial schools for girls	12
Homes/industrial schools for boys	6
Homes for penitents (Houses of Mercy)	26
Homes of protection for girls	7
Homes for business girls and governesses	13
Training homes for servants	18
Homes for servants out of place/working women out of employment	16
Crèches/day nurseries for infants	3
Homes for babies and illegitimate children	2
Homes for aged poor	32
Night refuges and homes of protection	10
Soup kitchens	7
Convalescent homes for women	12
Homes for children needing nursing care (includes education)	25
Hospitals	14
Nursing the sick poor in own homes	14
Visiting and relief of the poor	'Many'

Source: The Handbook of Catholic Charities and Social Works (London: Catholic Truth Society, 3rd edn, 1912)
* Detailed in Walsh, Appendix (x) b

Table 11. Certified Reformatories and Industrial Schools for Roman Catholics in England and Wales, 1857–97

	Reformatories			Industrial Schools		
	Boys	Girls	Total	Boys	Girls	Total
1857	1	1	2	–	–	–
1877	4	2	6	9	8	17
1897	4	2	6	12	11	23

Source: Inspectors' Annual Reports, P.P. 1897 [C.8566] XLI (official figures do not indicate the number of institutions administered by women religious)

Table 12. Undertakings and Activities of Three Congregations in England and Wales, 1887

Activity	SSP*	DVDP	Sisters of Mercy
parish schools, mixed	83	–	–
parish schools, girls	19	–	–
parish schools, infants	77**	–	–
day schools (government grant)	–	9	–
poor schools (infants), elementary schools	–	–	41
middle/day schools	–	2	–
select/middle-class boarding and day schools	23**	–	24
night schools	1	–	–
night schools/training workshops	–	6	5
blind asylum and school	–	1	–
deaf and dumb institute and school	–	1	–
day crèche for infants	–	3	–
training school for servants	–	–	2
home for workhouse boys	1	–	–
home for business girls/pupil-teachers	–	1	5
orphanages, mixed/industrial and reform schools	–	12	9
parish visiting/relief of poor and sick	47	12	11
night refuge	–	–	1
hospital	–	1	1
hospice for pilgrims	1	–	–
houses of mercy	–	–	6

Source: Anon., *The Religious Houses of the United Kingdom* (London: Burns & Oates, 1887)

* J.J. Scarisbrick, *Selly Park and Beyond* (Birmingham, 1997); in 1887 the number of sisters in this congregation was just under 400 (p. 87)

**Exact numbers are not clear in the wording employed for these two categories in the 1887 listings

Table 13. Religious Communities of Women and Growth of Convent Numbers 1857–1937: England and Wales

	Number of Orders and Congregations	Number of Locations
1857	31	100
1877	68	278
1897	105	469
1917	161	800
1937	175	956

Calculations based on: J. Murphy (1873), F. Steele (1902), H. Hohn (1912), P. Anson (1949) and the *Catholic Directories* for 1857–1937

Table 14. Convent Houses by Type and Growth Rates in England and Wales, 1857–1937

	1857		1877			1897			1917			1937		
	No.	%	No.	%	% rise	No.	%	% rise	No.	%	% rise	No.	%	% rise
Active	65	65.0	209	75.2	222	356	75.9	70	605	75.6	70	728	76.2	20
Mixed	18	18.0	42	15.1	133	85	18.1	102	149	18.7	75	155	16.2	4
Contemplative	14	14.0	24	8.6	71	27	5.8	13	45	5.6	67	70	7.3	55
No information*	3	3.0	3	1.1	–	1	0.2	–	1	0.1	–	3	0.3	–
Totals	100	100.0	278	100.0		469	100.0		800	100.0		956	100.0	

Sources: calculations based on J. Murphy (1873), F. Steele (1902), H. Hohn (1912), P. Anson (1949) and *Catholic Directories*, 1857–1937
* convent locations uncertain with regard to name or type

Table 15. Convent Houses Run by Active Sisters Prominent in Providing Social Care in England and Wales, 1857–1937

	1857	1877	1897	1917	1937
Sisters of Mercy	24	44	72	98	104
Charity of St. Paul	10	35	51	54	71
Daughters St. Vincent de Paul	–	17	35	50	65
Poor Sisters of Nazareth	–	6	12	22	25
Little Sisters of the Poor	–	10	17	19	18

Note: These indications have been compiled from the *Catholic Directories*, 1857–1937, and may be taken as being broadly accurate although possibly underestimated.

Table 16. Regional Distribution of Convents in England and Wales, 1857–1937

	1857		1877		1897		1917		1937	
	No.	%	No.	%	No.	%	No.	%	No.	%
London/South-East	31	31	97	35	184	39	351	44	416	44
East Anglia	–	–	4	1	6	1	14	2	22	2
South-West	8	8	28	10	40	9	79	10	93	10
Midlands	25	25	44	16	64	14	96	12	108	11
Wales	1	1	7	3	11	2	30	4	39	4
North-West	25	25	62	22	92	20	139	17	168	18
North-East	4	4	14	5	36	8	45	6	51	5
Yorkshire (ER/WR)	6	6	22	8	36	8	46	6	59	6
Totals	100	100	278	100	469	100	800	100	956	100

Source: extracted from Table 17; calculations based on J. Murphy (1873), F. Steele (1902), H. Hohn (1912), P. Anson (1949) and the *Catholic Directories* for 1857–1937 Regions as designated in Floud and McCloskey (eds), *The Economic History of Britain* (2nd edn, 1994), Vol.2, pp. 465–6

Table 17. Distribution of Convent Houses, 1857–1937

1857	No.	%	1877	No.	%	1897	No.	%
London	23	23.0	London	65	23.38	London	97	20.68
Lancs.	21	21.0	Lancs.	51	18.34	Lancs.	74	15.78
Staffs.	10	10.0	Yorks., WR	20	7.20	Yorks., WR	31	6.60
Warwicks.	7	7.0	Warwicks.	14	5.03	Sussex	23	4.90
Yorks. WR	6	6.0	Staffs.	11	3.95	Warwicks.	21	4.47
Gloucs.	4	4.0	Durham	8	2.87	Durham	17	3.62
Cheshire	3	3.0	Gloucs.	8	2.87	Kent	16	3.41
Dorset	2	2.0	Sussex	7	2.52	Essex	12	2.55
Derbys.	2	2.0	Kent	7	2.52	Staffs.	12	2.55
Sussex	2	2.0	Essex	7	2.52	Northumberland	11	2.34
Oxon	2	2.0	Devon	7	2.52	Cheshire	11	2.34
Notts.	2	2.0	Cheshire	6	2.16	Gloucs.	11	2.34
Durham	2	2.0	Northumberland	4	1.44	Middlesex	10	2.13
Middlesex	1	1.0	Somerset	4	1.44	Somerset	9	1.91
Kent	1	1.0	Glamorgan	4	1.44	Devon	9	1.91
Northumberland	1	1.0	Oxon	4	1.44	Hants.	8	1.70
Somerset	1	1.0	Cumberland	4	1.44	Yorks., NR	8	1.70
Glamorgan	1	1.0	Dorset	4	1.44	Notts.	7	1.49
Bucks.	1	1.0	Wilts.	4	1.44	Surrey	6	1.30

→

Table 17. Distribution of Convent Houses, 1857–1937 *(cont.)*

	1857			1877			1897	
	No.	%		No.	%		No.	%
Worcs.	1	1.0	Worcs.	3	1.08	Cumberland	6	1.30
Leics.	1	1.0	Leics.	3	1.08	Yorks., ER	5	1.07
Yorks., NR	1	1.0	Derbys.	3	1.08	Worc.	5	1.07
Cornwall	1	1.0	Hereford	3	1.08	Dorset	5	1.07
Cumberland	1	1.0	Northants.	3	1.08	Glamorgan	5	1.07
Hereford	1	1.0	Yorks., ER	2	0.72	Wilts.	5	1.07
Essex	1	1.0	Yorks., NR	2	0.72	Lincs.	4	0.86
Northants.	1	1.0	Suffolk	2	0.72	Oxon	4	0.86
Suffolk	–		Berks.	2	0.72	Hereford	4	0.86
Herts.	–		Notts.	2	0.72	Suffolk	4	0.86
Wilts.	–		Flint	2	0.72	Berks.	3	0.64
Flint	–		Surrey	1	0.36	Leics.	3	0.64
Yorks., ER	–		Hants.	1	0.36	I of W	3	0.64
Lincs.	–		Bucks.	1	0.36	Derbys.	3	0.64
I of W	–		Cornwall	1	0.36	Monmouth	2	0.43
Denbigh	–		Lincs.	1	0.36	Northants.	2	0.43
Devon	–		I of W	1	0.36	Herts.	2	0.43
Surrey	–		Monmouth	1	0.36	Salop	2	0.43
Hants.	–		Norfolk	1	0.36	Flint	2	0.43
Berks.	–		Salop	1	0.36	Norfolk	2	0.43
Pembroke	–		Westmorland	1	0.36	Rutland	1	0.21
Salop	–		Middlesex	1	0.36	Westmorland	1	0.21
Westmorland	–		Cambridge	1	0.36	Pembroke	1	0.21
Norfolk	–		Pembroke	–		Cornwall	1	0.21
Monmouth	–		Denbigh	–		Denbigh	1	0.21
Beds.	–		Herts.	–		Bucks.	–	
Caernarvon	–		Beds.	–		Beds.	–	
Cambridge	–		Caernarvon	–		Caernarvon	–	
Carthmarth.	–		Carthmarth	–		Carthmarth	–	
Angelsey	–		Angelsey	–		Angelsey	–	
Cardigan	–		Cardigan	–		Cardigan	–	
Merioneth	–		Merioneth	–		Merioneth	–	
Hunts.	–		Hunts.	–		Hunts.	–	
Rutland	–		Rutland	–		Cambridge	–	
Radnorshire	–		Radnorshire	–		Radnorshire	–	
Brecknockshire	–		Brecknockshire	–		Brecknockshire	–	
Montgomeryshire	–		Montgomeryshire	–		Montgomeryshire	–	
Totals	100	100	Totals	278	100	Totals	469	100

Table 17. Distribution of Convent Houses, 1857–1937 *(cont.)*

| | 1917 | | | 1937 | |
	No.	%		No.	%
London	152	19.00	London	169	17.67
Lancs.	114	14.25	Lancs.	136	14.23
Kent	43	5.38	Yorks., WR	50	5.23
Sussex	41	5.13	Sussex	46	4.81
Yorks., WR	39	4.88	Kent	44	4.60
Devon	28	3.50	Devon	36	3.77
Warwicks.	28	3.50	Warwicks.	35	3.66
Essex	24	3.00	Essex	30	3.14
Staffs.	23	2.88	Middlesex	27	2.82
Durham	22	2.76	Herts.	26	2.72
Middlesex	21	2.63	Staffs.	25	2.62
Cheshire	17	2.13	Durham	24	2.51
Somerset	17	2.13	Surrey	21	2.20
Hants.	16	2.00	Cheshire	21	2.20
Herts.	16	2.00	Hants.	19	1.99
Gloucs.	13	1.63	Gloucs.	18	1.88
Surrey	12	1.50	Northumberland	15	1.57
Northumberland	12	1.50	Somerset	15	1.57
Yorks., NR	11	1.38	Glamorgan	14	1.46
Worcs.	10	1.25	Oxon	12	1.26
Glamorgan	10	1.25	Yorks., NR	12	1.26
Oxon	8	1.00	Leics.	11	1.15
Leics.	8	1.00	Cumberland	10	1.05
Suffolk	8	1.00	Suffolk	10	1.05
Cornwall	8	1.00	Dorset	10	1.05
I of W	8	1.00	Yorks., ER	9	0.94
Yorks., ER	7	0.88	Norfolk	9	0.94
Cumberland	7	0.88	Bucks	7	0.73
Dorset	7	0.88	Cornwall	7	0.73
Wilts.	6	0.75	Derbys.	7	0.73
Berks.	6	0.75	Lincs.	7	0.73
Notts.	6	0.70	Wilts.	7	0.73
Norfolk	5	0.63	Worcs.	6	0.63
Derbys.	5	0.63	Berks.	6	0.63
Lincs.	4	0.50	Hereford	6	0.63
Hereford	4	0.50	I of W	6	0.63
Monmouth	4	0.50	Notts.	6	0.63
Flint	4	0.50	Pembroke	5	0.52
Northants.	4	0.50	Denbigh	4	0.41
Denbigh	3	0.37	Monmouth	4	0.41
Bucks.	3	0.37	Beds.	3	0.31

→

Table 17. Distribution of Convent Houses, 1857–1937 *(cont.)*

	1917 No.	%		*1937* No.	%
Caernarvon	3	0.37	Caernarvon	3	0.31
Salop	3	0.37	Cambridge	3	0.31
Pembroke	2	0.26	Carthmarth	3	0.31
Carthmarth	2	0.26	Flint	3	0.31
Beds.	1	0.12	Northants.	3	0.31
Cambridge	1	0.12	Salop	2	0.21
Angelsey	1	0.12	Angelsey	1	0.11
Cardigan	1	0.12	Cardigan	1	0.11
Rutland	1	0.12	Merioneth	1	0.11
Westmorland	1	0.12	Westmorland	1	0.11
Merioneth	–		Rutland	–	
Hunts.	–		Hunts.	–	
Radnorshire	–		Radnorshire	–	
Brecknockshire	–		Brecknockshire	–	
Montgomeryshire	–		Montgomeryshire	–	
Totals	800	100	Totals	956	100

Source: Compiled from the *Catholic Directories*, 1857–1937, Steele (1902), Hohn (1912), Anson (1949)

Table 18. Convents in Liverpool

	Contemplatives	*Mixed*	*Active*	*Total*
1857	–	2	4	6
1877	–	2	18	20
1897	–	3	22	25
1917	2	9	32	43
1937	3	10	33	46

Table 19. Convents in Manchester

	Contemplatives	*Mixed*	*Active*	*Total*
1857	–	2	4	6
1877	–	2	8	10
1897	–	2	17	19
1917	–	2	21	23
1937	–	2	28	30

Table 20. Balance Sheet for an Elementary Convent School in London, 1891

Income	£	s	d	Expenditure	£	s	d
Education grant	181	11	3	Mistresses' salaries	145	2	6
Voluntary contribution (one individual)	103	9	6	Assistant (needlework only)	14	0	0
Fees paid by scholars	84	15	7	Pupil-teachers' salaries	98	0	0
Fees paid by guardians	1	2	0	Teacher of cookery	5	5	0
Other sources (sale of needlework)	9	4	0	Books, apparatus, etc.	10	9	10
				Fuel, light and heating	19	14	3
				Rent (£30), rates and taxes	40	19	2
				Replacement of furniture and repairs	36	4	9
				Needlework materials	7	6	10
Total	380	2	4	Total	380	2	4

Source: Notre Dame de Namur Archives, ref. BS h/3

Table 21. Three Congregations of Active Sisters: New Entrants Subsequently Professed from England, Ireland, Scotland, Wales and Overseas, 1847–1926

	SSP	SND	SSHJM	
1847–56	46	106	–	
1857–66	92	169	–	
1867–76	123	166	32[*]	(1870–76)
1877–86	183	178	67	
1887–96	103	208	42	
1897–06	144	235	80	
1907–16	135	234	84	
1917–26	130	251	70	

Source: Congregation archives
[*] Not here before 1870

Table 22. Daughters of Charity of St. Vincent de Paul: New Entrants (Professed Sisters) from Ireland, 1847–1926

	Number
1847–56	19
1857–66	37
1867–76	58
1877–86	93
1887–96	147
1897–06	151
1907–16	167
1917–26	235
Total	907

Source: Congregation archives. Over the same period, about 800 Sisters are believed to have come from England, Scotland and Wales.

Table 23. Sisters of St. Paul the Apostle: Successful and Unsuccessful Entrants

	Successful Entrants	Unsuccessful Entrants	Total Intake	Percentage Successful	Percentage Unsuccessful
1877–86	183	88	271	68	32
1887–96	103	79	182	57	43
1897–06	144	41	185	78	22
1907–16	135	91	226	60	40
1917–26	130	108	238	55	45
Totals	956	562	1,518	[average: 64]	[average: 36]

Source: Congregation registers

Table 24. Three Congregations: Successful and Unsuccessful Entrants, 1914–26

	Total Intake	Professed Sisters	Left before Profession	Percentage Unsuccessful
SSP	315	170	145	46
SND	333	265	68	20
SSHJM	134	94	40	30

Source: Congregation archives

Table 25. (Professed) Sisters of St. Paul the Apostle: Country of Origin of Entrants, 1847–1926

	England and Wales	Ireland	Scotland	Abroad	Totals
1847–56	34 (74%)	10 (22%)	1 (2%)	1 (2%)	46
1857–66	61 (66%)	28 (31%)	1 (1%)	2 (2%)	92
1867–76	53 (43%)	60 (49%)	2 (1.6%)	8 (6.4%)	123
1877–86	66 (36%)	111 (60%)	3 (2%)	3 (2%)	183
1887–96	44 (43%)	59 (57%)	–	–	103
1897–1906	31 (21%)	113 (79%)	–	–	144
1907–16	45 (33%)	85 (63%)	4 (3%)	1 (1%)	135
1917–26	40 (31%)	83 (64%)	7 (5%)		130
Totals	374 (39.1%)	549 (57.4%)	18 (1.9%)	15 (1.6%)	956

Source: congregation archives; see bibliography for full details

Table 26. (Professed) Sisters of Notre Dame de Namur: Country of Origin of Entrants, 1847–1926

	England and Wales	Ireland	Scotland	Abroad	Unknown	Totals
1847–56	59 (56%)	20 (19%)	–	24 (22%)	3 (3%)	106
1857–66	106 (63%)	53 (32%)	4 (2%)	4 (2%)	2 (1%)	169
1867–76	120 (72%)	37 (22%)	7 (4%)	2 (2%)	–	166
1877–86	123 (65%)	45 (29%)	7 (4%)	–	3 (3%)	178
1887–96	147 (71%)	53 (25%)	8 (4%)	–	–	208
1897–1906	148 (63%)	56 (24%)	27 (11%)	4 (2%)	–	235
1907–16	157 (67%)	47 (20%)	29 (12%)	1 (1%)	–	234
1917–26	166 (66%)	26 (10%)	54 (21%)	4 (2%)	1 (1%)	251
Totals	1026 (66.3%)	337 (21.8%)	136 (8.8%)	39 (2.5%)	9 (0.6%)	1,547

Source: congregation archives; see bibliography for full details

Table 27. (Professed) Sisters of Sacred Hearts of Jesus and Mary: Country of Origin of Entrants, 1870–1926

	England and Wales	Ireland	Scotland	Abroad	Totals
1867–76*	6 (19%)	24 (75%)	2 (6%)	–	32
1877–86	13 (19%)	52 (78%)	2 (3%)	–	67
1887–96	7 (17%)	33 (78%)	2 (5%)	–	42
1897–06	14 (18%)	61 (76%)	5 (6%)	–	80
1907–16	7 (8%)	74 (88%)	3 (4%)	–	84
1917–26	12 (17%)	51 (73%)	4 (6%)	3 (4%)	70
Totals	59 (15.7%)	295 (78.7 %)	18 (4.8%)	3 (0.8%)	375

Source: congregation archives; see bibliography for full details
* The order was not present in the United Kingdom before 1870

Table 28. Birth Origins of English-/Scots-/Welsh-born Professed Sisters, 1845–1926

	SSP	%	SND	%	SSHJM*	%
Bedfordshire	0		3	0.3	0	
Berkshire	0		2	0.2	0	
Buckinghamshire	3	0.8	2	0.2	0	
Cambridgeshire	0		7	0.6	0	
Cheshire	10	2.6	26	2.3	1	2.3
Cornwall	2	0.5	6	0.5	0	
Cumberland	4	1.0	10	0.9	1	2.3
Derbyshire	4	1.0	11	1.0	0	
Devonshire	2	0.5	19	1.7	0	
Dorset	1	0.3	4	0.4	0	
Durham	**28**	**7.2**	19	1.7	1	2.3
Essex	4	1.0	6	0.5	0	
Gloucestershire	3	0.8	2	0.2	0	
Hampshire	1	0.3	16	1.4	1	2.3
Herefordshire	0		2	0.2	0	
Hertfordshire	0		1	0.05	0	
Huntingdonshire	0		0		0	
Isle of Wight	1	0.3	0		0	
Kent	3	0.8	8	0.7	1	2.3
Lancashire	**115**	**29.5**	**424**	**37.7**	**7**	**15.9**
Leicestershire	2	0.5	2	0.2	0	
Lincolnshire	4	1.0	3	0.3	0	
London/Middlesex	**27**	**6.9**	**180**	**16.0**	**14**	**31.8**
Norfolk	2	0.5	27	2.4	0	
Northamptonshire	0		14	1.2	0	
Northumberland	13	3.3	7	0.6	0	
Nottinghamshire	1	0.3	3	0.3	0	
Oxfordshire	16	4.1	6	0.5	1	2.3
Rutland	0		0		0	
Scotland **	**18**	**4.6**	**135**	**12.0**	**12**	**27.2**
Shropshire	1	0.3	7	0.6	0	
Somerset	1	0.3	2	0.2	0	
Staffordshire	**20**	**5.1**	26	2.2	0	
Suffolk	1	0.3	1	0.05	0	
Surrey	5	1.3	6	0.5	0	
Sussex	0		4	0.4	1	2.3
Wales **	3	0.8	20	1.8	0	
Warwickshire	**35**	**9.0**	25	2.2	2	4.5
Westmorland	2	0.5	3	0.3	0	
Wiltshire	0		4	0.4	0	
Worcestershire	18	4.6	6	0.5	0	
Yorkshire	**39**	**10.0**	**76**	**6.8**	2	4.5
Sub-totals	389	100	1,125	100	44	100
County not identified	2		37		27	
Totals	**391**		**1,162**		**71**	

Source: congregation archives, see bibliography for details; data confined to records with accurate county addresses

* SSHJM records commence in 1869

** counties in Scotland and Wales are not designated.

Table 29. Birth Origins of Irish-born Professed Sisters, 1845–1926

	SSP		DVDP		SND		SSHJM*	
	No.	%	No.	%	No.	%	No.	%
Antrim	3	0.6	13	1.5	3	1.1	0	
Armagh	4	0.7	8	0.9	1	0.3	1	0.5
Cavan	4	0.7	29	3.3	1	0.3	4	1.9
Carlow	17	3.1	7	0.8	3	1.1	5	2.3
Clare	7	1.3	42	4.8	5	1.8	3	1.4
Cork	**49**	**9.0**	**176**	**20.2**	**34**	**12.0**	**24**	**11.3**
Derry	0		13	1.5	1	0.3	1	0.5
Down	17	3.1	13	1.5	7	2.5	0	
Donegal	5	0.9	8	0.9	4	1.4	6	2.8
Dublin	**49**	**9.0**	**80**	**9.2**	**41**	**14.5**	**13**	**6.1**
Fermanagh	2	0.4	0		0		1	0.5
Galway	6	1.1	24	2.8	6	2.1	5	2.3
Kerry	8	1.5	30	3.5	7	2.5	7	3.3
Kildare	10	1.8	18	2.0	5	1.8	3	1.4
Kilkenny	**58**	**10.7**	20	2.3	10	3.5	5	2.3
Laois	21	3.9	13	1.5	11	3.9	**11**	**5.2**
Leitrim	2	0.4	4	0.4	1	0.3	0	
Limerick	**79**	**14.6**	22	2.5	**30**	**10.6**	9	4.2
Longford	1	0.2	1	0.1	2	0.7	0	
Louth	6	1.1	**69**	**8.0**	6	2.1	1	0.5
Mayo	6	1.1	21	2.4	7	2.5	1	0.5
Meath	11	2.0	**88**	**10.1**	7	2.5	6	2.8
Monaghan	6	1.1	10	1.2	1	0.3	3	1.4
Offaly	7	1.3	12	1.4	4	1.4	9	4.2
Roscommon	7	1.3	18	2.1	3	1.1	8	3.8
Sligo	9	1.8	15	1.8	6	2.1	1	0.5
Tipperary	**57**	**10.5**	**44**	**5.0**	**24**	**8.5**	**55**	**25.8**
Tyrone	1	0.2	8	0.9	3	1.1	3	1.4
Waterford	16	3.0	13	1.5	12	4.2	**15**	**7.0**
Westmeath	8	1.5	22	2.5	**16**	**5.7**	0	
Wexford	**62**	**11.4**	21	2.4	**19**	**6.7**	**13**	**6.1**
Wicklow	4	0.7	9	1.0	3	1.1	0	
Sub-totals	**542**	**100**	**871**	**100**	**283**	**100**	**213**	**100**
County not identified	7		36		54		82	
Totals	**549**		**907**		**337**		**295**	

Source: congregation archives, see bibliography; data confined to records with clearly identified county

* SSHJM records commence in 1869

**Table 30. Birth Origins of Professed Sisters from Ireland in Four
Congregations, 1845–1926★**

County	Number	Percentage
Cork	283	14.83
Dublin	183	9.59
Tipperary	180	9.43
Limerick	140	7.33
Wexford	115	6.02
Meath	112	5.87
Kilkenny	93	4.87
Louth	82	4.29
Laois	56	2.93
Waterford	56	2.93
Kerry	52	2.72
Westmeath	46	2.41
remainder (20 counties)	511	26.78
Sub-total	**1,909**	**(100.0)**
Counties not identified	149	
Total	2,058	

★ Confined to records with clearly identified county for the SSP, the SND, the
DVDP and the SSHJM

**Table 31. Sample of Irish Surnames among English-/Scots-/
Welsh-Born Entrants, 1911–26**

	SSP		SND		SSHJM	
	UK-born	Identifiable Irish Surname	UK-born	Identifiable Irish Surname	UK-born	Identifiable Irish Surname
Lancashire	19	8	107	35	6	2
Scotland	11	5	64	29	7	1
London	10	3	31	9	4	2
Yorkshire	3	3	20	7	–	–
Durham	7	4	5	2	–	–
Cheshire	3	3	7	2	1	–
Warwickshire	5	1	4	1	1	–
Northumberland	8	4	2	-	–	–
Others	11	4	40	6	12	1
Totals	**77**	**35**	**280**	**91**	**31**	**5**
		(c. 45%)		(c. 33%)		(c. 16%)

Source: congregation archives, see bibliography

Table 32. (Professed) Sisters of St. Paul: Proportion of Irish Surnames among English-/ Scots-/ Welsh-Born Entrants, 1847–1926

	UK-born	Identifiable Irish Surname
Lancashire	115	29
Scotland	18	7
London	27	6
Yorkshire	39	16
Durham	28	8
Cheshire	10	6
Warwickshire	35	11
Northumberland	13	7
Others	104	18
Total	389	108 (c. 28%)

Source: congregation archives, see bibliography

Table 33. Occupation of Fathers of (Professed) Sisters of St. Paul, 1847–1926

	English-, Scots- and Welsh-born Sisters	Percentage of Total English, Scots and Welsh	Irish-born Sisters	Percentage of Total Irish
Farmers/agricultural	33	8.42	335	61.02
Artisan/trades	155	39.54	52	9.47
Shopkeepers/commercial	66	16.84	47	8.56
Professions	14	3.57	5	0.91
Teachers	3	0.76	12	2.19
Police/army/maritime	2	0.51	17	3.10
Undefined or deceased	119	30.36	81	14.75
Totals	392	100.0	549	100.0

Source: Congregation archives; full listings in Tables 34 and 35

Table 34. Occupations of Fathers of English, Welsh and Scots SSP Entrants, 1847–1926

abstractor at Customs
   House
agent
architect
artists' colour maker
assistant (shop?)
auctioneer
bailiff
baker
barrister
blacksmith
bobbin maker
bookkeeper
bookseller
bootmaker
brass founder
brewer
bricklayer
builder
business
butcher
butler
[uncertain] blade
   manufacturer
cab proprietor
cabinetmaker
cabman
carpenter
chef
clerk
clerk of works
clock/watchmaker
cloth dealer
clothier
coachbuilder
coachman
coal dealer
coal merchant
coastguard/pensioner
colliery mason
commercial traveller
commercial clerk
compositor

corn dealer
Custom House [?official]
decorator
doctor and surgeon
draftsman
draper
draper's traveller
druggist
editor, *Manchester*
   Guardian
engine driver
engineer
farmer
fireman
foreman
forge builder
fork heer (?)
furniture broker
furniture dealer
gardener
gardener/groom
gas stoker
glasscutter
grocer
gunmaker
hairdresser
harness maker
hatter
hotel keeper
independent
Inland Revenue officer
insurance agent
invalid
ironmonger
ironworker
jeweller
joiner
labourer
lawyer
leather porter
manager
manager, paper-bag
   firm

manufacturer of
   wares
marble polisher
marine stores
mason
master baker
master tailor
mechanic
merchant
military bootmaker
miller and corn dealer
miner
moulder
musician
muslin manufacturer
newsagent and
   tobacconist
organist
outfitter
overseer of coal works
packer
packing-case maker
painter
painter and decorator
pawn broker
pensioner
plumber
police
porter
Post Office
postmaster
printer
prison warder
professional gunmaker
professor of music
provision business
provision merchant
publican
railway agent
reed maker
rent agent
retired mechanic
retired merchant

→

Table 34. Occupations of Fathers of English, Welsh and Scots SSP Entrants, 1847–1926 *(cont.)*

school attendance officer	slater	tailor and draper
schoolmaster	snuff merchant	tinplate maker
screw and nut manufacturer	soldier	tobacconist
serviceman in army	solicitor	tradesman
sexton	solicitor's clerk	traveller (commercial)
shears maker	stationmaster	warehouseman in CWS
ship block maker	steel worker	watchmaker
shipowner	stone cutter	wine and spirit merchant
shoemaker	stone mason	wire weaver
shopkeeper	surgeon/physician	wood sawyer
silver plater	surveyor in Inland Revenue	worker
	tailor	yarn agent

There were two or multiple numbers in the following categories (non-related entrants)

architect	coal merchant	merchant
agent	commercial traveller	miner
baker	draper	pensioner
blacksmith	engineer	porter
bootmaker	farmer	printer
brewer	gardener	professor of music
builder	grocer	publican
business	ironworker	schoolmaster
butler	joiner	stone mason
cabinetmaker	labourer	tailor
clerk	manager	traveller
coachman	mechanic	

Source: SSP congregation archives; see bibliography

Table 35. Occupations of Fathers of Irish SSP Entrants, 1847–1926

accountant	farrier/blacksmith	poulterer
agent	farrier/cooper	principal of academy
Army	flax merchant	proprietor of flour
artist	gardener	mill
baker	gentleman farmer	publican
bank manager	gentleman	rate collector
blacksmith	grocer	railway official
boot and shoe maker	herd	relieving officer
bootmaker	hospital registrar	restaurant keeper
builder	hotel keeper	saddler and
business	inspector of police	shopkeeper
butcher	inspector	schoolmaster
cabinet maker	insurance agent	sea captain
captain of Guard	ironmonger	seaman
captain	ironworker	shoemaker
carpenter	jeweller	shopkeeper
cattle dealer	labourer	silk merchant
clerk	land proprietor	slater
coachbuilder	landlord	solicitor's clerk
coachman	leather dresser	spirit merchant
coastguard sailor	magistrate	station master
coastguard/pensioner	mason	steward
commercial traveller	mason/plasterer	stonecutter
constable	master plumber	superannuated
contractor	merchant	superintendent
cooper	miller	tailor
distiller	military constabulary	teacher
distillery manager	overseer	tradesman
draper	painter	under agent
ex-head constable	pig dealer	warder, Richmond
farmer	police sergeant	Hospital

There were two or multiple numbers in the following categories (non-related entrants)

baker	coachbuilder	labourer
blacksmith	coachman	police constable
bookseller	commercial traveller	poulterer
bootmaker	contractor	schoolmaster/teacher
builder	draper	seaman
business	farmer	shopkeeper
cabinetmaker	grocer	tailor
cattle dealer	gardener	tradesman
clerk	herd	

Source: SSP congregation archives; see bibliography

Table 36. Socio-Economic Background of Entrants to Sisters of St. Paul from Co. Limerick, 1859–1926

	Number
Entrants (6 from same household)	118
Households traced	88
Farming households	80
Non-farming households	8
Extensive family clusters, tenants with land in Griffith's Valuation Lists or in Guy's Directory (principal farmers) before 1901*	34

*The following relate to households in 1901 and 1911 Census schedules**

	Number
Father's occupation 'Other' **	8
Household in Class 1 house	5
Household in Class 2 house	44
Household in Class 3 house	5
8–16 types of farm out-office	6
5–7 types of farm out-office	27
1–4 types of farm out-office	9
Farm out-offices not stated	46†
Households with servants	20
Households with adult siblings	37
Households with occupations for girls other than 'farmer's daughter'	2

Sources: Congregation archives; Griffith's Valuation Lists of 1850–57; Guy's Munster Directory, 1886; Census of Ireland, manuscript returns for Limerick, 1901 and 1911

* See Appendix III for explanation of sources and terminology and notes on the 1901 and 1911 census material

** Bank manager, boot and shoe maker, rate collector, saddler and shopkeeper, teacher, under agent, 'in business'

† mainly pre-1901 census dates

Terms Used with Reference
to the Census of Population of Ireland and Other Sources before 1901

EXTENSIVE FAMILY CLUSTERS AND PRINCIPAL FARMERS

ALMOST ALL archives accessed by the Public Record Office of Ireland were destroyed by fire and explosion during the Civil War in June 1922. These included all but fragments of the Irish Census of Population Returns for a few counties in the period 1821–51. For this reason, research focused on the mid to late nineteenth century must rely on a number of other recognised sources. These include the Primary or Griffith's Valuations of 1847–64 (on microfiche) which show the names of occupiers of land and buildings, the names of persons from whom these were leased and the amount and value of the property held. For periods covering the 1880s onwards a number of county directories (see Bibliography) may be used to identify and name commercial businesses and large (principal) farmers. Examination of these sources reveals many instances of localised family clusters which remained *in situ* over several generations, although experiencing a changeover from being tenant farmers to owner occupiers as a result of nineteenth-century Land Acts.

CENSUS OF POPULATION RETURNS FOR 1901 AND 1911

The 1901 and the 1911 Census of Population manuscript returns for all thirty-two counties are held in the National Archives, Dublin. Access to the original census manuscripts is provided for readers. Parliamentary Papers published in volume form contain the statistical abstracts.

TOWNLANDS EXPLAINED

The 1901 and the 1911 Irish census manuscript returns for each household in the thirty-two counties are arranged by townland or, in urban areas, by street. Townlands have been described thus:

Since at least the medieval period, every county and parish has been divided into small land units known generally as townlands . . . Despite frequent enlargement and division, the basic townland pattern has survived to the present day. Of varying area, townlands average 1.3km², large enough to contain a number of farms whose owners were kin and traditionally co-operated in various ways. Numbering over 60,000, the townlands no longer have significance as units of social and agrarian life, but in a country of dispersed rural settlements where farms lack individual names, the ancient units still have use for conveying topographical information and for postal addresses.

(F.H.A Aalen, K.Whelan and Matthew Stout [eds], *Atlas of
the Irish Rural Landscape* (Cork: University Press, 1997, p. 21)

ASSESSMENT OF FARMSTEADS AS ECONOMIC UNITS FROM DATA
CONTAINED IN THE CENSUSES OF 1901 AND 1911

Houses were categorised by class (1–4) which was calculated by the type of materials used for walls and roofs, and the number of rooms and windows. An extract from a footnote to the summary tables for the census provides further clarification of the criteria used for house classification:

Four classes have been adopted, and the result is that the lowest of the four classes are comprising houses principally built of mud or other perishable material, having only one room and window; in the third a better description of house, varying from one to four rooms and windows; in the second, what might be considered a good farm house, having from five to nine rooms and windows, and in the first class, all houses of a better description than the preceding.

Census of Ireland, 1901, *PP* [Cd 1058–III], HMSO, 1902, p. 69

A useful assessment of a farmstead as an economic unit of production can be based also on the numerator's listing of the number and type of out-offices (in rural areas these would include farm buildings described as cow- or calf-houses, dairies, piggeries, fowl houses, stables, barns and sheds, potato, turf and boiling houses).

Notes

CHAPTER ONE

1 The terms 'Roman Catholic' and 'Catholic' have been used interchangeably throughout. For the distinctions made between nuns and sisters see Appendix I.
2 Herbert Thurston in his preface to Francesca M. Steele, *The Convents of Great Britain* (London: Sands; Dublin: M.H. Gill, 1902) cites two additional but ambiguously named orders in a total of twenty-one convents, pp. xviii–xx.
3 J.J. Scarisbrick, *Selly Park and Beyond: the Story of Genevieve Dupuis and the Congregation of the Sisters of Charity of St. Paul the Apostle* (Birmingham: Sisters of St. Paul, 1997), *passim*, produced by the Sisters of St. Paul the Apostle is an excellent example of data well presented.
4 James Obelkevich, 'Religion', in F.L.M. Thompson (ed.), *The Cambridge Social History of Britain,1750–1950*, Vol. 3, *Social Agencies and Institutions* (London: Cambridge University Press, 1990), p. 342.
5 F.K. Prochaska, *Women and Philanthropy in Nineteenth-Century England* (Oxford: Clarendon Press, 1980), p. 224 and *passim*.
6 Discussed more fully in Chapter 3.
7 If not entirely ignored, references are often relegated to a footnote in definitive texts such as David Mathew, *Catholicism in England* (London: Eyre & Spottiswode, 1936; 3rd edn, 1955) and Denis Gwynn, *A Hundred Years of Catholic Emancipation, 1829–1929* (London: Longman, Green, 1929). More recently, E.R. Norman, *The English Catholic Church in the Nineteenth Century* (Oxford: Clarendon Press, 1984) presents a short litany of named congregations sourced from contributors in G.A. Beck (ed.), *The English Catholics, 1850–1950* (London: Burns & Oates, 1950), pp. 182–3 (see list in n. 8). John Bossy, *The English Catholic Community, 1570–1850* (London: Darton, Longman & Todd 1978) in the chapter on the restoration of the English hierarchy and developments within the Catholic community contains nothing on the contribution made by the work undertaken by nuns and sisters.
8 John Bennett, 'The Care of the Poor' (pp. 559–89); W.J. Battersby, 'Educational Work of the Religious Orders of Women: 1850–1950' (pp. 335–64); and Edward Cruise, 'The Development of the Religious Orders' (pp. 442, 448–52, 472–74), all in Beck (ed.), *The English Catholics*.
9 Susan Mumm, 'Lady Guerillas of Philanthropy: Anglican Sisterhoods in Victorian England', PhD thesis, University of Sussex, 1992, p. 3.

10 Cornelia Connolly's Society of the Holy Child Jesus is remembered because of the colourful nature of her story; Janet Erskine Stuart and the Society of the Sacred Heart for her much-quoted saintly writings; several 'Sisters of Charity', however, remain but shadowy token figures mostly relegated to footnotes.

11 Jo Ann Kay Macnamara, *Sisters in Arms: Catholic Nuns through Two Millennia* (Cambridge, MA and London: Harvard University Press, 1996). The thrust of her final chapters are mainly concerned with developments of women's religious institutions in America and elsewhere. References to communities in England and Ireland are embedded in Chapters 19 and 20.

12 Mary Heimann, *Religious Devotion in Victorian England* (Oxford: Clarendon Press, 1995), pp. 63, 68–9, 97, 144, 156, 167.

13 Susan O'Brien, 'Terra Incognita: the Nun in Nineteenth-Century England', *Past and Present*, 121 (November 1988), pp. 110–40; idem, '10,000 Nuns: Working in Convent Archives', *Journal of Catholic Archives*, 9 (1989), pp. 27–33; 'Lay Sisters and Good Mothers: Working Class Women in English Convents, 1840–1910', in W.J. Sheils and D. Wood, *Women in the Church: Ecclesiastical History Society Papers, 1989/90* (London: Blackwell, 1990), pp. 453–65; 'Making Catholic Spaces: Women, Décor and Devotion in the English Catholic Church, 1840–1900', in D. Wood, (ed.), *The Church and the Arts*, Studies in Church History, Ecclesiastical History Society, 28 (London: Blackwell, 1992), pp. 449–64; and 'French Nuns in Nineteenth-Century England', *Past and Present*, 154 (February 1997), pp.142–80.

14 Maria G. McClelland, *The Sisters of Mercy, Popular Politics and the Growth of the Roman Catholic Community in Hull, 1855–1930* (Lampeter; Lewiston, NY; Queenston, Ontario: Edwin Mellen Press, 2000).

15 Many of these studies have largely redressed the omission in respect of Ireland and were inspired by Margaret MacCurtain, former Lecturer in History, UCD, Dublin. See MacCurtain, 'Late in the Field: Catholic Sisters in Twentieth Century Ireland and the New Religious History', *Journal of Women's History*, Special Double Issue, 6, 4 and 7, 1 (Winter/Spring, 1995), pp. 47–63. Important unpublished theses include: Tony Fahey, 'Female Asceticism in the Catholic Church: A Case Study of Nuns in the Nineteenth Century', PhD thesis, University of Illinois at Urbana-Champaign, 1982; Mary Peckham, 'Catholic Female Congregations and Religious Change in Ireland 1770–1870', PhD thesis, University of Wisconsin-Madison, 1993; and Jacintha Prunty, 'The Geography of Poverty, Dublin 1850–1900: The Social Mission of the Church with Particular Reference to Margaret Alyward and Co-workers', PhD thesis, University College, Dublin, 1992.

16 Caitriona Clear, *Nuns in Nineteenth-Century Ireland* (Dublin: Gill & Macmillan, 1987), Introduction, p. xvii, and Maria Luddy, *Women and Philanthropy in Nineteenth-Century Ireland* (Cambridge: Cambridge University Press, 1995).

17 For example, Suellen Hoy, 'The Journey Out: the Recruitment and Emigration of Irish Religious Women to the United States 1812–1914', *Journal of Women's History*, Special Double Issue, 6, 4 and 7, 1 (Winter/Spring, 1995), pp. 64–98.

18 Fintan Geser, OSB, *The Canon Law Governing Communities of Sisters* (St. Louis, MO and London: Herder, 1938), cites Canon Law 488 §7 which states 'Religious are all those who have taken vows in a religious congregation. Regulars are those who have taken vows in an order, Sisters are religious women who have taken simple vows. Nuns are religious women who have taken solemn vows', p. 28. Some congregations of sisters adopted the alternative title of an institution or a society for their foundation.

19 To achieve a reasonable level of clarity for analysis, the few instances of orders of nuns which took in a small number of boarding pupils or women on retreat have remained categorised as contemplatives; to do otherwise would distort the criteria on which analysis is based. A note to this effect is given in the discussion of the work of religious communities in Chapter 3.

20 The number of congregations *without* class divisions rose from 28 per cent of all religious in 1857 to almost 50 per cent in 1937, which may indicate the influence of an increasingly egalitarian society. It is an aspect of convent life which is deserving of more research.

21 It may be puzzling to find, for example, references to the work of the Sisters of the Most Holy Cross and Passion in Manchester being cited on dates several years before their official foundation in 1863.

22 Geser, *Canon Law Governing Communities of Sisters*, defines the particular distinctions made between diocesan institutes and papal institutes and the minutiae of rulings applicable, pp. 41–51. The involvement of members of the English hierarchy was therefore a necessity in the case of new English foundations. See Chapters 2 and 5 for discussion of the level of involvement.

23 Battersby, 'Educational Work of the Religious Orders of Women', in Beck (ed.), *The English Catholics*, p. 359.

24 Full explanations of housing and farm building classification and townland divisions are provided in Appendix III.

CHAPTER TWO

1 While indices of growth are calculated with as much accuracy as possible, some allowance has been made for small errors and discrepancies found within the sources used. Data have been calculated from records of convent addresses compiled in the annual publications of the *Catholic Directories* 1857–1937, a source sometimes regarded as being of dubious reliability; these were found to be sufficiently accurate when allowance was made for the lapse of up to a year for new entries. Minor errors in designation were corrected by supplementary consultation of several general guides on the religious life, for the most part contemporary or near-contemporary publications. These include: John Murphy, *Terra Incognita; or, the Convents of the United Kingdom* (London: Longman, Green, 1873); the anonymously compiled *The Religious Houses of the United Kingdom: Containing a Short History of Every Order and House* (London: Burns & Oates, 1887); Francesca M. Steele, *The Convents of Great Britain* (London: Sands; Dublin: M.H. Gill, 1902); Herman Hohn, *Vocations:*

Conditions of Admission to Convents (London: Washbourne, 1912); Peter F. Anson, *The Religious Orders and Congregations of Great Britain and Ireland*, (Worcester: Stanbrook Abbey Press, 1949).

2　For example, Table 1 lists the Sisters of Mercy with a first arrival in London in 1839. These sisters were drawn from the community in Cork. Subsequent separate foundations of Sisters of Mercy in England emanated from the convent communities of Carlow, Tullamore, Dublin, Kinsale and Wexford, and, in Scotland, from communities in Limerick and Derry. See Shiela Lunney, 'Mercy', Dublin: Mercy International Archives, Ref. 271.92, 1983, pp. 196–7. See also the foundations of the Sisters of Mercy, published privately by the Mercy Institute, *Trees of Mercy: Sisters of Mercy of Great Britain from 1839* (London: privately published, 1993). The Ursulines have been treated likewise, being made up of several autonomous communities each of which arrived at a later date, although sharing the same root and rule with the Ursulines who came to London in 1851. In 1900 the majority of these communities were united under one Union. See Mary Winefride Sturman, *The Ursulines in England 1851–1981* (London: Ursulines of the Roman Union, 1981).

3　See Appendix I.

4　See Chapter 4.

5　See Chapter 1, n.2. Thurston is unclear in his designation of at least two communities and convent addresses, pp. xvii–xx.

6　There were several communities of Benedictines, Carmelites and Poor Clares. Thurston's identification of the Dames Bernadine, however, does not concur with Steele, *Convents of Great Britain*, p. 167; Anson, *Religious Orders*, p. 180 and the *Catholic Directory* place the date of this order's first foundation in England as 1897. See reference to difficulties encountered by other researchers over the clarification of communities' titles in Chapter 1.

7　The Institute of the Blessed Virgin Mary (IBVM) founded by the Yorkshire woman Mary Ward (1585–1645). See Anson, *Religious Orders*, pp. 318–19.

8　A definition of what is meant by a 'mixed' community is given in Chapter 1 and Appendix I. Although this community of Canonesses of the Lateran returned to Bruges in 1802, both Steele and Anson describe as mixed their re-established foundation here some eighty years later. See Table 1.

9　Anson, *Religious Orders*, maintains that eighty communities of women religious 'came into being in England between the years 800 and 1535', p. 163.

10　Anson cites examples which include: the Arundels, who offered homes to the Carmelites, p. 201 and Lord Stourton, who helped the Canonesses of the Holy Sepulchre, p. 194. The welcome extended to the Benedictines by the Prince Regent (later George IV) has been attributed to the influence of Mrs Fitzherbert, p. 171.

11　Exact numbers are shadowy. Graham Davis, *The Irish in Britain 1815–1914* (Dublin: Gill & Macmillan, 1991), cites Williamson's calculations that the Irish share of the British labour force went up from 3.4 to 8.8 per cent between 1821 and 1861, p. 92. Davis also cites F. Neal's figure of 296,231 Irish arriving in Liverpool between January and December 1847, p. 153.

12 For a précis of Newman's influence and conversion see Denis Gwynn, *A Hundred Years of Catholic Emancipation 1829–1929* (London: Longman, Green), pp. 20–62.

13 See Table 1. The Canonesses of Lateran had moved to Bruges by 1802.

14 Anson, *Religious Orders*, p. 262. Also see Steele, *Convents of Great Britain*, who describes the Faithful Companions of Jesus as 'mixed not enclosed', p. 201.

15 Anson, *Religious Orders*, p. 375.

16 Lunney, 'Mercy', p. 196.

17 Her own account of this campaign from the letters of Sister Mary Aloysius (later decorated with the Royal Red Cross Medal by Queen Victoria) may be found in James J. Walsh, *These Splendid Sisters* (New York, NY: Sears, 1927), pp. 140–63.

18 Florence Nightingale writing to Cardinal Manning is cited by Susan O'Brien in 'Terra Incognita: The Nun in Nineteenth-Century England', *Past and Present*, 121 (November 1988), p. 115.

19 The chaplain working beside the sisters in the Crimea was Edward Bagshawe, later Bishop of Nottingham, was to be instrumental in the setting up of the nursing sisters, the Little Company of Mary (1877) and the Sisters of St. Joseph of Peace (1884). Fanny Taylor, a former Crimean nurse, founded the nursing Congregation of the Poor Servants of the Mother of God in 1868.

20 Discussed at greater length in Chapter 3.

21 The work in Houses of Refuge, Houses of Mercy or Magdalen Asylums will be addressed in Chapter 3.

22 Steele, *Convents of Great Britain*, described them as being 'active and enclosed' p. 222.

23 Sisters of Notre Dame, *The English Foundations of the Sisters of Notre Dame de Namur* (Liverpool: Philip, Son & Nephew, 1895), pp. 1–25.

24 Anson, *Religious Orders*, p. 283 and O'Brien, 'Terra Incognita', pp. 122–3. Connolly has been considered to have been highly influential and innovative in the setting up of high standards of education for girls and accounts of the unusual circumstances surrounding her choice of the religious life, her former marriage, her husband's court proceedings seeking restitution of conjugal rights and her curious treatment of her younger children (who were put into care so that she could pursue the religious life) is well documented in histories of the Congregation of the Holy Child Jesus and in almost every piece of writing on religious life for women.

25 Anson, *Religious Orders*, p. 390.

26 George V. Hudson, *Mother Genevievre Dupuis, Foundress of the English Congregation of the Sisters of Charity of St. Paul the Apostle* (London: Sheed & Ward, 1929), pp. 55–66.

27 Discussed in more detail in Chapter 5.

28 This was the designated term then used: a 'mission' was in effect a 'parish' although many were not regularised under Canon Law as such until 1918.

29 Susan O'Brien, 'French Nuns in Nineteenth-Century England', *Past and Present*, 154 (February 1997), pp. 163–4, seems not completely convinced on

this issue, although citing Edna Hamer, *Elizabeth Prout 1820–1864: Foundress of the Most Holy Cross and Passion* (Bath: Downside Abbey, 1994) in regard to the experience of the Sisters of Cross and Passion, p. 149.

30 O'Brien, 'French Nuns', p. 163. This issue is discussed in depth in Chapter 6.

31 See list of Mercy convents (1931) in Barbara M. Walsh, 'A Social History of Roman Catholic Nuns and Sisters in Nineteenth and Early Twentieth Century England and Wales: The Veiled Dynamic', PhD thesis, University of Lancaster, 1999, Appendix xi.

32 Caitriona Clear, *Nuns in Nineteenth-Century Ireland* (Dublin: Gill & Macmillan, 1987), *passim*, provides a comprehensive history of the development of the role they played within Irish society. Also Emmet Larkin, 'The Devotional Revolution in Ireland 1850–75', *American Historical Review*, 77 (June 1972), pp. 625–52, argued for acknowledgement of the lead provided by Ireland's religious revival affecting wider social and cultural issues which, in turn, contributed to the development of Catholic education and social care in England and the USA through the recruitment and emigration of Irish nuns and priests.

33 Anson, *Religious Orders*, p. 320.

34 Sturman, *Ursulines in England*, p. 17.

35 Anson, *Religious Orders*, p. 256.

36 The histories of many congregations contain detailed accounts of the involvement of male orders or senior churchmen, and it cannot be doubted that their influence was often crucial to the successful initial foundation or development of a great number of the communities.

37 See individual accounts in Steele, *Convents of Great Britain*; Hohn, *Vocations*; Anson, *Religious Houses*.

38 Rosemary Clerkin, *A Heart for Others* (Chigwell: Sisters of the Sacred Hearts of Jesus and Mary, 1983), pp. 27–50. By 1906 the Servants of the Sacred Heart of Jesus were divided into two separate communities. One became an English institution, renamed as the Sisters of the Sacred Hearts of Jesus and Mary, pp. 59–60. Selected for particular reference, these congregations are discussed in more detail in Chapters 3 and 6.

39 Anson, *Religious Orders*, p. 161.

40 An account of how Mother Hallahan purchased a tavern, The Hand and Trumpet, to accommodate hospital patients is related with some amusement in Frances R. Drane, *The Life of Mother Mary Hallahan* (London: Longmans, Green, Reader & Dwyer 1869), p. 284. Published originally without acknowledgement of its author but now identified as one of Margaret Hallahan's assistants. Drane is mentioned in Steele, *Convents of Great Britain*, p. 46.

41 Hamer, *Elizabeth Prout*, p. 84. O'Brien, 'Terra Incognita', p. 127, infers that much of their difficulty arose because they were caught in the acrimonious territorial crossfire between the regular clergy of Manchester and Prout's spiritual mentors, the Passionist Fathers.

42 Anson, *Religious Orders*, p. 373.

43 Ibid., p. 269.

44 Ibid., p. 323 (see also references to this congregation in Chapters 3 and 5).

45 Ibid., p. 186.

46 Ibid., p. 270.

47 Ibid., p. 272.

48 Ibid., p. 273.

49 Ibid., p. 276.

50 Ibid., p. 303; Steele, *Convents of Great Britain*, p. 317; Hohn, *Vocations*, p. 314.

51 A paper on the reassessment of Margaret Anne Cusack was given by Avril Reynolds at the Irish Women's History Association Conference in Galway University, 1994. Mary O'Dowd, 'Women Historians in Ireland from the 1790s to the 1990s', in Maryann G.Valiulis and Mary O'Dowd (eds), *Women and Irish History* (Dublin: Wolfhound Press, 1997), pp. 38–58, recommends Irene Ffrench Eager, *Margaret Anna Cusack: One Woman's Campaign for Women's Rights, a Biography* (Dublin: Arlen House,1970; revised edn, 1979), fn p. 43. An account of events leading to these sisters' arrival in Grimsby, acknowledging Cusack, is provided by William Bedford and Michael Knight, *Jacob's Ladder: The Rise of a Catholic Community 1848–1913* (Grimsby: St. Mary on the Sea, NRCDT, 1996), pp. 102–11, 133–43.

52 Edward G. Bagshawe is cited by Paul Misner, *Social Catholicism in Europe* (London: Darton, Longman & Todd, 1991), p. 192, as having written 'a clearly anti-capitalist book' *Mercy and Justice to the Poor: The True Political Economy* (London: Kegan Paul, Trench, 1885).

53 Cusack is also mentioned in Chapter 5.

54 Revd Fr. Paul, OSFC, *The British Church from the Days of Cardinal Allen* (London: Burns, Oates & Washbourne, 1929), describes him as 'having many troubles in his old age, brought on him through the largesse of his charitable heart, which allowed him to see nothing but good in others; as a consequence, he was sadly imposed upon', p. 93.

55 Adrian Dansette (trans. John Dingle), *The Religious History of Modern France* (Edinburgh and London: Herder, 1961), Vol.2, p. 204.

56 See Table 1.

57 Dansette, *Religious History of Modern France*, p. 57.

58 Illustrated in more detail in Chapter 3.

59 I am grateful to Sr. Jean Bunn, SND, Provincial Archivist, Sisters of Notre Dame de Namur, Liverpool, and to Sr. Anne Cunningham, SSP, Archivist, Sisters of St. Paul the Apostle, Birmingham, for this information.

60 It would seem to be mostly attributed to the number of new Carmelite and Poor Clare communities. Forty-three Carmelite monasteries and dates of their establishment, dispersal and amalgamation have been listed by Sr. Helen of Jesus, ODC, 'The Carmels of Great Britain: A Check List', *Journal of the Catholic Archives Society*, 20 (2000), pp. 38–42.

61 In detail beyond the scope of this book, it is none the less intriguing to reflect that, while numbers of active and mixed congregations subsequently suffered dramatic disintegration in the second half of the twentieth century, the number of contemplative orders remained small but contained and showed no signs of incipient decline.

62   Because of their high Catholic population, the northern counties have been called the Catholic heartland, see Walsh, thesis, Appendices v–vii, reproducing the map and statistics for 1851 in John D. Gay, *The Geography of Religion in England* (London: Duckworth, 1971), p. 282; and the map for 1892 taken from the anonymously compiled *The Position of the Catholic Church in England and Wales during the Last Two Centuries: Retrospect and Forecast*, edited for the XV Club (but written by Thomas Murphy) (London: Burns & Oates, 1892), p. 98a; and the reproduction of the 1929 map in Gwynn, *A Hundred Years of Catholic Emancipation*, p. xxxii.

63   Walsh, thesis, Chapter 1.

64   Philip Hughes, 'The English Catholics in 1850', in G.A. Beck (ed.), *The English Catholics 1850–1950* (London: Burns & Oates, 1950), p. 68.

65   Cardinal Wiseman, 'Appeal to the English People', a pamphlet which appeared in five London daily papers on 20 November 1850. Cited by John Bennett, 'The Care of the Poor', in G.A. Beck (ed.), *The English Catholics*, p. 559.

66   Anson, *Religious Orders*, p. 306.

67   Bennett, 'Care of the Poor', pp. 581–2.

68   An autobiographical comment made by Manning expressing his philosophy of life and 'practical Christianity'. M.G. McClelland, *Cardinal Manning: His Public Life and Influence, 1865–1892* (London: Oxford University Press, 1962), p. 10.

69   Sisters of Nazareth, *The Sisters of Nazareth* (London: privately published, 1933), p. 22.

70   Vaughan was particularly dismissive of Manning's support for workers in the 1889 London docks strike. See McClelland, *Cardinal Manning*, p. 146.

71   Susan Mumm, 'Lady Guerillas of Philanthropy: Anglican Sisterhoods in Victorian England', PhD thesis, University of Sussex, 1992, p. 349, holds that the sisterhoods were entirely outside the direct hierarchical control of the Anglican Church.

72   Peter Coman, *Catholics and the Welfare State* (London: Longman, 1977), p. 4.

73   Ibid.

74   Cited in E.S. Purcell, *Life of Cardinal Manning* (London: Macmillan, 1896), Vol. II and also by Denis Gwynn, 'The Irish Immigration', in Beck (ed.), *The English Catholics*, pp. 585–614.

75   Gay, *The Geography of Religion in England*, provides a map of the distribution of Roman Catholics in 1851 based on the religious census of 1851, p. 282.

76   Hughes, 'The English Catholics in 1850', in Beck (ed.), *The English Catholics*, p. 45.

77   J.A. Jackson, *The Irish in Britain* (London: Routledge & Kegan Paul; Cleveland, OH: Western Reserve University Press, 1963), p. 11.

78   Brenda Collins, 'The Irish in Britain', in B.J. Graham and L.J. Proudfoot (eds), *An Historical Geography of Ireland* (London and New York, NY: Academic Press, 1993), p. 372.

79   Davis, *The Irish in Britain*, pp. 61–2.

80   Ibid., p. 62.

81   Ibid., p. 132. See also Thomas Burke, *The Catholic History of Liverpool* (Liverpool: Tingling, 1910), p. 203 and Owen Chadwick, *The Victorian Church* (London: A. & C. Black, 2nd edn, 1972), Part II, p. 411.

82 McClelland, *Cardinal Manning*, gives a succinct account of the controversies surrounding grants for schools, pp. 24–86.

83 J.J. Scarisbrick, *Selly Park and Beyond : the Story of Genevieve Dupuis and the Congregation of the Sisters of Charity of St. Paul the Apostle* (Birmingham: Sisters of St. Paul, 1997), 'Sisters Reminisce', p. 61.

84 Murphy, *Terra Incognita*, p. 77. The North Western Division of England is given here as embracing Lancashire, Cheshire, Shropshire and North Wales.

85 Ibid., pp. 480–2.

86 Convent-based schools and teacher training colleges are discussed more fully in Chapter 3.

87 Coman, *Catholics and the Welfare State*, p. 4.

88 Mary Peckham, 'Catholic Female Congregations and Religious Change in Ireland 1770–1870', PhD thesis, University of Wisconsin-Madison, 1993, pp. 45–6.

89 Jose Harris, *Private Lives, Public Spirit, Britain 1870–1914* (London: Oxford University Press, 1993), p. 198.

90 Ian Levitt, 'Poor Law and Pauperism', in J. Langton and R.J. Morris (eds), *Atlas of Industrializing Britain 1780–1914* (London: Methuen, 1986), pp. 161–2. See also Chapter 3 on welfare care of the poor.

91 Karel Williams, *From Pauperism to Poverty* (London: Routledge & Kegan Paul, 1981), pp. 158–62 (Table 4.5).

92 Levitt, 'Poor Law and Pauperism', p. 161.

93 Mumm, 'Lady Guerrillas of Philanthropy', p. 164.

94 More fully examined and discussed in Chapter 3.

CHAPTER THREE

1 John Murphy, *Terra Incognita; or, the Convents of the United Kingdom* (London: Longmans Green, 1873), p. 516. Quoted as 'Opinions of the Press'. The precise date for the citation was not provided.

2 F.K. Prochaska, *Women and Philanthropy in Nineteenth-Century England* (Oxford: Clarendon Press, 1980), pp. 222–30. Also see Margaret Simey, *Charitable Effort in Liverpool in the Nineteenth Century* (Liverpool: Liverpool University Press, 1951), pp. 62–80, and John Bennett, 'The Care of the Poor', in G.A. Beck (ed.), *The English Catholics 1850–1950* (London: Burns & Oates, 1950), pp. 559–84. Maria Luddy, *Women and Philanthropy in Nineteenth-Century Ireland* (Cambridge: Cambridge University Press, 1995), pp. 21–67, draws attention to the work of women within Bible societies and the close ties between London-based charities such as the YWCA and their Irish counterparts. Ireland's Catholic lay women, however, were 'confined in their activities by the acceptance of nuns as the ideal providers of Catholic relief.'

3 Bennett, 'The Care of the Poor', p. 563.

4 Eve Healy, *The Life of Mother Mary Potter: Foundress of the Congregation of the Little Company of Mary* (London: Sheed & Ward, 1935), p. 179.

5   J.J. Scarisbrick, *Selly Park and Beyond: the Story of Genevieve Dupuis and the Congregation of the Sisters of Charity of St. Paul the Apostle* (Birmingham: Sisters of St. Paul, 1997), pp. 62, 64.

6   Manning's overt support of religious communities of women has been already illustrated.

7   M.G. McClelland, *Cardinal Manning: His Public Life and Influence 1865–92* (London: Oxford University Press, 1962), p. 19.

8   See Chapter 1.

9   Virginia Berridge, 'Health and Medicine', in F.L.M. Thompson, *The Cambridge Social History of Britain,1750–1950*, Vol. 3, *Social Agencies and Institutions* (London: Cambridge University Press, 1990), p. 183, makes a brief generalised reference to Anglican religious sisterhoods by citing S.W.F. Holloway, 'The All Saints' Sisterhood at University College Hospital, 1862–1899', *Medical History*, 3 (1959), pp. 146–56, but this research would seem not to have been followed up nor acknowledged by others.

10 Celia Davis (ed.), *Rewriting Nursing History* (London: Croom Helm, 1980), pp. 44–5.

11 Sisters of Mercy, *Trees of Mercy: Sisters of Mercy of Great Britain from 1839* (London: privately published, 1993), p. 23.

12 Brian Abel-Smith, *The Hospitals, 1800-1948* (London: Heinemann,1964), p. 9.

13 Ibid., *A History of the Nursing Profession* (London: Heinemann, 1960), p. 5 (fn). Other works on nursing history by Robert Dingwall, Anne Marie Rafferty and Charles Webster (eds), *An Introduction to the Social History of Nursing* (London: Routledge, 1988) and Christopher Maggs (ed.), *Nursing History: The State of the Art* (London and Sydney: Croom Helm, 1987) make no reference to input by female religious communities other than to mention sisters nursing in the Crimea and the early training given to Florence Nightingale by the Protestant Deaconesses of Kaiserswerth. The Nightingale school is now considered as having been over-publicised and of marginal value.

14 A welcome insight may be found in Margaret Ó hÓgartaigh, 'Flower Power and Mental Grooviness: Nurses and Midwives in Ireland in the Early Twentieth Century', in Bernadette Whelan (ed.), *Women and Paid Work in Ireland 1500–1930* (Dublin: Four Courts Press, 2000), pp. 133–57, in which she draws attention to attitudes which continued to align professional nursing training standards to the rigorous requirements of a religious vocation in hospitals in England as well as Ireland.

15 Examples include: David Fitzpatrick, 'The Irish in Britain, 1871–1921', in W.E. Vaughan (ed.), *A New History of Ireland*, VI, *Ireland under the Union*, II, *1870–1921* (Oxford: Clarendon Press, 1996), pp. 653–702; Graham Davis, *The Irish in Britain, 1815–1914* (Dublin: Gill & Macmillan, 1991); and M.A.G. O'Tuathaigh, 'The Irish in Nineteenth-Century Britain: Problems of Integration', *Transactions of the Royal Historical Society*, 5th Ser., 31 (1981), pp. 149–73. Sheridan Gilly 'The Catholic Faith of the Irish Slums: London 1840–70', in H.J. Dyos and M. Wolff (eds), *The Victorian City: Images and Realities*, Vol. 2 (London: Routledge & Kegan Paul, 1973), pp. 837–53, concentrates sole attention on the role of male clergy in the organisation of education and social care.

16 Susan O'Brien, 'Terra Incognita: The Nun in Nineteenth-Century England', *Past and Present*, 121 (November 1988), pp. 110–40, also 'Lay Sisters and Good Mothers: Working-Class Women in English Convents, 1840–1910', *Women in the Church: Ecclesiastical History Society Papers, 1989/90* (London: Blackwell, 1990), pp. 453–65; and 'French Nuns in Nineteenth-Century England', *Past and Present*, 154 (February 1997), pp. 142–80.

17 Susan Mumm, 'Lady Guerillas of Philanthropy. Anglican Sisterhoods in Victorian England', PhD thesis, University of Sussex, 1992.

18 Ibid., Chapters 4 and 5.

19 H.C.B. Stone, 'Constraints on the Foundresses: Contrasts in Anglican and Roman Catholic Religious Headships in Victorian England', PhD thesis, University of Leeds, 1993.

20 Caitriona Clear, *Nuns in Nineteenth-Century Ireland* (Dublin: Gill & Macmillan, 1987) and Luddy, *Women and Philanthropy*.

21 *The Catholic Directories*, 1857–1937; Murphy, *Terra Incognita*, Francesca M. Steele, *The Convents of Great Britain* (London: Sands; Dublin: M.H. Gill, 1902); Herman Hohn, *Vocations: Conditions of Admission to Convents* (London: Washbourne, 1912); Peter F. Anson, *The Religious Orders and Congregations of Great Britain and Ireland* (Worcester: Stanbrook Abbey Press, 1949); and *Handbook of Catholic Charitable and Social Works* (London: Catholic Truth Society, 1912).

22 The *Catholic Directories* contain a variety of non-consistent headings under which charitable and other institutions are listed and statistical information is patchy. The deficiencies inherent in these data have been balanced and corrected by consulting other sources such as *The Handbook of Catholic Charities and Social Works*.

23 Listed in Table 12. Data extracted from the anonymously-compiled *The Religious Houses of the United Kingdom: Containing a Short History of Every Order and House* (London: Burns & Oates, 1887), pp. 125–32, 134–8.

24 See also an excellent account of the provision of schools at many levels in Lancashire in 1852–58 in Edna Hamer, *Elizabeth Prout 1820–1864: Foundress of the Sisters of the Most Holy Cross and Passion* (Bath: Downside Abbey, 1994), pp.107–19.

25 Murphy, *Terra Incognita*, p. 462.

26 Mary Linscott, *Quiet Revolution* (Glasgow: Burns, 1966), p. 149.

27 Commentary on past trends and influences is contained in a report of the Consultative Committee to the Board of Education, 1919, cited by Felicity Hunt, in Hunt (ed.), *Lessons for Life: The Schooling of Girls and Women, 1850–1950* (London: Basil Blackwell, 1987), p. 18.

28 Ibid., p. xxv.

29 Gillian Sutherland, 'Education', in F.L.M. Thompson (ed.), *The Cambridge Social History of Britain,1750–1950*, Vol. 3, *Social Agencies and Institutions* (London: Cambridge University Press, 1990), p. 158.

30 Advertisement in the *Catholic Directory*, 1920, p. 705, inserted by the Daughters of the Cross, Carshalton, Surrey.

31 Advertisement in the *Catholic Directory*, 1920, p. 652, inserted by the Sisters of St. Joseph, Clifton, Bristol.

32   Hunt, *Lessons for Life*, p. 150.

33   O'Brien, 'French Nuns in Nineteenth-Century England', p. 179.

34   Ibid., citing Penny Summerfield, 'Cultural Reproduction in the Education of Girls: a Study of Girls' Secondary Schooling in Two Lancashire Towns, 1900–1950', in Hunt (ed.), *Lessons for Life*, p. 162. Also W.J. Battersby, 'Educational Work of the Religious Orders of Women: 1850–1950', in G.A. Beck (ed.), *The English Catholics 1850–1950* (London: Burns & Oates, 1950), cites the findings of a special commission in 1948, which reported that 43 per cent of the places in convent schools then occupied by non-Catholics, pp. 360–1.

35   Advertisement in the *Catholic Directory*, 1920, p. 670, inserted by the Nuns of the Nativity from St. Germain-en-Laye, relocated in Leicester.

36   Advertisement in the *Catholic Directory*, 1920, p. 664, inserted by the Sisters of Mercy, Hull.

37   XV Club (edited for the Club, but written by Thomas Murphy), *The Position of the Catholic Church in England and Wales during the Last Two Centuries: Retrospect and Forecast* (London: Burns & Oates, 1892), p. 95.

38   Mary Winefride Sturman, *The Ursulines in England 1851–1981* (London: Ursulines of the Roman Union, 1981), p. 122.

39   Ibid.

40   Ibid.

41   Ibid.

42   Ibid., p. 123.

43   I am indebted to Sr. Jean Bunn, archivist, Notre Dame de Namur in Liverpool, for pointing out that the volume of work generated by elementary teaching has been largely overlooked because so much archival material is now lost, whereas high school and college records were usually well-preserved.

44   Provincial Archives of the Sisters of Notre Dame de Namur, Liverpool (see bibliography).

45   Linscott, *Quiet Revolution*, p. 152.

46   Provincial Archives of the Sisters of Notre Dame de Namur, Liverpool. Folder marked Leeds no.3, 1911–21.

47   Tony Fahey, 'Nuns in the Catholic Church in Ireland in the Nineteenth Century', in Mary Cullen (ed.), *Girls Don't Do Honours: Irish Women in Education in the 19th and 20th Centuries* (Dublin: Women's Educational Bureau, 1987), p. 23.

48   A general discourse on teacher training is contained in Alexander Wall, 'The Supply of Certified Teachers to the Roman Catholic Elementary Schools of Britain 1848–1870', MPhil thesis, University of Lancaster, 1983.

49   Linscott, *Quiet Revolution*, p. 50.

50   A full account of the development of the Endsleigh College may be found in Maria G. McClelland, *The Sisters of Mercy: Popular Politics and the Growth of the Roman Catholic Community in Hull, 1855–1930* (Lampeter; Lewiston, NY; Queenston, Ontario: Edwin Mellen Press, 2000), Chapters 7 and 8.

51   Ibid., p. 111.

52   Murphy, *Terra Incognita*, pp. 485–6. Murphy designates Lancashire, Cheshire and North Wales as the North-West. See also Barbara M. Walsh, 'A Social

History of Roman Catholic Nuns and Sisters in Nineteenth and Early Twentieth Century England and Wales: The Veiled Dynamic', PhD thesis, University of Lancaster, 1999, Table (3:3).

53 References to the system allowing for school half-timers may be found in J.K. Walton, *Lancashire: a Social History: 1558-1939* (Manchester: Manchester University Press, 1987), pp. 202, 288, 308; and ibid., 'The North West', in F.L.M. Thompson (ed.), *The Cambridge Social History of Britain, 1750–1950*, Vol. 1, *Regions and Communities* (London: Cambridge University Press, 1990), pp. 388, 393.

54 An argument recently explored by O'Brien in 'French Nuns in Nineteenth-Century England'.

55 The numbers quoted are taken from the *Catholic Directories* and should be read as underestimated.

56 Full listings from this handbook are contained in Walsh, thesis, Appendix (x) b.

57 Jules Kosky and Raymond J. Lunnon, *Great Ormond Street and the Story of Medicine* (London: Granta, 1991), p. 4.

58 Scarisbrick, *Selly Park and Beyond*, pp. 42–3.

59 Figures supplied by Mary Gandy of the Catholic Child Welfare Council in a paper delivered at the Catholic Archive Society Conference, Durham, 1995.

60 For older boys, reformatory work was undertaken at first by the Cistercian Fathers and Christian Brothers.

61 Bennett, 'The Care of the Poor', pp. 561–2.

62 Rosemary Clerkin, *A Heart for Others* (London: Sisters of the Sacred Hearts of Jesus and Mary, 1983), p. 72.

63 Alice Vowe Johnson, 'The Problem of the Feeble-minded', *The Crucible: A Catholic Magazine of Higher Education for Women*, 6, 23 (December 1910), pp.142–9.

64 Clerkin, *A Heart for Others*, p. 62.

65 The *Handbook of Catholic Charitable and Social Works*, passim. See also Walsh, thesis, Appendix (x) b for details of all diocesan charitable undertakings as described therein.

66 Sourced from: *The Religious Houses of the United Kingdom*.

67 Ibid. and Scarisbrick, *Selly Park and Beyond*, p. 87.

68 Scarisbrick, *Selly Park and Beyond*, pp. 73–86.

69 Steele, *The Convents of Great Britain*, p.111; Hohn, *Vocations*, p. 258; Anson, *The Religious Orders*, p. 206 and *The Religious Houses of the United Kingdom*, p. 125.

70 Anonymously-compiled *Sisters of Charity of St. Vincent de Paul* (London, Catholic Truth Society, 1924), p. 11.

71 The *cornette* was based on seventeenth-century Normandy peasant head-dress.

72 Early activities given in *The Religious Houses of the United Kingdom*, p. 179; Steele, *The Convents of Great Britain*, p. 226; Anson, *The Religious Orders*, p. 330; see also Sisters of Mercy, *Trees of Mercy*, passim.

73 Details are listed in Walsh, thesis, Appendix (xi), which outlines the exact level of activity reached by 1931.

74 Mary Josephine Gately, *Supplementary Manual to the Sisters of Mercy: Historical Sketches 1831-1931* (New York, NY: Macmillan, 1931), pp. 30–44. Also Sisters of Mercy, *Trees of Mercy*, for one example of a convalescent home for war veterans, p. 94.

75 See Walsh thesis, Appendix (x) (b) for data relating to charitable undertakings in 1912.

76 S. Constantine, *Social Conditions in Britain 1918–1939* (London: Methuen, 1983), p. 21.

77 Sisters of Mercy, *Trees of Mercy*, p. 88.

78 Murphy, *Terra Incognita*, pp. 319–20.

79 Prochaska, *Women and Philanthropy*, p. 153.

80 Michel Foucault (trans. Alan Sheridan), *Discipline and Punish: the Birth of the Prison,* (London: Penguin, 1991), p. 211.

81 Pat Thane, 'Government and Society in England and Wales 1750–1914', in F.L.M. Thompson (ed.), *The Cambridge Social History of Britain,1750–1950*, Vol. 3, *Social Agencies and Institutions* (London: Cambridge University Press, 1990), p. 38.

82 Clerkin, *A Heart for Others*, pp. 51–2.

83 The numbers quoted are taken from the *Catholic Directories* and should be read as underestimated.

84 Jose Harris, *Private Lives, Public Spirit: Britain 1870–1914* (London: Oxford University Press, 1993), p. 29.

85 Ibid.

86 These figures, compiled from the *Catholic Directories* for 1857, 1877, 1897, 1917 and 1937, are at best only approximations of hospital and convalescent nursing.

87 Sisters of Mercy, *Trees of Mercy*, pp. 22–5, 54. The date of transfer to St. John's Wood is given in David Mathew, *Catholicism in England* (London: Eyre & Spottiswode, 1936; 2nd edn, 1948), p. 250.

88 Kosky and Lunnon, *Great Ormond Street*, p. 1. Of interest is the fact that Dr West published an instructional handbook, *How to Nurse*, in 1854.

89 Shiela Lunney, 'Mercy', Dublin: Mercy International Archives, Ref. 271.92, 1983, thus describes the children's ward, p. 197. The hospital for incurables was cited by Murphy, *Terra Incognita*, p. 360 and in *The Religious Houses of the United Kingdom*, p. 186.

90 *The Catholic Directory*, 1897, advertising section for institutions, societies, etc., p. 498.

91 For example as cited by Kosky and Lunnon, *Great Ormond Street*, p. 22.

92 See the illustration of advertised hospital and nursing services above.

93 Edmund M. Hogan, *The Irish Missionary Movement: A Historical Survey, 1830–1980* (Dublin: Gill & Macmillan, 1990), pp. 106–7.

94 Ibid.

95 Healy, *Life of Mother Mary Potter*, p. 180. Her patron, Bishop Bagshawe, by contrast, had approved, but was overruled by the need to conform to the Cardinal's application of Canon Law.

96 Hogan, *Irish Missionary Movement*, cites *Notes and Queries*, IER 5th ser., xlviii (1936), 427, p. 107 (fn). See also Margaret MacCurtain, 'Late in the Field:

Catholic Sisters in Twentieth-Century Ireland and the New Religious History', *Journal of Women's History*, 6, 4 and 7, 1 (Winter/Spring 1995), for an account of the many other congregations and individuals engaged in the struggle for change, pp. 40–1.

97 Mary Martin's argument may also be seen as hinged on a threat to withdrawn her support of the African missions, where there was a chronic need of doctors and maternity nurses and whose success relied on supervision provided by female members of religious communities.

98 Figures extracted from Obelkevich, James Obelkevich, 'Religion', in F.L.M. Thompson (ed.), *The Cambridge Social History of Britain, 1750–1950*, Vol. 3, *Social Agencies and Institutions* (London: Cambridge University Press, 1990), p. 335 and G.A. Beck, 'To-day and To-morrow', in G.A. Beck (ed.), *The English Catholics 1850–1950* (London: Burns & Oates, 1950), p. 387. Beck notes the problem inherent in the accurate calculation of the Catholic population because of the large number of 'lapsed' members whose existence only re-emerges within statistics of funerals, p. 392.

99 Clerkin, *A Heart for Others*, thus describes the apostolate of the Sisters of the Sacred Hearts of Jesus and Mary, p. 52.

100 Clear, *Nuns*, p. 165, quoting a member of the Irish Sisters of Charity, *The Life and Work of Mary Aikenhead* (New York, NY and London: Longman, Green, 1924), fn, p. 174.

CHAPTER FOUR

1 Alan Deacon and Michael Hill, Alan Deacon and Michael Hill, 'The Problem of "Surplus Women" in the Nineteenth-Century: Secular and Religious Alternatives', in M. Hill (ed.), *A Sociological Yearbook of Religion in Britain*, Vol. 5 (London: SCM Press, 1972), cites a typical pamphlet written by Mr Newdegate, p. 95.

2 A study of these campaigns may be found in W.L. Arnstein, *Protestant versus Catholic in Mid-Victorian England: Mr. Newdegate and the Nuns* (Columbia, MO and London: University of Missouri Press, 1982).

3 For example, foundations of Sisters of Mercy were originally established as branch houses sent out from time to time from one of five different mother houses in Ireland. In my categorisation of 'newly arrived' foundations (Table 1), only the first batch of Sisters of Mercy was listed.

4 The only qualification that must be added here is the number of new contemplative communities of Carmelites between 1907 and 1937. See Peter F. Anson, *The Religious Orders and Congregations of Great Britain and Ireland* (Worcester: Stanbrook Abbey Press, 1949), p.204.

5 Sisters of Mercy, *Trees of Mercy: Sisters of Mercy of Great Britain from 1839* (London: privately published, 1993), pp.10-12. See also Chapter 3.

6 With a novitiate here for intake from these islands until 1885, after which time an English province and novitiate were established in London.

7   Francesca M. Steele, *The Convents of Great Britain* (London: Sands; Dublin: M.H. Gill, 1902), p. xi, writing in 1902, favoured twelve.

8   Convent records marked: ref. MP. Sector C, Community Lists for 1878–1980. Sisters of Notre Dame Provincial Archive Office, Liverpool.

9   George V. Hudson, *Mother Genevieve Dupuis. Foundress of the Sisters of Charity of St. Paul the Apostle* (London: Sheed & Ward, 1929), p.258.

10 Mary Josephine Gately, *Supplementary Manual to the Sisters of Mercy: Historical Sketches 1831–1931* (New York, NY: Macmillan, 1931), pp. 30–44. See Barbara M. Walsh, 'A Social History of Roman Catholic Nuns and Sisters in Nineteenth and Early Twentieth Century England and Wales: The Veiled Dynamic', PhD thesis, University of Lancaster, 1999, Appendix (xi) with table of 1931 figures.

11 For a complete series of maps displaying five twenty-year time spans see Walsh, thesis, Chapter 1.

12 Dudley Baines, 'Population, Migration and Regional Development 1870–1930', in R. Floud and D. McCloskey (eds), *The Economic History of Britain since 1700*, Vol.2, *1860–1939* (London: Cambridge University Press, 2nd edn, 1994), p. 52, identifies the eight largest towns in the Midlands and the North, 1841–1911, as Manchester, Liverpool, Birmingham, Leeds, Sheffield, Leicester, Hull and Nottingham.

13 See maps in Walsh, thesis, Appendices (v), (vi) and (vii).

14 London is defined by the city postal districts, see note 20.

15 Details of exact percentages are in Table 17.

16 A single convent is shown in Rutland for 1897 and 1917 only.

17 See Walsh, thesis, Chapter 1, in which maps F and G relate to census figures for 1871 and 1891.

18 Martha Vicinus, *Independent Women: Work and Community, 1850–1920* (Edinburgh and London: Nelson, 1961; Chicago, IL: Virago, 1985), p.50 cites A.M. Allchin, *The Silent Rebellion: Anglican Religious Communities* (London: SCM Press, 1958), p.100.

19 Susan Mumm, 'Lady Guerillas of Philanthropy. Anglican Sisterhoods in Victorian England', PhD thesis, University of Sussex, 1992, pp. 15–16.

20 By 1877 the *Catholic Directory* cites convent addresses under London postal districts. To achieve some consistency within the tabled statistics the designation 'London' has been based on inner postal divisions up to 1937. London's county boroughs were formed in 1889. The distribution of convents within London's spreading suburbs is indicated in the detailed county figures in Walsh, thesis, Table (1:10).

21 P.L. Garside, 'London and the Home Counties', in F.L.M. Thompson (ed.), *The Cambridge Social History of Britain, 1750–1950*, Vol. 1, *Regions and Communities* (London: Cambridge University Press, 1993), p. 505, cites H. McLeod, *Class and Religion in the Late-Victorian City* (London: Croom Helm, 1974), p. 2.

22 Ibid., p. 508, citing S.J. Low, 'The Rise of the Suburbs', *Contemporary Review*, 60 (1891), p. 546.

23 Walsh, thesis, Appendix (iii) and accompanying map sequences H (i)–(vi),

contains more detailed analysis demonstrating changes within twenty-year time spans, 1857-1937.

24 See examples of illustrated advertisements for schools in Chapter 3.

25 Thus described in the anonymously compiled *The Religious Houses of the United Kingdom: Containing a Short History of Every Order and House* (Burns & Oates, 1887).

26 See illustrations of advertisements in Chapter 3.

27 David Mathew, *Catholicism in England* (London: Eyre & Spottiswode, 1936; 2nd edn, 1948), p. 257.

28 In 1929 it was estimated that there were only 20,000 Catholics in the Roman Catholic diocese of Northampton (Norfolk, Suffolk, Northamptonshire, Huntingdonshire, Cambridgeshire, Buckinghamshire and Bedfordshire.) See Walsh, thesis, calculations and map, Appendix (vi).

29 Susan O'Brien, 'French Nuns in Nineteenth-Century England', *Past and Present*, 154 (February 1997), p.179, reflects on the increasing numbers of bourgeois Anglican families who favoured convent school education for their daughters.

30 John Murphy, *Terra Incognita, or the Convents of the United Kingdom* (London: Longmans Green, 1873), p. 334.

31 D.W. Howell and C. Barber, 'Wales', in F.L.M. Thompson (ed.), *The Cambridge Social History of Britain, 1750–1950*, Vol. 1, *Regions and Communities* (London: Cambridge University Press, 1993), p. 313. See also comments on the Irish in Britain in Chapter 2.

32 In other words, the number of convents in Northumberland, Durham, Cumberland, Westmorland, Cheshire and the three Yorkshire Ridings, if all added together, would barely double the number found in Lancashire alone.

33 J.K. Walton, *Lancashire, a Social History:1558–1939* (Manchester: Manchester University Press, 1987), p. 226.

34 The unknown compiler of *The Religious Houses of the United Kingdom* (1887) states their object as 'care of the sick, rich or poor, in their own homes, without distinction of creed', p. 118.

35 *Catholic Directory* for 1897, p. 498. See also the illustrated advertisements for nursing in Chapter 5.

36 Meg Whittle, 'Philanthropy in Preston: the Changing Face of Charity', PhD thesis, University of Lancaster, 1990, pp. 309–12. Discussed further in Chapter 5.

37 Mentioned in more detail in Chapter 5.

38 Their full history may be found in Sr. Mary P. Darbyshire, CSA, 'The Archives of the Canonesses of Saint Augustine, Boarbank Hall, Grange-over-Sands', *Journal of the Catholic Archives Society*, 21 (2001), pp. 45–52.

39 O'Brien, 'French Nuns in Nineteenth-Century England' highlights the diversity of French cultural influences, pp. 142–80.

40 The impact of the sheer size and economic wealth of London and the sprawl of suburban areas into the adjoining counties has been commented upon above and is demonstrated in Maps D to F.

CHAPTER FIVE

1   Mary Linscott, *This Excellent Heritage: An Introduction to the Constitutions of the Sisters of Notre Dame* (Liverpool: Sisters of Notre Dame, 1989), p. 4.

2   Ibid.

3   Caitriona Clear, *Nuns in Nineteenth-Century Ireland* (Dublin: Gill & Macmillan, 1987), p. 76.

4   Ibid.

5   Maria G. McClelland, *The Sisters of Mercy: Popular Politics and the Growth of the Roman Catholic Community in Hull, 1855–1930* (Lampeter; Lewiston, NY; Queenston, Ontario: Edwin Mellen Press, 2000), p. 286.

6   Mary Linscott, *Towards Revised Constitutions: a Historical Perspective* (Liverpool: Sisters of Notre Dame, 1976), p. 10.

7   L.G. Fanfani and K.D. O'Rourke, OP, *Canon Law for Religious Women* (Dubuque, IA: Priory Press, 1961), p. 132.

8   Edna Hamer, *Elizabeth Prout 1820–1864: Foundress of the Sisters of the Most Holy Cross and Passion* (Bath : Downside Abbey, 1994), p.122.

9   Sisters of Notre Dame, *The English Foundations of the Sisters of Notre Dame de Namur* (Liverpool: Philip, Son & Nephew, 1895), p. 32.

10   Linscott, *This Excellent Heritage*, p. 18.

11   Ibid. Further modifications to their Constitution took place in 1948 and 1965.

12   Sheridan Gilley in his introduction to McClelland, *The Sisters of Mercy*, p. xvii.

13   For example, evidence drawn from convent account books provides great strength of argument in Mary Margaret Kealy, 'The Dominican Nuns of Channel Row, 1717–1820', MA dissertation, University of Lancaster, September 1998.

14   Even international publicity accompanying scandals, for instance, the death of Roberto Calvi and the collapse of the Italian bank Banco Ambrosiano in 1982, which reputedly deeply involved Vatican financiers, has failed to uncover details of the closely guarded church accounts.

15   Under new British legislation relating to charitable funds introduced in the early 1990s, the Roman Catholic archdioceses of England and Wales are now required to register details of diocesan accounts which may be scrutinised on payment of a fee. (I am indebted to the Catholic Press Office, Dublin for this information.)

16   I am grateful to Sr. Jean Bunn, SND for alerting me to this fact.

17   The archives of the English Province of the Sisters of Notre Dame de Namur in Liverpool are well organised and contain a wealth of detail for each of their convent houses and training colleges.

18   Archives of the Sisters of St. Paul, Selly Park, Birmingham. Balance Sheet of Receipts and Expenses, 1883–93.

19   Gilly in his introduction to McClelland, *The Sisters of Mercy*, p. xv.

20   *The Constitutions of the Sisters of Notre Dame de Namur* (1948). Rules approved by His Holiness Pope Benedict XV, 27 November 1921, Third Part. The Government of the Congregation. Ch. XIV. Authority in the Congregation, Article 221, p. 90 and Article 244, p. 98.

21 Archives of the Sisters of Notre Dame de Namur, WG h/1 in BH5, letter to the Institute's Provincial Treasurer, Sr. Bernard, 20 October 1930.

22 See further discussion and comment in this chapter.

23 Discussed more fully later.

24 Maria McClelland, 'The First Hull Mercy Nuns: a Nineteenth-Century Case Study', *Recusant History*, 22, 2, October 1994, pp. 199–221, thus describes her (p.208). See also McClelland, *The Sisters of Mercy*, Ch. 3 and 4. Accounts of *Saurin* vs. *Starr & Another* may be found also in W.A. Arnstein, *Protestant versus Catholic in Mid-Victorian England: Mr. Newdegate and the Nuns* (Columbia, MO and London: University of Missouri Press, 1982), pp. 108–22.

25 McClelland, 'First Hull Mercy Nuns' , p. 217.

26 Referred to in George V. Hudson, *Mother Genevieve Dupuis. Foundress of the Sisters of Charity of St. Paul the Apostle* (London: Sheed & Ward, 1929), pp. 298–305, and in J.J. Scarisbrick, *Selly Park and Beyond: the Story of Genevieve Dupuis and the Congregation of the Sisters of Charity of St. Paul the Apostle* (Birmingham: Sisters of St. Paul, 1997), p. 25.

27 This was not an unusual occurrence. Rome grew more and more reticent to grant active religious communities the status of 'true religious' and a twenty-years' or more wait was not exceptional.

28 Susan O'Brien, 'Lay Sisters and Good Mothers: Working-Class Women in English Convents, 1840–1910', *Women in the Church: Ecclesiastical History Society Papers, 1989/90* (London: Blackwell, 1990), pp. 463–4.

29 Hudson, *Mother Genevieve Dupuis*, p. 133.

30 Ibid.

31 Scarisbrick, *Selly Park and Beyond*, p. 25.

32 Ibid.

33 Eve Healy, *The Life of Mother Mary Potter: Foundress of the Congregation of the Little Company of Mary* (London: Sheed & Ward, 1935), p. 137.

34 Ibid., pp. 138–9.

35 Maria Luddy, *Women and Philanthropy in Nineteenth-Century Ireland* (Cambridge: Cambridge University Press, 1995), p. 27.

36 Cecil Kerr, *A Memoir of a Sister of Charity: Lady Ethelreda Fitzalan-Howard* (London: Burns, Oates & Washbourne, 1928), p. 53 (Lady Cecil Kerr, Marchioness of Lothian, was a prominent convert and writer).

37 Mary Peckham, 'Catholic Female Congregations and Religious Change in Ireland 1770–1870', PhD thesis, University of Wisconsin-Madison, 1993, p. 55.

38 As, for example, the rehabilitation of Margaret Anna Cusack as the true founder of the Sisters of St. Joseph of Peace which took place only after Vatican II. An account of the early days of her Sisters in Grimsby can be found in William Bedford and Michael Knight, *Jacob's Ladder: The Rise of a Catholic Community 1848–1913* (Grimsby: St. Mary on the Sea, 1996); also see Hamer, *Elizabeth Prout*, and Hope Stone, 'Constraints on the Foundresses: Contrasts in Anglican and Roman Catholic Religious Headships in Victorian England', PhD thesis, University of Leeds, 1993.

39 Mary Winefride Sturman, *The Ursulines in England 1851–1981* (London: Ursulines of the Roman Union, 1981), p. 61.

40   Ibid., p. 91.

41   Taped interview with the late Sr. Ruth Duckworth, DHS, Talbot Library, Preston, 1996. In the 1890s there is a similar instance of a convent setting up a laundry as a regular source of income, described by Rosemary Clerkin, *A Heart for Others* (London: Sisters of the Sacred Hearts of Jesus and Mary, 1983), p. 40. There are numerous other such examples of convent laundries to be found in the histories of women's religious institutions.

42   For example, in the personnel records of the SND and the SSP.

43   Gillian Sutherland, 'Education', in F.L.M. Thompson (ed.), *The Cambridge Social History of Britain,1750–1950*, Vol. 3, *Social Agencies and Institutions* (London: Cambridge University Press, 1990), p.121.

44   Ibid.

45   For example, 'Popular Education' (Ch. IV, in Hamer, *Elizabeth Prout*). Similarly, the statistical data presented in M. Linscott, SND, 'The Educational Work of the Sisters of Notre Dame in Lancashire since 1850', MA thesis, University of Liverpool, 1964, and in Linscott, 'The Educational Experience of the Sisters of Notre Dame de Namur, 1804-1964', PhD thesis, University of Liverpool, 1964, although useful, take a non-interpretative approach. See also Mary Linscott, *Quiet Revolution* (Glasgow: Burns, 1966)

46   Issues which are discussed more fully in Chapter 2 and 3.

47   Hudson, *Mother Genevieve Dupuis*, p. 165.

48   Ibid.

49   Alexander Wall, 'The Supply of Certificated Teachers to the Roman Catholic Elementary Schools of Britain, 1848–1870', MPhil thesis, University of Lancaster, 1983, p. 471.

50   Tony Fahey, 'Nuns in the Catholic Church in the Nineteenth Century', in Mary Cullen (ed), *Girls Don't Do Honours: Irish Women in Education in the 19th and 20th Centuries* (Dublin: Women's Educational Bureau, 1987), p. 20.

51   Hudson, *Mother Genevieve Dupuis*, illustrates examples of her 'endless tact and patience' in correspondence with a parish priest in Bradford in 1868, and in the 1880 agreement negotiated with the missioner in Holywell, pp. 166–7.

52   A.C.F. Beales, 'The Struggle for the Schools', in G.A. Beck (ed.), *The English Catholics 1850–1950* (London: Burns & Oates, 1950), p. 377.

53   Hamer, *Elizabeth Prout*, p. 99, citing Linscott, MA thesis, pp. 31–2.

54   *Catholic Directory*, 1857, advertisement section for ladies' schools in communities, p. 182.

55   See further discussion of subsidisation.

56   *Catholic Directory*, 1857, p. 181.

57   The term 'pension' was used to indicate boarding charges, *Catholic Directory*, 1897, advertisement section for convent schools, etc., p. 448.

58   Ibid., p. 453.

59   *Catholic Directory* for 1897 contains examples of how the niceties of class distinction were punctiliously observed for the education of pupils. The convent of Notre Dame de Sion in Holloway in north London, with a boarding and day school for young ladies advertised that their 'middle school for Day Scholars is attached to the Convent but is *entirely separated* from the

Ladies' School' [my italics], p. 439. A similar arrangement was advertised by the Picpus Sisters of St. John's convent in Trowbridge, p. 449.

60 Archives of the SND, CL h/5, Property and Accounts.

61 For example, entries in the *Catholic Directory* of 1897, advertisement section for institutions, societies, etc., pp. 504–5.

62 Hamer, *Elizabeth Prout*, p. 85 and Hudson, *Mother Genevieve Dupuis*, p. 163.

63 Clerkin, *A Heart for Others*, pp. 63–4.

64 Archives of the SND. NH h/3 in BH3.

65 John Murphy, *Terra Incognita, or the Convents of the United Kingdom* (London: Longmans Green, 1873), p. 391.

66 Herman Hohn, *Vocations: Conditions of Admission to Convents* (London: Washbourne, 1912), cites only two communities which rarely granted a dispensation.

67 See Appendix I for clarification of the distinction between choir and lay sisters.

68 K.H. Connell, 'Peasant Marriage in Ireland: Its Structure and Development since the Famine', *Economic History Review*, 14 (1961–62), p. 504. See also Clear, *Nuns in Nineteenth-Century Ireland*, p. 87.

69 Ibid.

70 Registers of Postulants and Novices, 1869–1926, Archives of the Sisters of the Sacred hearts of Jesus and Mary, Chigwell, Essex (see Bibliography).

71 Other congregations designated as Sisters of Charity which were not so constrained include: Sisters of St. Paul the Apostle, Daughters of St. Vincent de Paul, Sisters of Mercy, Irish Sisters of Charity, Sisters of Our Lady of Mercy, Sisters of Our Lady of Charity and Refuge, Sisters of Charity of Jesus and Mary, Sisters of Charity of Providence, Sisters of Charity of St. Louis and Sisters of Charity of Notre Dame d'Evron.

72 Extracted from Canon Law 1010, issued in 1896 and 1908. See F. Geser, OSB, *The Canon Law Governing Communities of Sisters* (St. Louis, MO and London: Herder, 1938), p. 316. The humiliation of having to 'beg' was embraced by the sisters as a worthy penitential exercise.

73 Murphy, *Terra Incognita*, gives a full account of the work of the Little Sisters, pp. 277–82 and quotes at length from a Protestant 'witness' writing of the 'liberal contributions' proffered by his co-religionists in support of the sisters in a contemporary issue of the *London Review* (no date).

74 Clerkin, *A Heart for Others*, p. 33.

75 The French distrust of the English Poor Laws is an issue recently explored by Timothy B. Smith, 'The Ideology of Charity: The Impact of the English Poor Law and Debates over the Right of Assistance in France 1830–1905', *Historical Journal*, 40, 4 (December 1997), pp. 997–1032.

76 Ibid., pp.999 and 1002.

77 Sisters of Notre Dame, *Sr. Mary of St. Francis: Hon. Laura Stafford Jerningham* (London: Burns, Oates & Washbourne, 1951), p. 43.

78 Sisters of Notre Dame, *Sr. Marie des Saint Anges: Mary Elizabeth Townley* (London: Burns, Oates & Washbourne, 1950); these missions are cited by the author as being in Empandeni and Embakwe in the former Southern

Rhodesia, in Chikuni in the former Northern Rhodesia and in Kroonstad in the former Orange Free State, p. 7.

79   Ibid.

80   Contained in the archives of the SND English province in Liverpool.

81   Archives of the SND; property and finance files in sections designated to British houses and training colleges.

82   Archives of the SND. CL h/5 in BH2, Property and Accounts.

83   Bedford and Knight, *Jacob's Ladder*, p. 137.

84   See previous reference to her in Chapter 2.

85   Denis Gwynn, *A Hundred Years of Catholic Emancipation 1829–1929* (London: Longmans Green, 1929), p. xvii.

86   Clerkin, *A Heart for Others*, p. 30.

87   *The Tablet*, 13 March 1875, p.347 and 19 June 1875, p. 795 concerning similar charitable appeals.

88   Anon., *The Poor Servants of the Mother of God* (London: Catholic Truth Society, 1928), pp. 35–9.

89   T.J. Walsh, *Nano Nagle and the Presentation Sisters* (Dublin: Gill & Son, 1959), unlike all other sources, gives the year to be 1835, p. 259.

90   Archives of the SND, MP h/15 in MPC. Bequests and Legacies, 1910–76.

91   Arnstein, *Protestant versus Catholic*, also adds 205 army officers, 39 naval officers, 129 lawyers, 60 doctors and 162 literary men and women to this list, p. 42.

92   Arnstein drew from W. Gordon Gorman, *Converts to Rome: A Biographical List of the More Notable Converts to the Catholic Church in the United Kingdom during the Last Sixty Years* (London: Sands, 4th edn, 1899). First published in 1878, there were many editions of this work, including an enlarged, updated edition which appeared in 1910.

93   David Mathew 'Old Catholics and Converts', in G.A. Beck (ed.), *The English Catholics 1850–1950* (London: Burns & Oates, 1950), p. 237.

94   Ibid., pp. 350–1. See also John Bennett, 'The Care of the Poor', in the same work, p. 564. Also Peter F. Anson, *The Religious Orders and Congregations of Great Britain and Ireland* (Worcester: Stanbrook Abbey Press, 1949), p. 373.

95   Clerkin, *A Heart for Others*, p. 41.

96   Ibid.

97   Meg Whittle, 'Philanthropy in Preston: The Changing Face of Charity', PhD thesis, University of Lancaster, 1990, p. 309.

98   Ibid., p. 130.

99   Ibid., pp. 130, 132.

100   Ibid., p. 130.

101   Ibid., p. 132.

102   Ibid., p. 131.

103   S.G. Snead-Cox, *Life of Cardinal Vaughan* (London: Burns & Oates, 2 vols, 1910), Vol.1, p. 293.

104   For an account of these events see ibid., pp. 275–93.

105   Andrew White and Michael Winstanley, *Victorian Terraced Houses in Lancaster*, (Lancaster: Centre for North-West Regional Studies, Lancaster University, 1996), pp. 52–3.

106 Scarisbrick, *Selly Park and Beyond*, pp. 73–86.

107 Hudson, *Mother Genevieve Dupuis*, p. 133.

108 Ibid.

109 Sisters of Mercy, *Trees of Mercy: Sisters of Mercy of Great Britain from 1839* (London: privately published, 1993), *passim*.

110 Mary Josephine Gately, *The Sisters of Mercy: Historical Sketches 1831–1931* (New York, NY: Macmillan, 1931), p. 101. See also Sisters of Mercy, *Trees of Mercy*, p. 13. The convent was designed by Pugin, for whom Hardman worked almost exclusively.

111 F.K. Prochaska, *Women and Philanthropy in Nineteenth-Century England* (Oxford: Clarendon Press, 1980), p. 224 and *passim*.

112 Ibid., p. 226.

113 Ibid., p. 224. Prochaska cites a statistical survey carried out by Louisa Hubbard and Angela Burdett-Coutts in 1893.

114 E.R. Norman, *The English Catholic Church in the Nineteenth Century* (Oxford: Clarendon Press, 1984), p. 189.

115 See ibid., *Anti-Catholicism in Victorian England* (London: Allen & Unwin, 1968), for the full report of the Convent enquiry of 1871 which came later, pp. 202–11.

116 Morgan V. Sweeney, 'Diocesan Organization and Administration', in G.A. Beck (ed.), *The English Catholics 1850–1950* (London: Burns & Oates, 1950), p. 126.

117 Norman, *The English Catholic Church*, p. 190.

118 Ibid., p. 191. See also Gwynn, *A Hundred Years of Catholic Emancipation*, pp. 264–5.

119 Evidence contained in the archives of the SND, MP h/16, Architects, for example. There are records, accounts and correspondence relating to building or repair work carried out by all the convent houses of this institution.

120 Archives of the SND, CL h/5 in BH2. Property and Accounts.

121 Ibid.

122 Ibid., NC h/3 in Bh3, correspondence files 1 and 3, for example.

123 As were the purchase of land and property. Archives of the SND, MP h/7, for example.

124 Archives of the SND, English Account Annual Summaries Register, 1905–54.

125 Ibid. NC h/3 in BH 3. File 3, 1910–23.

126 During the Second World War many religious houses suffered damage by air raids.

127 McClelland, *The Sisters of Mercy*, p. 275.

128 Archives of the SND, SF h/3 in BH4. Files 1860–1914, Properties, land, etc.

129 Ibid.

130 Ibid.

131 Ibid. BS h/3. File 4, 1869–1900.

132 Ibid. The file contains many sketched plans and letters exchanged between Chas. A. Buckler and Sr. Mary of St. Francis. One convent annalist noted that the building of the Battersea convent in 1868–70 is mentioned in Eastlake, *A History of the Gothic Revival* (1872).

133 Archives of the Sisters of St. Paul, Selly Park, Birmingham.

134 Run on similar lines to the Army and Navy Stores and thus described by Bill Lancaster, *The Department Store* (London, 1995), p. 88 The Civil Service Supply Association had been founded by the clerks in the General Post office in 1864. Traditionally, the CWS was founded mainly to serve the needs of working-class customers but this firm provided a thrifty, bulk-purchasing and deposit savings facility for customers of the professional classes.

135 Clear, *Nuns in Nineteenth-Century Ireland,* p. 166, cites a paper delivered by Tony Fahey, 'The Feminism of the Catholic Church in Ireland in the Nineteenth Century', to the Conference of Sociologists' Association of Ireland, Ballyvaughan, 1983.

CHAPTER SIX

1 Susan O'Brien, 'Terra Incognita: The Nun in Nineteenth-Century England', *Past and Present,* 121 (November 1988), pp. 110–40; ibid., 'Lay Sisters and Good Mothers: Working-Class Women in English Convents, 1840–1910', *Women in the Church: Ecclesiastical History Society Papers, 1989/90* (London: Blackwell, 1990), pp. 453–65; ibid., 'French Nuns in Nineteenth-Century England', *Past and Present,* 154 (February 1997), pp. 142–80; Caitriona Clear, *Nuns in Nineteenth-Century Ireland* (Dublin: Gill & Macmillan, 1987); Mary Peckham, 'Catholic Female Congregations and Religious Change in Ireland 1770–1870', PhD thesis, University of Wisconsin-Madison, 1993; H.C.B. Stone, 'Constraints on the Foundresses: Contrasts in Anglican and Roman Catholic Religious Headships in Victorian England', PhD thesis, University of Leeds, 1993; and Susan Mumm, 'Lady Guerillas of Philanthropy. Anglican Sisterhoods in Victorian England', PhD thesis, University of Sussex, 1992.

2 Lay sisters are briefly referred to in Chapters 1 and 5.

3 O'Brien, 'Terra Incognita', p. 123.

4 Ibid., p. 128. One was a countess, another a convert and former head-mistress who entered at the age of 47. Third was the daughter of a prominent Dublin lawyer.

5 Ibid., p. 131.

6 O'Brien, 'French Nuns in Nineteenth-Century England', also notes that they opened a house in Kilcullen, Co. Kildare in 1878, p. 164.

7 Ibid., p. 146.

8 Ibid., p. 151.

9 See n.63 for the process and sources employed to identify Irish roots.

10 O'Brien, 'French Nuns in Nineteenth-Century England', p. 163.

11 Ibid., 'Terra Incognita', p. 119.

12 Ibid., p. 140.

13 Clear, *Nuns in Nineteenth-Century Ireland,* pp. 168–74.

14 Peckham, 'Catholic Female Congregations'; Stone, 'Constraints on the Foundresses'.

15 Peckham, 'Catholic Female Congregations', pp. 155–7.

16   Mumm, 'Lady Guerillas of Philanthropy'.

17   Suellen Hoy, 'The Journey Out: The Recruitment and Emigration of Irish Religious Women to the United States 1812–1914', *Journal of Women's History*, 6, 4 and 7, 1 (Winter/Spring 1995), pp. 64–98.

18   Raised by O'Brien, 'Terra Incognita', p. 138; her footnote suggests the need for further careful analysis as to how typical were her findings that one-third of all postulants in the congregations she studied might have left in their first few months.

19   Ralph Gibson, 'The Christianization of the Countryside in Western Europe in the Nineteenth Century', in J.-P. Massaut and M.-E. Hebbeau (eds), *La christianisation des campagnes*, Vol. II (Brussels and Rome: Institut Historique Belge de Rome/Belgisch Historisch Instituut te Rome, 1996), pp. 485–509 and statistical tables.

20   Ibid.

21   O'Brien, 'Lay-sisters and Good Mothers', p. 454, has drawn attention to the subtle lines of demarcation she found in at least one community. Documentary evidence to confirm instances of how this discrimination existed has come to light within my own research.

22   Although a broadly general figure for the total intake into the English Province has been supplied by Sr. Judith Greville, Provincial Archivist of the Daughters of Charity of St. Vincent de Paul, Mill Hill, London.

23   Discussed more fully in Chapter 3.

24   See n.22.

25   Herman Hohn, *Vocations: Conditions of Admission to Convents* (London: Washbourne, 1912), *passim*.

26   Maria Luddy, *Women and Philanthropy in Nineteenth-Century Ireland* (Cambridge: Cambridge University Press, 1995), p. 27.

27   Cecil Kerr, *A Memoir of a Sister of Charity: Lady Ethelreda Fitzalan-Howard* (London: Burns, Oates & Washbourne, 1928), p. 55. Sr. Mary (c. 1850–1926) was the daughter of the 14th Duke of Norfolk.

28   J.J. Scarisbrick, *Selly Park and Beyond: the Story of Genevieve Dupuis and the Congregation of the Sisters of Charity of St. Paul the Apostle* (Birmingham: Sisters of St. Paul, 1997), pp. 88–7.

29   Luddy, *Women and Philanthropy*, p. 30.

30   Clear, *Nuns in Nineteenth-Century Ireland*, p. 79.

31   Sisters of Charity of St. Paul the Apostle, Generalate Archive Office, Selly Park, Birmingham. Registers of Postulants and Novices, 1847–1926: Ref. boxes 26, 27 and 37.

32   Ibid., box 37.

33   Sisters of the Sacred Hearts of Jesus and Mary, Chigwell, Essex. Register of Professions 1870–1926 and Register of Postulants 1903–26.

34   F. Geser, OSB, *The Canon Law Governing Communities of Sisters* (St. Louis, MO and London: Herder, 1938), covers all aspects of departure and dismissal, pp. 337–77.

35   For an analysis of entry ages between 1847 and 1926, see Barbara M. Walsh, 'A Social History of Roman Catholic Nuns and Sisters in Nineteenth and

Early Twentieth Century England and Wales: The Veiled Dynamic', PhD thesis, University of Lancaster, 1999, Tables (4:4) and (4:5).

36 Luddy, *Women and Philanthropy*, p. 30.

37 Peckham, 'Catholic Female Congregations', p. 154.

38 O'Brien, 'Terra Incognita', 'Lay Sisters and Good Mothers' and 'French Nuns in Nineteenth-Century England'.

39 Jose Harris, *Private Lives, Public Spirit: Britain 1870–1914* (London: Oxford University Press, 1993), draws attention to the lack of marriage dowries in the middle and lower classes in England in comparison with their importance in Ireland, p. 69. Social and economic factors affecting Irish rural families are dealt with later in this chapter in the context of regional patterns of recruitment. See also the discussion on dowries in Chapter 5.

40 Influences affecting choice and recruitment methods used will be discussed in more detail later in this chapter.

41 Dudley Baines, 'Population, Migration and Regional Development 1870–1930', in R. Floud and D. McCloskey (eds), *The Economic History of Britain since 1700*, Vol.2, *1860–1939* (London: Cambridge University Press, 2nd edn, 1994) pp. 39–40.

42 Timothy W. Guinnane, *The Vanishing Irish: Households, Migration, and the Rural Economy in Ireland, 1850–1914* (Princeton, NJ: Princeton University Press, 1997), p. 95. See also Cormac O'Grada, *Ireland: A New Economic History, 1780–1939* (Oxford: Clarendon Press, 1994), p. 215, citing Fitzpatrick and Vaughan.

43 Sheila Jeffreys, *The Spinster and Her Enemies. Feminism and Sexuality 1880–1930* (London: Pandora, 1985), pp. 88–9.

44 Alan Deacon and Michael Hill, 'The Problem of "Surplus Women" in the Nineteenth-Century: Secular and Religious Alternatives', in M. Hill (ed.), *A Sociological Yearbook of Religion in Britain*, Vol. 5 (London: SCM Press, 1972), p. 100.

45 Jeffreys, *The Spinster and Her Enemies*, examined the period 1801–1931 and found 1911 to be the year at which marriage was least popular, pp. 88–9.

46 Barbara Leigh Smith, *Women and Work* (London: Bosworth & Harrison, 1857), p. 9.

47 Mary Carbery, *The Farm by Lough Gur* (London: 1937; reprinted Dublin: Mercier, 1987), p. 47.

48 Mumm, 'Lady Guerillas of Philanthropy', p. 94. Her choir sisters lived marginally longer than the lay-sisters.

49 T.H. Hollingworth, 'A Demographic Study of British Ducal Families', in Michael Drake (ed.), *Population in Industrialization* (London: Methuen, 1969), p. 82.

50 O'Brien, 'Terra Incognita', pp. 139–40 (fn).

51 Ibid., citing E.A. Wrigley and R.S. Scofield, *The Population History of England, 1541–1871* (London: Edward Arnold, 1981), Table A14.1, p. 709.

52 As shall be shown when familial and economic pressures and the appeal of arguments presenting the ultimate spiritual superiority of the religious life are discussed later (see n.112) the limited availability of any other equally stress-free lifestyle brought its own benefits.

53 Unique enough to have been thought worthy of photographic display in DVDP Provincial Archives, Blackrock, Co. Dublin.

54 Clear, *Nuns in Nineteenth-Century Ireland*, p. 146.

55 Peckham, 'Catholic Female Congregations', pp. 155–7.

56 Interview with the late Sr. Ruth Duckworth, Talbot Library, Preston, 1995.

57 North-West Regional Oral History Archive, University of Lancaster. Interview conducted by Elizabeth Roberts with 'Miss C.4P', Preston, 1979.

58 Data collected for this book can only provide broad indications of this practice. It may be an interesting topic for further research.

59 See Tables 28 and 29.

60 *The Commission on Emigration and Other Population Problems 1948–54:Reports*, PR 2541, (Dublin, 1955), Table 34, p. 325, does not provide divisions by sex, but established research practice regards at least half all emigrants to have been female. Care is needed when comparing the Commission's statistics with those presented by Rita M. Rhodes, *Women and the Family in Post-Famine Ireland* (New York, NY and London: Garland Publishing, 1992). The difficulty may be that her comments were focused on emigration to America. For example, pp. 244–5, in citing Vaughan and Fitzpatrick's percentage proportion of provincial statistics, she presents a different pattern from that by the Commission's Report.

61 *The Commission on Emigration and Other Population Problems*, Table 34, p. 325.

62 Colin G. Pooley and Jean Turnbull, 'Leaving Home: The Experience of Migration from the Parental Home in Britain since c.1770', *Journal of Family History*, 22, 4 (October 1997), p. 416.

63 Edward McLysaght, *Irish Families: Their Names, Arms and Origins* (Dublin: Hodges Figgis, 1957) is the standard reference work. I have placed reliance on identifying Irish surnames on the following criteria: Names beginning with O' and names very common in Ireland, or in particular Irish regions, such as Kelly, Murphy, Walsh, Ryan and Byrne; also further confirmed if an entrant had a parent with the first name Patrick, Bridget or Kathleen. Although care has to be taken not to confuse Scottish parentage, some surnames common in particular regions of Ireland beginning with Mac have also been selected.

64 Archives of the SND, ref. Dowanhill, Box.2, F.2, Item (3). Letter from Sr. Mary of St. Wilfrid to Sr. Mary des Saint Anges, dated Glasgow, 11 September 1896.

65 Internal divisional structures of choir and lay sisters are not relevant nor examined here.

66 O'Brien, 'Lay Sisters and Good Mothers', p. 454.

67 See earlier notes on heiresses in Chapter 5.

68 Memoirs of Sr. Mary Benedicta, 1979, SND Provincial Archives, Liverpool.

69 O'Brien, 'Lay Sisters and Good Mothers', pp. 453–5.

70 Ibid.

71 Scarisbrick, *Selly Park and Beyond*, 'Sisters Reminisce', p. 61.

72 The data made available for the DVDP are insufficient to allow for comment.

73   T. Jones Hughes, 'Landholding and Settlement in County Tipperary in the Nineteenth Century', in W. Nolan and T. McGrath (eds), *Tipperary History and Society* (Dublin: Geography Publications, 1985), p. 351.

74   English and Irish censuses differ considerably in the amount and nature of the data made available for research. See notes and explanations in Appendix III.

75   David Fitzpatrick, 'Irish Farming Families before the First World War', *Comparative Studies in Society and History*, 25, 3 (1983), pp. 339–80, carries data in Table 2, 'Irish Household Composition, 1841–1911'(p.349) that are congruent with my findings.

76   These were all respectable middle-class occupations: bank manager, rate collector, under agent, boot- and shoe-maker, saddler, shopkeeper, teacher, and one described as being 'in business'.

77   Griffith's Valuation Lists of 1850–7 and *Guy's Munster Directory* (Cork, 1886), Gilbert Library, Dublin.

78   Census manuscripts for townlands in Limerick, Tipperary and Wexford, 1901 and 1911, National Archives of Ireland, Bride Street, Dublin. For an explanation of the term 'townlands' see Appendix III.

79   J.J. Lee, *The Modernisation of Irish Society 1848–1918* (Dublin: Gill & Macmillan, 1989), pp. 3–5. Also the exchange of interpretations of the stem family system instigated by P.Gibbon and C.Curtin, 'The Stem Family in Ireland', *Comparative Studies in Society and History*, 20, 3 (July 1978), pp. 429–53 and Fitzpatrick, 'Irish Farming Families', pp. 339–80.

80   Patrick Hickey, 'The Famine in the Skibbereen Union (1845–1851)', in Cathal Poirteir (ed), *The Great Irish Famine* (Dublin: RTE/Mercier Press, 1995), p. 203.

81   This conclusion has been drawn from examination of the census manuscripts for townland addresses of entrants from Limerick, Tipperary and Wexford, National Archives of Ireland, Bride Street, Dublin. See also Rhodes, *Women and the Family*, who comments at length on social mores applicable to women from Irish farm households in chapters on 'Mothers and Daughters' and 'Women and Emigration'.

82   Mss. Collection, Irish Folklore Commission, University College Dublin, D. IV. Vol. 107, p. 316.

83   Tony Fahey, 'Female Asceticism in the Catholic Church: A Case Study of Nuns in the Nineteenth Century', PhD thesis, University of Illinois at Urbana-Champaign, 1982, pp. 90–2.

84   See discussion in Chapter 5 on finance.

85   Kevin Whelan, 'The Catholic Church, 1700–1900' (in Nolan and McGrath (eds), *Tipperary History and Society*, p. 244), cites W.J. Smyth, 'Clogheen-Burncoat: a Social History of a Co. Tipperary Parish', PhD thesis, National University of Ireland, 1969.

86   See the more general discussion in Chapter 5 on the topic of the amount of dowry payments expected.

87   W.J. Smyth, 'The Making of Ireland: Agendas and Perspectives in Cultural Geography', in B.J. Graham and J. Proudfoot (eds), *A Historical Geography of Ireland* (London and New York, NY: Academic Press, 1993), p. 431.

88   L.P. Curtis, 'Ireland in 1914', in W.E. Vaughan (ed.), *A New History of Ireland*, VI, *Ireland under the Union*, II, *1870–1921* (Oxford: Clarendon Press, 1996), p. 156.

89   Joanna Bourke, 'Dairywomen and Affectionate Wives: Women in the Irish Dairy Industry, 1890–1914', *Agricultural History Review*, 38, II (1990), pp. 149–64. George H. Bassett, *County Tipperary One Hundred Years Ago: A Guide and Directory* (Dublin, 1889, reprint, Belfast, 1991), commented on the establishment 'lately' of fifteen new butter factories, p. 29.

90   Joanna Bourke, *Husbandry to Housewifery: Women, Economic Change and Housework in Ireland, 1890–1914* (Oxford: Clarendon Press, 1993), p. 169.

91   Ibid., pp.110–41; see also Anne Rossiter, 'Bringing the Margins into the Centre', in Ailbhe Smyth (ed.), *Irish Women's Studies Reader* (Dublin: Attic Press, 1993), p. 183, who cites J.J. Lee, 'Women and the Church since the Famine', in M. McCurtain and D. O'Corrain (eds), *Women in Irish Society: The Historical Dimension* (Dublin: Arlen Press, 1978), p. 37.

92   Bourke, *Husbandry to Housewifery*, p. 69.

93   Rossiter, 'Bringing the Margins into the Centre', p. 188, cites David Fitzpatrick, 'A Share of the Honeycomb: Education, Emigration and Irishwomen', *Continuity and Change*, 1, 2 (1989), pp. 217–34.

94   Declan Kiberd, *Inventing Ireland* (London: Jonathan Cape, 1995), pp. 23–4.

95   Rossiter, 'Bringing the Margins into the Centre', p. 180, cites Janet A. Nolan, *Ourselves Alone: Women's Emigration from Ireland, 1885–1920*, (Lexington, , KY: University of Kentucky Press, 1989), p. 100. See also Walsh, thesis, for the analysis of the age of emigrant women, Table 12.

96   *The Commission on Emigration and Other Population Problems Report*, Table 91, p. 122, contains figures tabled by sex for emigration to the USA, Canada, Australia and destinations outside Europe, but a qualification warns that these figures do 'not include movements between Britain and Ireland', p. 314. However, the compiler of Table 94, p. 125, does provide statistics for emigration to 'England and Wales'; see n.98.

97   Pauric Travers, 'Emigration and Gender: The Case of Ireland 1922–60', Mary O'Dowd and Sabrine Wichet (eds), *Chattel, Servant or Citizen: Women's Status in Church, State and Society*, Historical Studies XIX (Belfast: Queen's University Institute of Irish Studies, 1995), pp. 188, 190. See also Rossiter 'Bringing the Margins into the Centre', p. 180.

98   *The Commission on Emigration and Other Population Problems Report*, Table 94,'The Total Emigration from the 26 [sic] Counties and the 6 [sic] Counties according to Destination, 1876–1921', p. 125, provides no indication as to how these figures were calculated. See also Walsh, thesis, Appendix (x).

99   Letter from the Bishop of Galway to the Bishop of Southwark, who had written on behalf of the sisters, August 1934. SND Provincial Archives, ref. Dowanhill: Box 20, item 30.

100 Rosemary Clerkin, *A Heart for Others* (London: Sisters of the Sacred Hearts of Jesus and Mary, 1983), pp. 68, 78.

101 Archives of the SND, ref. Dowanhill, Box.2, F.2, Item (3). Letter from Sr. Mary of St. Wilfrid to Sr. Mary des Saint Anges.

102   O'Brien's research has been cited and discussed earlier in this chapter.

103   Kate O'Brien, *Land of Spices* (London: Heinemann, 1941; Dublin: Arlen House, 1982), *passim* and Carbery, *The Farm by Lough Gur*, pp. 94–105, 134–41.

104   Hoy, 'The Journey Out', p. 79.

105   Ibid., p. 64.

106   Ibid., p. 65.

107   Already discussed above, O'Brien, 'Terra Incognita', p. 123.

108   Sharon Lambert, 'Female Emigration from Post-Independence Ireland: an Oral History of Irish Women in Lancashire, c.1922–1960', PhD thesis, University of Lancaster, 1997.

109   The Catholic Truth Society was founded in London in 1884. The Catholic Truth Society of Ireland was founded in Dublin in 1899.

110   The notorious horror stories of Maria Monk or of Barbara Ubryk, the 'Nun of Cracow', and similar tales which contained highly salacious accounts of convent life were most usually written anonymously.

111   For example, the anonymously published *The Religious Houses of the United Kingdom: Containing a Short History of Every Order and House* (London: Burns & Oates, 1887); Francesca M. Steele, *The Convents of Great Britain* (London: Sands; Dublin: M.H. Gill, 1902); and Hohn, *Vocations*.

112   Variations on the six advantages of the religious life for the soul can be found in M.D. Forrest, SJ, *The Pearl of Great Price, or the Religious Life* (London: Catholic Truth Society, 1922) and *Come Follow Me* (Dublin: Catholic Truth Society of Ireland, 1930), 'The soul of a religious lives more purely; falls more rarely; rises more speedily; enjoys the dews of comforting grace more frequently; dies more confidently; and is purified more quickly in the flames of purgatory.' (From *Pearl*, pp. 12–16 and *Come Follow Me*, pp. 13–15.)

113   F.L.M. Thompson, 'Town and City', *The Cambridge Social History of Britain, 1750–1950*, Vol. 1, *Regions and Communities* (London: Cambridge University Press, 1993), p. 65.

114   Ibid., pp. 64–5.

115   As we have shown, the greatest number were drawn from the 'strong farmer class' in rural Ireland.

116   See earlier reference to statistics in Gibson, 'The Christianisation of the Countryside'.

117   Michel Foucault, *Discipline and Punish: The Birth of the Prison* (London: Penguin, 1991), p. 211.

118   James Miller, *The Passion of Michel Foucault* (London: Flamingo, 1994), p. 236.

119   Scarisbrick, *Selly Park and Beyond*, p. 88. This figure should not be confused with the data contained in this chapter, which is mainly concerned with the number of entrants who applied each year and who were subsequently accepted.

CONCLUSION

1 Susan Mumm, 'Lady Guerillas of Philanthropy. Anglican Sisterhoods in Victorian England', PhD thesis, University of Sussex, 1992, p. 280.

2 Caitriona Clear, *Nuns in Nineteenth-Century Ireland* (Dublin: Gill & Macmillan, 1987), p. 35.

3 Sheridan Gilly, in Maria G. McClelland, *The Sisters of Mercy: Popular Politics and the Growth of the Roman Catholic Community in Hull, 1855–1930* (Lampeter; Lewiston; Queenston: Edwin Mellen Press, 2000), p. xvii.

4 A theme running throughout Jo Ann Kay Macnamara, *Sisters in Arms: Catholic Nuns through Two Millennia* (London and Cambridge, MA: Harvard University Press, 1996), see, for example, pp. 4 and 613–14. Feminist works include Margaret Brennan, 'Enclosure: Institutionalising the Invisibility of Women in Ecclesiastical Communities', *Concilium*, 182 (1985), pp. 38–48; Helen Rose Ebaugh, 'Patriarchal Bargains and Latent Avenues of Social Mobility: Nuns in the Roman Catholic Church', *Gender and Society*, 7, 3 (September 1993), pp. 400–14; Mary Audrey Kopp, 'Bureaucratic Dysfunction in American Convents', in M.C. Borromeo, CSC (ed.), *The New Nuns* (London and Sydney: Sheed & Ward, 1968); Mary Loudon, *Unveiled: Nuns Talking* (London: Vintage, 1992).

Bibliography

PRIMARY SOURCES

MANUSCRIPTS: CONVENT ARCHIVES

Sisters of Charity of St. Paul the Apostle, Generalate Archive Office, Selly Park, Birmingham

Registers of Postulants and Novices, 1847–1926
Box numbers: 26, 27 and 37
Deposit account book: Civil Service Supply Association Ltd, 1886–91
Balance sheet of receipts and expenses, 1883–93

Sisters of Notre Dame de Namur, Provincial Archives, Liverpool

The Constitution of the Sisters of Notre Dame of Namur (1948)
Personnel records
    Registers of Professed Sisters for the British Province, 1845–1926
    Records of Postulants and Novices British Province, 1915–26
Notre Dame Convent Records
    BS h/3 File 4, 1869–1900
    CL h/5 in BH2. Correspondence, Property and Accounts
    NC h/3 in BH3. Ledger 1847–50. Correspondence, Files 1, 2 and 3
    NH h/3 in BH3. Correspondence
    MP h/7 Finance
    MP h/15 Bequests and Legacies
    MP h/16 Architects
    SF h/3 in BH4. Properties, land, buildings, etc.
    WG h/1 in BH5 Annals and correspondence, file 3
English Account Annual Summaries Register, 1905–54
Provincial Bursar's Office
Dowanhill
    Box 2. F.2, Item 3
    Letter from Sr. M. des St. Anges to Sr. M. Wilfrid, 11 September 1896
    Box.20. Item 30
    Letter from Bishop of Galway, 21 August 1934
    Letter from Bishop of Southwark, 27 August 1934

Leeds
No.3, 1911–21
Correspondence from Education Department, Leeds, April 1921
Confidential Report of the Inspectors, October 1921
Manchester
1924–37 (Ref. 382) Yearly Lists of Sisters
Mount Pleasant
Ref. MP. Sector C, Community Lists for 1878–1980
MSS memoirs: 'A few Memoirs of Sister Mary Benedicta for Sister Dorothy McCaffrey'

Sisters of Sacred Hearts of Jesus and Mary, Chigwell, Essex (formerly the English Province of the Servants of the Sacred Heart)

Register of Professions, 1870–1926
Register of Postulants, 1903–26

Daughters of Charity of St. Vincent de Paul, Archives, Provincial House, Blackrock, Co. Dublin

Register of Irish Sisters, 1847–1926

Census of Population of Ireland, 1901 and 1911, Manuscript Returns

Census of Population of Ireland Manuscript Returns for Co. Limerick, Co. Tipperary and Co. Wexford, National Archives, Dublin

Primary (or Griffith's) Valuations, 1847–64

National Archives and Griffith's Library, Pearse Street, Dublin (microfiches)

NINETEENTH- AND EARLY TWENTIETH-CENTURY PRINTED REFERENCE SOURCES

Catholic Directory (London: Burns & Oates, 1857, 1877, 1897 and 1917)
Catholic Directory (London: Burns, Oates & Washbourne, 1937)
Catholic Directory of Ireland (Dublin: Burns & Oates, 1877 and 1897)
Guys Munster Directory (Cork: 1886)
Land Owners in Ireland: Return of Owners of Lands of One Acre and Upwards (Dublin: HMSO, Alex Thom, 1876)
General Alphabetical Index to the Towns and Townlands of Ireland: Based on the Census of 1851 (Dublin: Thom, 1861; reprinted: Baltimore, MD: Genealogical Publishing, 1995)

NINETEENTH-CENTURY NEWSPAPERS AND PERIODICALS

The Tablet, 13 March 1875, p. 347; 19 June 1875, p. 795

NINETEENTH-CENTURY BOOKS

Anon., *The Religious Houses of the United Kingdom: Containing a Short History of Every Order and House* (London: Burns & Oates, 1887)

Edward G. Bagshawe, *Mercy and Justice to the Poor: The True Political Economy* (London: Kegan Paul, Trench, 1885)

George H. Bassett, *Wexford County: A Guide and Directory* (Dublin, 1885; reprinted Dublin: Hibernian Imprints, 1991)

—, *Tipperary County One Hundred Years Ago: A Guide and Directory* (Dublin, 1889; reprinted Belfast: Friars Bush Press, 1991)

Arthur Devine, *Convent Life, or the Duties of Sisters Dedicated in Religion to the Service of God* (London: Washbourne; Dublin: M.H. Gill, 4th edn, 1897)

Frances R. Drane, *Life of Mother Mary Hallahan* (London: Longmans, Green, Reader & Dwyer, 1869)

W. Gordon Gorman, *Converts to Rome: A Biographical List of the More Notable Converts to the Catholic Church in the United Kingdom during the Last Sixty Years* (London: Sands, 4th edn, 1899)

John Murphy, *Terra Incognita; or, the Convents of the United Kingdom* (London: Longman, Green, 1873)

Sisters of Notre Dame, *The English Foundations of the Sisters of Notre Dame de Namur* (Liverpool: Philip, Son & Nephew, 1895)

E.S. Purcell, *Life of Cardinal Manning*, Vol. II (London: Macmillan, 1896)

W.A. Shaw, *Manchester Old and New* (London: Cassell, 1894)

Barbara Leigh Smith, *Women and Work* (London: Bosworth & Harrison, 1857)

XV Club (edited for the Club, but written by Thomas Murphy), *The Position of the Catholic Church in England and Wales during the Last Two Centuries: Retrospect and Forecast* (London: Burns & Oates, 1892)

NINETEENTH- AND EARLY TWENTIETH-CENTURY PAMPHLETS

Anon., *Archbishop Ullathorne (1806-89)* (London: Catholic Truth Society, 1898)

Anon., *Of What Use Are Nuns?* (London: Catholic Truth Society, 1908)

Anon., *Minnie Murphy's Mendacities: or How the Non-Catholic Press Exploits 'Escaped' Nuns* (London: Catholic Truth Society, 1913)

Anon., *The True History of Maria Monk* (London: Catholic Truth Society, 1894)

G. Elliot Anstruther, *Edith O'Gorman and Her Book* (London: Catholic Truth Society, 1913)

Dom Norbert Birt, OSB, *'In the Net' or, Advertisement by Libel* (London: Catholic Truth Society, 1906)

James Britten, KSG, *Mr. S.J. Abbott and the Convent Enquiry Society* (London: Catholic Truth Society, 1900)

—, *Nuns and Convents* (London: Catholic Truth Society, 1899)

—, *Convent Inspection* (London: Catholic Truth Society, 1913)

—, *The Truth about Convents* (London: Catholic Truth Society, 1898)

—, *A 'True Story of a Nun'* (London: Catholic Truth Society, 1911)

Very Revd Canon Foran, *About Monks and Nuns* (London: Catholic Truth Society, 1894)

M.D. Forrest, SJ, *Come, Follow Me* (Dublin: Catholic Truth Society of Ireland, 1930)

—, *The Pearl of Great Price, or the Religious Life* (London: Catholic Truth Society, 1922)

Mrs Conor Maguire, *The Cloistered Nun* (Dublin: Catholic Truth Society of Ireland, 1924)

Sydney F. Smith, SJ, *Calumnies against Convents* (London: Catholic Truth Society, 1894)

—, *Ellen Golding, the Rescued Nun* (London: Catholic Truth Society, 1894)

—, *The Escaped Nun from East Bergholt* (London: Catholic Truth Society, 1910)

—, *The True Story of Barbara Ubryk* (London: Catholic Truth Society, 1897)

H. Thurston, SJ, *The Immuring of Nuns* (London: Catholic Truth Society, 1892)

—, *The Myth of the Walled-up Nun* (London: Catholic Truth Society, 1902)

William B. Ullathorne, *The Origin of Conventual Life* (London: Catholic Truth Society, 1910)

—, *The Spirit of Conventual Life* (London: Catholic Truth Society, 1911)

—, *The Work of Conventual Life* (London: Catholic Truth Society, 1910)

—, *The Conventual Life* (St. Pauls, MN: Paulist Press, 1914)

NINETEENTH-CENTURY PARLIAMENTARY PAPERS

Census of England and Wales, 1871, Population Abstracts. Ages, Civil Conditions, Occupations and Birthplaces of the People, Vol. III, Table 13. Professional Occupations 3 (C. 872, 1873)

Census of England and Wales, 1891, Ages, Condition as to Marriage, Occupations, Birthplaces, and Infirmities, Vol. III, Table 7. Professional Occupations 3 (C.7058, 1893)

Reformatories and Industrial Schools, Inspectors' Annual Reports, 40th Report for 1896 (C.8566, 1897)

IRISH PUBLIC RECORDS

Commission on Emigration and Other Population Problems, 1948–54: Reports, PR.2541 (Dublin, 1955)

ORAL HISTORY

The North-West Regional Studies Oral History Archive, Lancaster University
Mss. Collection, Irish Folklore Commission 1935–71, Department of Irish Folklore, University College, Dublin
Interview with the late Sr. Ruth Duckworth, DHS, Talbot Library, Preston. Lancs.

SECONDARY SOURCES

BOOKS AND BOOK EXTRACTS

Anon., *Handbook of Catholic Charitable and Social Works* (London: Catholic Truth Society, 1912)

Anon., *The First Fifty Years, 1899–1949, Golden Jubilee Record* (Dublin: Catholic Truth Society of Ireland, 1949)

Anon., *Sisters of Charity of St. Vincent de Paul* (London, Catholic Truth Society, 1924)

Anon., *The Poor Servants of the Mother of God* (London: Catholic Truth Society, 1928)

F.H.A. Aalen, K. Whelan and Matthew Stout (eds), *Atlas of the Irish Rural Landscape* (Cork: University Press, 1997)

Brian Abel-Smith, *A History of the Nursing Profession* (London: Heinemann, 1960)

—, *The Hospitals, 1800–1948* (London: Heinemann, 1964)

Gordon Albion, 'The Restoration of the Hierarchy, 1850', in G.A. Beck (ed.), *The English Catholics 1850–1950* (London: Burns & Oates, 1950)

A.M. Allchin, *The Silent Rebellion: Anglican Religious Communities* (London: SCM Press, 1958)

Peter F. Anson, *The Religious Orders and Congregations of Great Britain and Ireland* (Worcester: Stanbrook Abbey Press, 1949)

W.A. Arnstein, *Protestant versus Catholic in Mid-Victorian England: Mr. Newdegate and the Nuns* (Columbia, MO and London: University of Missouri Press, 1982)

Automobile Association, *Ordinance Survey Illustrated Atlas of Victorian and Edwardian Britain* (London: Automobile Association, 1991)

Dudley Baines, 'Population, Migration and Regional Development 1870–1930', in R. Floud and D. McCloskey (eds), *The Economic History of Britain since 1700*, Vol. 2, *1860–1939* (London: Cambridge University Press, 2nd edn, 1994)

W.J. Battersby, 'Educational Work of the Religious Orders of Women: 1850–1950', in G.A. Beck (ed.), *The English Catholics 1850–1950* (London: Burns & Oates, 1950)

Jenny Beale, *Women In Ireland: Voices of Change* (Dublin: Gill & Macmillan, 1986)

A.C.F. Beales, 'The Struggle for the Schools', in G.A. Beck (ed.), *The English Catholics 1850–1950* (London: Burns & Oates, 1950)

G.A. Beck (ed.), *The English Catholics 1850–1950* (London: Burns & Oates, 1950)

William Bedford and Michael Knight, *Jacob's Ladder: The Rise of a Catholic Community 1848–1913* (Grimsby: St. Mary on the Sea, NRCDT, 1996)

Mark Bence-Jones, *The Catholic Families* (London: Constable, 1995)

John Bennett, 'The Care of the Poor', in G.A. Beck (ed.), *The English Catholics 1850–1950* (London: Burns & Oates, 1950)

Marcelle Bernstein, *Nuns* (London: Collins, 1976)

Virginia Berridge, 'Health and Medicine', in F.L.M. Thompson, *The Cambridge Social History of Britain, 1750–1950*, Vol. 3, *Social Agencies and Institutions* (London: Cambridge University Press, 1990)

Evelyn Bolster, *The Sisters of Mercy in the Crimea* (Cork: Mercier Press, 1994)

John Bossy, *The English Catholic Community, 1570–1850* (London: Darton, Longman & Todd, 1978)

Joanna Bourke, *Husbandry to Housewifery: Women, Economic Change, and Housework in Ireland, 1890–1914* (Oxford: Clarendon Press, 1993)

Barry Bruff (ed.), *The Village Atlas: The Growth of Manchester, Lancashire and North Cheshire, 1840–1912* (Edmonton: Village Press, 1989)

Thomas Burke, *Catholic History of Liverpool* (Liverpool: Tingling, 1910)

S. Campbell-Jones, *In Habit: An Anthropological Study of Working Nuns* (London: Faber, 1979)

Mary Carbery, *The Farm by Lough Gur* (London: 1937; reprinted Dublin: Mercier, 1987)

Owen Chadwick, *The Victorian Church*, Part I (London: A. & C. Black, 3rd edn, 1971); Part II (London: A. & C. Black, 2nd edn, 1972)

Caitriona Clear, *Nuns in Nineteenth-Century Ireland* (Dublin: Gill & Macmillan, 1987)

Rosemary Clerkin, *A Heart for Others* (Chigwell: Sisters of the Sacred Hearts of Jesus and Mary, 1983)

Sally Cline, *Women, Celibacy and Passion* (London: Andre Deutsch, 1993; Optima, 1994)

Brenda Collins, 'The Irish in Britain', in B.J. Graham and L.J. Proudfoot (eds), *An Historical Geography of Ireland* (London and New York, NY: Academic Press, 1993)

Peter Coman, *Catholics and the Welfare State* (London: Longman, 1977)

S. Constantine, *Social Conditions in Britain 1918–1939* (London: Methuen, 1983)

Edward Cruise, 'The Development of the Religious Orders', in G.A. Beck (ed.), *The English Catholics 1850–1950* (London: Burns & Oates, 1950)

L.M. Cullen, *The Formation of the Irish Economy* (Dublin: Mercier, 1969)

Mary Cullen (ed.), *Girls Don't Do Honours: Irish Women in Education in the 19th and 20th Centuries* (Dublin: Women's Educational Bureau, 1987)

Mary Cullen and Maria Luddy (eds), *Women, Power and Consciousness in Nineteenth-Century Ireland* (Dublin: Attic Press, 1995)

C. Curtin, H. Donnan and T.M. Wilson (eds), *Irish Urban Cultures* (Belfast: Institute of Irish Studies, Queen's University, 1993)

C. Curtin, P. Jackson and B. O'Connor (eds), *Gender in Irish Society* (Galway: University Press, 1987)

L.P. Curtis, 'Ireland in 1914', in W.E. Vaughan (ed.), *A New History of Ireland*, VI, *Ireland under the Union*, II, *1870–1921* (Oxford: Clarendon Press, 1996)

Mary E. Daly, *Women and Work in Ireland*, Studies in Irish Economic and Social History, No.7 (Dublin: Economic and Social History Association of Ireland, 1997)

Adrian Dansette, *The Religious History of Modern France*. Vol. II (trans. John Dingle) (Edinburgh and London: Herder, 1961)

Celia Davis (ed.), *Rewriting Nursing History* (London: Croom Helm, 1980),

Charles Davis, *Religion and the Making of Society* (Cambridge: Cambridge University Press, 1994)

Graham Davis, *The Irish in Britain, 1815–1914* (Dublin: Gill & Macmillan, 1991)

Alan Deacon and Michael Hill, 'The Problem of "Surplus Women" in the Nineteenth-Century: Secular and Religious Alternatives', in M. Hill (ed.), *A Sociological Yearbook of Religion in Britain*, Vol. 5 (London: SCM Press, 1972)

A. Digby, C. Feinstein and D. Jenkins (eds), *New Directions in Economic and Social History*, Vol. II (London: Macmillan, 1992)

Robert Dingwall, Anne Marie Rafferty and Charles Webster (eds), *An Introduction to the Social History of Nursing* (London: Routledge, 1988)

William Doyle, SJ., *Vocations* (Dublin: Irish Messenger, 19th edn, 1928)

Irene Ffrench Eager, *Margaret Anna Cusack: One Woman's Campaign for Women's Rights, a Biography* (Dublin: Arlen House, 1970; revised edn, 1979)

Tony Fahey, 'Nuns in the Catholic Church in Ireland in the Nineteenth Century', in Mary Cullen (ed.), *Girls Don't Do Honours: Irish Women in Education in the 19th and 20th Centuries* (Dublin: Women's Educational Bureau, 1987), pp. 7–30.

L.G. Fanfani and K.D. O'Rourke, OP, *Canon Law for Religious Women* (Dubuque, IA: Priory Press, 1961)

David Fitzpatrick, 'The Irish in Britain, 1871–1921', in W.E. Vaughan (ed.), *A New History of Ireland*, VI, *Ireland under the Union*, II, *1870–1921* (Oxford: Clarendon Press, 1996)

John Fitzsimons, *Manning: Anglican and Catholic* (London: Burns & Oates, 1951)

R. Floud and D. McCloskey (eds), *The Economic History of Britain since 1700*, Vol. 2, *1860–1939* (London: Cambridge University Press, 2nd edn, 1994)

M.D. Forrest, SJ, *The Pearl of Great Price, or the Religious Life* (London: Catholic Truth Society, 1922)

Michel Foucault (trans. Alan Sheridan), *Discipline and Punish: The Birth of the Prison* (London: Penguin, 1991)

P.L. Garside, 'London and the Home Counties', in F.L.M. Thompson (ed.), *The Cambridge Social History of Britain, 1750–1950*, Vol. 1, *Regions and Communities* (London: Cambridge University Press, 1993)

Mary Josephine Gately, *The Sisters of Mercy: Historical Sketches 1831–1931* (New York, NY: Macmillan, 1931)

—, *Supplementary Manual to the Sisters of Mercy: Historical Sketches 1831–1931* (New York, NY: Macmillan, 1931)

John D. Gay, *The Geography of Religion in England* (London: Duckworth, 1971)

—, 'Some Aspects of the Social Geography of Religion in England: the Roman Catholics and the Mormons', in M. Hill (ed.), *A Sociological Yearbook of Religion in Britain* (London: SCM Press, 1968)

Fintan Geser, OSB, *The Canon Law Governing Communities of Sisters* (St. Louis, MO and London: Herder, 1938)

Ralph Gibson, *A Social History of French Catholicism 1789–1914* (London and New York, NY: Routledge, 1989)

—, 'The Christianization of the Countryside in Western Europe in the Nineteenth Century', in J.-P. Massaut and M.-E. Hebbeau (eds), *La christianisation des campagnes*, Vol. II (Brussels and Rome: Institut Historique Belge de Rome/Belgisch Historisch Instituut te Rome, 1996), pp. 485–509.

Sheridan Gilly, 'Catholic Faith of the Irish Slums: London, 1840–70', in H.J. Dyos and M. Wolff (eds), *The Victorian City: Images and Realities*, Vol. 2 (London: Routledge & Kegan Paul, 1973)

S. Glynn and A. Booth, *Modern Britain: An Economic and Social History* (London: Routledge, 1996)

Erving Goffman, *Asylums* (London: Doubleday, 1961; Penguin, 1968)

B.J. Graham and J. Proudfoot, *An Historical Geography of Ireland* (London and New York, NY: Academic Press, 1993)

Timothy W. Guinnane, *The Vanishing Irish: Households, Migration, and the Rural Economy in Ireland, 1850–1914* (Princeton, NJ: Princeton University Press, 1997)

Denis Gwynn, *A Hundred Years of Catholic Emancipation, 1829–1929* (London: Longman, Green, 1929)

—, 'Growth of the Catholic Community', in G.A. Beck (ed.), *The English Catholics 1850–1950* (London: Burns & Oates, 1950)

—, 'The Irish Immigration', in G.A. Beck (ed.), *The English Catholics 1850–1950* (London: Burns & Oates, 1950)

Edna Hamer, *Elizabeth Prout 1820–1864: Foundress of the Sisters of the Most Holy Cross and Passion* (Bath: Downside Abbey, 1994)

Jose Harris, *Private Lives, Public Spirit: Britain 1870–1914* (London: Oxford University Press, 1993)

Adrian Hastings (ed.), *Bishops and Writers* (Wheathampstead: Anthony Clarke, 1977)

Eve Healy, *The Life of Mother Mary Potter: Foundress of the Congregation of the Little Company of Mary* (London: Sheed & Ward, 1935)

Mary Heimann, *Religious Devotion in Victorian England* (Oxford: Clarendon Press, 1995)

Hugh Heinrick, *A Survey of the Irish in England* (ed. Alan O'Day) (London: Hambledon Press, 1990; originally published 1872)

John Hickey, *Urban Catholics* (London: Chapman, 1967)

Patrick Hickey 'The Famine in the Skibbereen Union (1845–51)', in Cathal Poirteir (ed.), *The Great Irish Famine* (Dublin: RTE/Mercier Press, 1995), pp. 185–203.

J.A. Hilton, *Catholic Lancashire* (London: Phillimore, 1994)

Edmund M. Hogan, *The Irish Missionary Movement: A Historical Survey, 1830–1980* (Dublin: Gill & Macmillan, 1990)

Herman Hohn, *Vocations: Conditions of Admission to Convents* (London: Washbourne, 1912)

Lee Holcombe, *Victorian Ladies at Work* (Newton Abbot: David & Charles, 1973)

T.H. Hollingworth, 'A Demographic Study of British Ducal Families', in Michael Drake (ed.), *Population in Industrialization* (London: Methuen, 1969)

Derek Holmes, *More Roman than Rome* (London: Burns & Oates, 1978)

M.P. Hornsby-Smith, *The Changing Parish* (London: Routledge, 1989)

D.W. Howell and C. Barber, 'Wales', in F.L.M. Thompson, *The Cambridge Social History of Britain, 1750–1950*, Vol. 1 (London: Cambridge University Press, 1990)

George V. Hudson, *Mother Genevieve Dupuis. Foundress of the Sisters of Charity of St. Paul the Apostle* (London: Sheed & Ward, 1929)

Olwen Hufton, *The Prospect before Her: A History of Women in Western Europe, 1500–1800* (London: HarperCollins, 1995)

Philip Hughes, 'The English Catholics in 1850' and 'The Coming Century', in G.A. Beck (ed.), *The English Catholics 1850–1950* (London: Burns & Oates, 1950)

T. Jones Hughes, 'Landholding and Settlement in County Tipperary in the Nineteenth Century', in W. Nolan and T. McGrath (eds), *Tipperary History and Society* (Dublin: Geography Publications, 1985)

Felicity Hunt (ed.), *Lessons for Life: The Schooling of Girls and Women 1850–1950* (London: Basil Blackwell, 1987)

Tom Inglis, *Moral Monopoly: The Catholic Church in Modern Irish Society* (Dublin: Gill & Macmillan, 1987)

J.A. Jackson, *The Irish in Britain* (London: Routledge & Kegan Paul; Cleveland, OH: Western Reserve University Press, 1963)

Sheila Jeffreys, *The Spinster and Her Enemies. Feminism and Sexuality 1880–1930* (London: Pandora, 1985)

R.E. Kennedy, *The Irish: Emigration, Marriage, and Fertility* (Berkeley, CA and London: University of California Press, 1973)

Cecil Kerr, *A Memoir of a Sister of Charity: Lady Ethelreda Fitzalan-Howard* (London: Burns, Oates & Washbourne, 1928)

Declan Kiberd, *Inventing Ireland* (London: Jonathan Cape, 1995)

Mary Audrey Kopp, 'Bureaucratic Dysfunction in American Convents', in M.C. Borromeo, CSC (ed.), *The New Nuns* (London and Sydney: Sheed & Ward, 1968)

Jules Kosley and Raymond J. Lunnon, *Great Ormond Street and the Story of Medicine* (London: Hospitals for Sick Children/Granta, 1991)

Bill Lancaster, *The Department Store* (London and New York, NY: Leicester University Press, 1995)

J. Langton and R.J. Morris (eds), *Atlas of Industrializing Britain 1780–1914* (London: Methuen, 1986)

J.J. Lee, *The Modernisation of Irish Society 1848–1918* (Dublin: Gill & Macmillan, 1989)

—, 'Women and the Church since the Famine', in M. McCurtain and D. O'Corrain (eds), *Women in Irish Society: The Historical Dimension* (Dublin: Arlen Press, 1978)

Lynn Hollen Lees, *Exiles of Erin: Irish Migrants in Victorian London* (Manchester: Manchester University Press, 1979)

Etienne Lelong, *The Nun, Her Character and Work* (trans. by Mme Cecelia) (London: Kegan Paul, Trench & Trubner, 1925)

Lynda Letford and Colin C. Pooley, 'Geographies of Migration and Religion: Irish Women in Mid-Nineteenth-Century Liverpool', in P. O'Sullivan (ed.), *Irish Women and Irish Migration*, Vol. 4 (London and New York, NY: Leicester University Press, 1995)

Ian Levitt, 'Poor Law and Pauperism', in J. Langton and R.J. Morris (eds), *Atlas of Industrializing Britain 1780–1914* (London: Methuen, 1986)

Mary Linscott, *Quiet Revolution* (Glasgow: Burns, 1966)

—, *Towards Revised Constitutions: a Historical Perspective* (Liverpool: Sisters of Notre Dame, 1976)

—, *This Excellent Heritage: An Introduction to the Constitutions of the Sisters of Notre Dame* (Liverpool: Sisters of Notre Dame, 1989)

Mary Loudon, *Unveiled: Nuns Talking* (London: Chatto & Windus, 1992)

Maria Luddy, *Women and Philanthropy in Nineteenth-Century Ireland* (Cambridge: Cambridge University Press, 1995)

M. Luddy and C. Murphy (eds), *Women Surviving: Studies in Irish Women's History in the Nineteenth and Twentieth Centuries* (Dublin: Poolbeg, 1989)

Maria G. McClelland, *The Sisters of Mercy: Popular Politics and the Growth of the Roman Catholic Community in Hull, 1855–1930* (Lampeter; Lewiston, NY; Queenston, Ontario: Edwin Mellen Press, 2000)

M.G. McClelland, *Cardinal Manning: His Public Life and Influence 1865–92* (London: Oxford University Press, 1962)

—, *English Roman Catholics and Higher Education 1830–1903* (Oxford: Clarendon Press, 1973)

M. McCurtain and D. O'Corrain (eds), *Women in Irish Society: the Historical Dimension* (Dublin: Arlen Press, 1978)

Hugh McLeod, *Religion and the People of Western Europe 1789–1970* (London: Oxford University Press, 1981)

—, 'Class, Community and Region: The Religious Geography of Nineteenth-Century England', in M. Hill (ed.), *A Sociological Yearbook of Religion in Britain*, No. 6 (London: SCM Press, 1973)

—, *Class and Religion in the Late-Victorian City* (London: Croom Helm, 1974)

—, *Religion and the Working Class in Nineteenth-Century Britain* (London: Macmillan, 1984)

Edward McLysaght, *Irish Families: Their Names, Arms and Origins* (Dublin: Hodges Figgis, 1957)

Jo Ann Kay Macnamara, *Sisters in Arms: Catholic Nuns through Two Millennia* (London and Cambridge, MA: Harvard University Press, 1996)

Christopher Maggs (ed.), *Nursing History: The State of the Art* (London and Sydney: Croom Helm, 1987)

Sara Maitland, *A Map of the New Country. Women and Christianity* (London: Routledge & Kegan Paul, 1983)

Mother Marie Therese, SHCJ, *Cornelia Connolly* (London: Burns & Oates, 1963)

David Mathew, *Catholicism in England* (London: Eyre & Spottiswode, 1936; 3rd edn, 1955)

—, 'Old Catholics and Converts', in G.A. Beck (ed.), *The English Catholics 1850–1950* (London: Burns & Oates, 1950)

James Miller, *The Passion of Michel Foucault* (London: Flamingo, 1994)

Kerby A. Miller, David N. Doyle and Patricia Kelleher, 'For Love and Liberty: Irish Women and Domesticity in Ireland and America, 1815–1920', in P. O'Sullivan (ed.), *Irish Women and Irish Migration*, Vol. 4 (London and New York, NY: Leicester University Press, 1995)

Paul Misner, *Social Catholicism in Europe* (London: Darton, Longman & Todd, 1991)

Maud Monahan, *The Life and Letters of Janet Erskine Stuart: Superior General of the Society of the Sacred Heart 1857–1914* (London: Longmans Green, 1922)

Frank Neal, *Sectarian Violence: The Liverpool Experience, 1819–1914* (Manchester: Manchester University Press, 1986)

Janet A. Nolan, *Ourselves Alone: Women's Emigration from Ireland, 1885–1920* (Lexington, KY: University of Kentucky Press, 1989)

W. Nolan and T. McGrath (eds), *Tipperary History and Society* (Dublin: Geography Publications, 1985)

E. Ni Chuilleanain (ed.), *Irish Women: Image and Achievement* (Dublin: Arlen House, 1985)

Edward Norman, *Anti-Catholicism in Victorian England* (London: Allen & Unwin, 1968)

—, *The English Catholic Church in the Nineteenth Century* (Oxford: Clarendon Press, 1984)

James Obelkevich, 'Religion', in F.L.M. Thompson (ed.), *The Cambridge Social History of Britain, 1750–1950*, Vol. 3, *Social Agencies and Institutions* (London: Cambridge University Press, 1990)

Kate O'Brien, *Land of Spices* (London: Heinemann, 1941; Dublin: Arlen House, 1982)

Mary O'Dowd, 'Women Historians in Ireland from the 1790s to the 1990s', in Maryann G. Valiulis and Mary O'Dowd (eds), *Women and Irish History* (Dublin: Wolfhound Press, 1997)

Mary O'Dowd and Sabine Wichert (eds), *Chattel, Servant or Citizen Women's Status in Church, State and Society*, Historical Studies XIX (Belfast: Queen's University Institute of Irish Studies, 1995)

Cormac O'Grada, *Ireland: A New Economic History, 1780–1939* (Oxford: Clarendon Press, 1994)

Margaret Ó hÓgartaigh, 'Flower Power and Mental Grooviness: Nurses and Midwives in Ireland in the Early Twentieth Century', in Bernadette Whelan (ed.), *Women and Paid Work in Ireland 1500–1930* (Dublin: Four Courts Press, 2000).

Gerald Parsons (ed.), *Religion in Victorian Britain*, Vol. II, *Controversies* (Manchester: Open University, 1988)

Revd Fr. Paul, OSFC, *The British Church from the Days of Cardinal Allen* (London: Burns, Oates & Washbourne, 1929)

Joan Perkin, *Women and Marriage in Nineteenth-Century England* (London: Routledge, 1989)

Cathal Poirteir (ed.), *The Great Irish Famine* (Dublin: Thomas Davis Lecture Series, RTE/Mercier Press, 1995)

Avey Pounder, *The Ursuline Chronicle 1892–1992* (London: Ursulines of the Roman Union, 1992)

F.K. Prochaska, *Women and Philanthropy in Nineteenth-Century England* (Oxford: Clarendon Press, 1980)

Rita M. Rhodes, *Women and the Family in Post-Famine Ireland* (New York, NY and London: Garland Publishing, 1992)

Michael E. Rose, *The Relief of Poverty 1834–1914* (London: Macmillan, 1972)

Anne Rossiter, 'Bringing the Margins into the Centre', in Ailbhe Smyth (ed.), *Irish Women's Studies Reader* (Dublin: Attic Press, 1993)

J.J. Scarisbrick, *Selly Park and Beyond: the Story of Genevieve Dupuis and the Congregation of the Sisters of Charity of St. Paul the Apostle* (Birmingham: Sisters of St. Paul, 1997)

M.A. Schaldenbrand, SSJ, 'Asylums: Total Societies and Religious Life', in M.C. Borromeo, CSC (ed.), *The New Nuns* (London and Sydney: Sheed & Ward, 1968)

J.M. Scott, SJ, *Convent Life: The Meaning of a Vocation* (New York, NY: Kennedy, 1919)

W.J. Shiels and D. Wood (eds), *Studies in Church History: Women in the Church*, Ecclesiastical History Society papers, 1989/90 (London: Blackwell, 1990)

Margaret Simey, *Charitable Effort in Liverpool in the Nineteenth Century* (Liverpool: Liverpool University Press, 1951)

Sisters of Mercy, *Trees of Mercy: Sisters of Mercy of Great Britain from 1839* (London: privately published, 1993)

Sisters of Nazareth, *The Sisters of Nazareth* (London: privately published, 1933)

Sisters of Notre Dame, *Sr. Marie des Saint Anges: Mary Elizabeth Townley* (London: Burns, Oates & Washbourne, 1950)

—, *Sr. Mary of St. Francis: Hon. Laura Stafford Jerningham* (London: Burns, Oates & Washbourne, 1951)

—, *The Memoirs of Mother Frances Blin de Bourdon* (Westminster, MD: Trinity College, 1975)

Ailbhe Smyth (ed.), *Irish Women's Studies Reader* (Dublin: Attic Press, 1993)

W.J. Smyth, 'The Making of Ireland: Agendas and Perspectives in Cultural Geography', in B.J. Graham and J. Proudfoot (eds), *A Historical Geography of Ireland* (London and New York, NY: Academic Press, 1993)

S.G. Snead-Cox, *Life of Cardinal Vaughan* (London: Burns & Oates, 2 vols, 1910)

Francesca M. Steele, *The Convents of Great Britain* (London: Sands; Dublin: M.H. Gill, 1902)

Mary Winefride Sturman, *The Ursulines in England 1851–1981* (London: Ursulines of the Roman Union, 1981)

Penny Summerfield, 'Cultural Reproduction in the Education of Girls: a Study of Girls' Secondary Schooling in Two Lancashire Towns, 1900–1950', in Felicity Hunt (ed.), *Lessons for Life: The Schooling of Girls and Women, 1850–1950* (London: Basil Blackwell, 1987)

Ann Summers, 'A Home from Home: Women's Philanthropic Work in the Nineteenth Century', in Sandra Burman (ed.), *Fit Work for Women* (London: Croom Helm, 1979)

Gillian Sutherland, 'Education', in F.L.M. Thompson (ed.), *The Cambridge Social History of Britain, 1750–1950*, Vol. 3, *Social Agencies and Institutions* (London: Cambridge University Press, 1990)

Morgan V. Sweeney, 'Diocesan Organization and Administration', in G.A. Beck (ed.), *The English Catholics 1850–1950* (London: Burns & Oates, 1950)

R. Swift and S. Gilly, *The Irish in Britain 1815–1939* (London: Pinter, 1989)

Pat Thane, 'Government and Society in England and Wales 1750–1914', in F.L.M. Thompson (ed.), *The Cambridge Social History of Britain, 1750–1950*, Vol. 3, *Social Agencies and Institutions* (London: Cambridge University Press, 1990)

F.L.M. Thompson (ed.), *The Cambridge Social History of Britain, 1750–1950*, Vol.1. *Regions and Communities*; Vol. 3. *Social Agencies and Institutions* (London: Cambridge University Press, 1990)

Pauric Travers, '"There Was Nothing for Me There": Irish Female Emigration, 1922–71', in P. O'Sullivan (ed.), *Irish Women and Irish Migration*, Vol. 4 (London and New York, NY: Leicester University Press, 1995)

—, 'Emigration and Gender: The Case of Ireland 1922–60', in Mary O'Dowd and Sabrine Wichet (eds), *Chattel, Servant or Citizen: Women's Status in Church, State and Society*, Historical Studies XIX (Belfast: Queen's University Institute of Irish Studies, 1995)

Ursuline Sisters, *The Ursulines, Greenwich, 1877–1977* (London: Ursulines of the Roman Union, 1977)

Maryann G. Valiulis and Mary O'Dowd, *Women and Irish History: Essays in honour of Margaret MacCurtain* (Dublin: Wolfhound Press, 1997)

W.E. Vaughan (ed.), *A New History of Ireland*, VI. *Ireland under the Union*, II, *1870–1921* (Oxford: Clarendon Press, 1996)

Martha Vicinus, *Independent Women: Work and Community, 1850–1920* (Edinburgh and London: Nelson, 1961; Chicago, IL: Virago, 1985)

James J. Walsh, *These Splendid Sisters* (New York, NY: Sears, 1927)

T.J. Walsh, *Nano Nagle and the Presentation Sisters* (Dublin: Gill & Son, 1959)

J.K. Walton, *Lancashire, a Social History: 1558–1939* (Manchester: Manchester University Press, 1987)

—, 'The North West', in F.L.M. Thompson (ed.), *The Cambridge Social History of Britain, 1750–1950*, Vol. 1, *Regions and Communities* (London: Cambridge University Press, 1990)

Bernadette Whelan (ed.), *Women and Paid Work in Ireland 1500–1930* (Dublin: Four Courts Press, 2000)

Kevin Whelan, 'The Catholic Church, 1700–1900', in W. Nolan and T. McGrath (eds), *Tipperary History and Society* (Dublin: Geography Publications, 1985)

Andrew White and Michael Winstanley, *Victorian Terraced Houses in Lancaster* (Lancaster: Centre for North-West Regional Studies, Lancaster University, 1996)

Karel Williams, *From Pauperism to Poverty* (London: Routledge & Kegan Paul, 1981)

Margaret Williams, *The Society of the Sacred Heart* (London: Darton, Longman & Todd, 1978)

Adrian Wilson (ed.), *Re-thinking Social History: English Society and Its Interpretation, 1570–1920* (Manchester: Manchester University Press, 1993)

E.A. Wrigley and R.S. Scofield, *The Population History of England, 1541–1871* (London: Edward Arnold, 1981)

Stephen Yeo, *Religion and Voluntary Organisations in Crisis* (London: Croom Helm, 1976)

JOURNAL ARTICLES

Margaret Brennan, 'Enclosure: Institutionalising the Invisibility of Women in Ecclesiastical Communities', *Concilium*, 182 (1985), pp. 38–48

Joanna Bourke, 'Dairywomen and Affectionate Wives: Women in the Irish Dairy Industry, 1890–1914', *Agricultural History Review*, 38, II (1990), pp. 149–64

Jean Bunn, SND, 'The Archives of Notre Dame de Namur in Britain', *Journal of the Catholic Archives Society*, 13 (1993), pp. 3–12

Susan P. Casteras, 'Virgin Vows: The Early Victorian Artists' Portrayal of Nuns and Novices', *Victorian Studies*, (Winter 1981), pp. 157–84

K.H. Connell, 'Peasant Marriage in Ireland: Its Structure and Development since the Famine', *Economic History Review*, 14 (1961–62), pp. 502–23

Gerard Connolly, 'The Transubstantiation of Myth: Towards a New Popular History of 19th Century Catholicism in England', *Journal of Ecclesiastical History*, 35, 1 (January 1984), pp. 78–104

Mary P. Darbyshire, CSA, 'The Archives of the Canonesses of Saint Augustine, Boarbank Hall, Grange-over Sands', *Journal of the Catholic Archives Society*, 21 (2001), pp. 45–52

Helen Rose Ebaugh, 'Patriarchal Bargains and Latent Avenues of Social Mobility: Nuns in the Roman Catholic Church', *Gender and Society*, 7, 3 (September 1993), pp. 400–14

David Fitzpatrick, 'Women, Gender and the Writing of History', *Irish Historical Studies*, 27, 107 (May 1991), pp. 267–73

—, 'Irish Farming Families before the First World War', *Comparative Studies in Society and History*, 25, 3 (1983), pp. 339–80

—, 'A Share of the Honeycomb: Education, Emigration and Irishwomen', *Continuity and Change*, 1, 2 (1989), pp. 217–34

P. Gibbon and C. Curtin, 'The Stem Family in Ireland', *Comparative Studies in Society and History*, 20, 3 (July 1978), pp. 429–53

Sheridan Gilly, 'Heretic London, Holy Poverty and the Irish Poor: 1830–1870', *Downside Review*, 89 (1971), pp. 64–89

Judith Greville, 'Records of the Children's Homes of the Daughters of Charity of St. Vincent de Paul', *Journal of the Catholic Archives Society*, 15 (1995), pp. 3–12

Suellen Hoy, 'The Journey Out: The Recruitment and Emigration of Irish Religious Women to the United States 1812–1914', *Journal of Women's History*, Special Double Issue, 6, 4 and 7, 1 (Winter/Spring 1995), pp. 64–98

Philip Ingram, 'Protestant Patriarchy and the Catholic Priesthood in Nineteenth-Century England', *Journal of Social History*, (1991), pp. 783–97

Sr. Helen of Jesus, ODC, 'The Carmels of Great Britain: A Check List', *Journal of the Catholic Archives Society*, 20 (2000), pp. 38–42

Alice Vowe Johnson, 'The Problem of the Feeble-minded', *The Crucible: A Catholic Magazine of Higher Education for Women*, 6, 23 (December 1910), pp. 142–9

Liam Kennedy, 'Farm Succession in Modern Ireland: Elements of a Theory of Inheritance', *Economic History Review*, 44, 3 (1991), pp. 477–99

Emmet Larkin, 'The Devotional Revolution in Ireland 1850–75', *American Historical Review*, 77 (June 1972), pp. 625–52

Lynn Lees, 'Mid-Victorian Migration and the Irish Family Economy', *Victorian Studies*, 20, 1 (Autumn 1976), pp. 25–43

Maria Luddy, 'An Agenda for Women's History in Ireland. Part II. 1800–1900', *Irish Historical Studies*, 28, 109 (May 1992), pp. 19–37

Maria G. McClelland, 'The First Hull Mercy Nuns: A Nineteenth-Century Case Study', *Recusant History*, 22, 2 (October 1994), pp. 199–221

V.A. McClelland, 'Two Book Reviews on Education of Victorian and Edwardian England', *Victorian Studies*, 27, 1 (Autumn 1983), pp. 106–8

Margaret MacCurtain, 'Late in the Field: Catholic Sisters in Twentieth-Century Ireland and the New Religious History', *Journal of Women's History*, Special Double Issue, 6, 4 and 7, 1 (Winter/Spring 1995), pp. 47–63

Dennis and Joan Mills 'Farms, Farmers and Farm Workers in the Nineteenth-Century Census Enumerators' Books: A Lincolnshire Case Study, *Local Historian*, 27, 3 (August 1997), pp. 130–43

Michelle Motherway, LMC, 'Archives of the Little Company of Mary, *Journal of the Catholic Archives Society*, 14 (1994) pp. 12–19

Susan O'Brien, 'Terra Incognita: The Nun in Nineteenth-Century England', *Past and Present*, 121 (November 1988), pp. 110–40

—, '10,000 Nuns: Working in Convent Archives', *Journal of the Catholic Archives Society*, 9 (1989), pp. 27–33

—, 'Lay Sisters and Good Mothers: Working-Class Women in English Convents, 1840–1910', in W.J. Shiels and D. Wood (eds), *Women in the Church: Ecclesiastical History Society Papers, 1989/90* (London: Blackwell, 1990), pp. 453–65

—, 'French Nuns in Nineteenth-Century England', *Past and Present*, 154 (February 1997), pp. 142–80

—, 'Making Catholic Spaces: Women, Decor and Devotion in the English Catholic Church, 1840–1900', in Diana Wood (ed.), *The Church and the Arts*, Studies in Church History, Ecclesiastical History Society, 28 (London: Blackwell, 1992), pp. 449–64

M.A.G. O'Tuathaigh, 'The Irish in Nineteenth-Century Britain: Problems of Integration', *Transactions of the Royal Historical Society*, 5th Ser., 31 (1981), pp. 149–73

Colin G. Pooley and Jean Turnbull, 'Leaving Home: The Experience of Migration from the Parental Home in Britain since c.1770', *Journal of Family History*, 22, 4 (October 1997), pp. 390–424

Timothy B. Smith, 'The ideology of Charity: The Impact of the English Poor Law and Debates over the Right of Assistance in France 1830–1905', *Historical Journal*, 40, 4 (December 1997), pp. 997–1032

UNPUBLISHED THESES, DISSERTATIONS AND PAPERS

Tony Fahey, 'Female Asceticism in the Catholic Church: A Case Study of Nuns in the Nineteenth Century', PhD thesis, University of Illinois at Urbana-Champaign, 1982

Mary Gandy, 'Sending Children to Canada: A Search for Records Requested by the Catholic Child Welfare Council', paper presented to the Catholic Archives Society, Annual Conference, Durham, 1995

Mary Margaret Kealy, 'The Dominican Nuns of Channel Row, 1717–1820', MA dissertation, University of Lancaster, 1998

Sharon Lambert, 'Female Emigration from Post-Independence Ireland: An Oral History of Irish Women in Lancashire, c.1922–1960', PhD thesis, University of Lancaster, 1997

M. Linscott, SND, 'The Educational Work of the Sisters of Notre Dame in Lancashire since 1850', MA dissertation, University of Liverpool, 1964

—, 'The Educational Experience of the Sisters of Notre Dame de Namur, 1804–1964', PhD thesis, University of Liverpool, 1964

Shiela Lunney, 'Mercy', Dublin: Mercy International Archives, Ref. 271.92, 1983

Susan Mumm, 'Lady Guerillas of Philanthropy. Anglican Sisterhoods in Victorian England', PhD thesis, University of Sussex, 1992

Mary Peckham, 'Catholic Female Congregations and Religious Change in Ireland 1770–1870', PhD thesis, University of Wisconsin-Madison, 1993

Jacintha Prunty, 'The Geography of Poverty, Dublin 1850–1900: The Social Mission of the Church with Particular Reference to Margaret Alyward and Co-workers', PhD thesis, University College, Dublin, 1992

Avril Reynolds, 'A Re-assessment of Margaret Anne Cusack', paper presented to the Irish Women's History Association Conference, Galway University, 17 September 1994

W.J. Smyth, 'Clogheen-Burncoat: A Social History of a Co. Tipperary Parish', PhD thesis, National University of Ireland, 1969

H.C.B. Stone, 'Constraints on the Foundresses: Contrasts in Anglican and Roman Catholic Religious Headships in Victorian England', PhD thesis, University of Leeds, 1993

Alexander Wall, 'The Supply of Certificated Teachers to the Roman Catholic Elementary Schools of Britain, 1848–1870', MPhil thesis, University of Lancaster, 1983

Barbara M. Walsh, 'A Social History of Roman Catholic Nuns and Sisters in Nineteenth and Early Twentieth Century England and Wales: The Veiled Dynamic', PhD thesis, University of Lancaster, 1999

Meg Whittle, 'Philanthropy in Preston: The Changing Face of Charity', PhD thesis, University of Lancaster, 1990

Index